ATONEMENT THEORIES

ATONEMENT THEORIES

A Way through the Maze

BEN PUGH

CASCADE *Books* · Eugene, Oregon

ATONEMENT THEORIES
A Way through the Maze

Cascade Books
An Imprint of Wipf and Stock Publishers
199 W. 8th Ave., Suite 3
Eugene, OR 97401

www.wipfandstock.com

ISBN 13: 978-1-62032-853-8

Cataloguing-in-Publication data:

Pugh, Ben.

Atonement theories : a way through the maze / Ben Pugh.

xiv + 190 pp. ; 23 cm. Includes bibliographical references and index.

ISBN 13: 978-1-62032-853-8

1. Atonement. 2. Theology of the cross. 3. Jesus Christ—Crucifixion. I. Title.

BT265.3 P844 2014

Manufactured in the U.S.A.

Chapter 1 of Part 1 has been adapted from my "'Kicking the Daylights out of the Devil': The Re-appropriation of the Victory Motif in Some Recent Atonement Theology" *European Journal of Theology* 23.1 (2014), 32–42. Used by permission.

Parts of chapter 2 of Part 3 have been adapted from my "The Mind of the Spirit: Explorations in the Reciprocal Relationship between the Work of the Spirit and the Work of the Son," *Journal of the European Pentecostal Theological Association* 32.1 (2012) 41–60, and from my, "The Spirit and the Cross: Insights from Barth and Moltmann into the Holy Spirit's Relationship to the Cross of Christ," *Evangelical Review of Theology* 36.4 (2012) 292–301. Both used by permission.

To Barry Taylor, the very first person to introduce me to what has proven to be the richest seam in theology: Atonement theories.

Contents

Acknowledgments   ix

Introduction   xi

PART ONE: *Christus Victor*

1   The Ransom to Satan   3

2   Recapitulation and *Theosis*   26

PART TWO: *Objective Theories*

3   Satisfaction Guaranteed: Anselm   45

4   Luther and Calvin   63

5   The Nineteenth Century   83

6   Twentieth- and Twenty-First-Century Developments   93

PART THREE: *Subjective Theories*

7   The Cross as Transformative Revelation   125

8   "The Spirit Comes from the Cross": The Pneumatological Synthesis   144

PART FOUR: *A New Option? Anthropological Theories*

9   The Story of Nonviolent Atonement   153

10   The Way through the Maze: Some Initial Deductions   162

Conclusion   164

Bibliography   167

Index   189

Acknowledgments

WERE IT NOT FOR MATTERSEY Hall, I would never have had the chance to write an entire MA module called "Contemporary Issues in Atonement Theology," which I delivered over a memorable week in January 2012. The students who gathered there, in the conservatory sitting around on the sofas, to discuss atonement theology for several hours every day were a delight. That module grew into this book. I am indebted to Dr. Ben Fulford of Chester University for creating the opportunity to try out parts of the book as papers presented at conferences there in October 2012 and January 2013. I am also very indebted to Dr. Stephen Skuce, Academic Dean of Cliff College (my boss), for allowing me to work away from the office throughout the July and August of 2013, which is when most of the book was written. Thanks to him I don't need to include that "thanks for letting me neglect you all" bit, where the author thanks his or her long-suffering spouse and children for tolerating long periods of absence. I have enjoyed the company of my wife Pearl and my children Abigail, Gracie, and Reuben as much as always over this time. Finally, a word of thanks to my editor, Dr. Robin Parry: an extremely easy-going and supportive editor while I struggled to finish the manuscript.

Introduction

IF YOU ARE A BEGINNING student doing a degree in theology or religious studies and you want a fairly friendly guide that will get you from knowing almost nothing, because the lecturer sent you to sleep that day, to gaining a pretty good level of mastery of the subject over the space of a few hours of reading, this book is for you. If that is you then you will probably need to ignore the footnotes and just keep reading. I have tried to make this like one of those encyclopedias full of lovely pictures that make you feel that you have the complete subject in your hands. Good encyclopedias make you feel really clever when you put them down because each article sums up, in an accessible way, the very latest research that is normally accessible only to the experts. Yet, you have grasped it. This is an encyclopedia of the atonement. It does not contain references to everything that has ever been said on the subject within theology, but it covers everything you really need to know, and does so exhaustively, yet simply. It is a compendium on the subject. You are not likely to be caught out on anything you should know if you have read this.

If you are not a beginning undergraduate student but are a postgraduate student or a beginning researcher of any kind, this book is for you. The only difference is that you do need to read the footnotes—and the bibliography. The footnotes have been designed to give you access to the very latest research in as exhaustive a way possible. And, if this book goes into further revisions, I fully intend to keep adding to that. For you, this book is a repository, a bibliographical resource.

It will also stimulate your thinking. Each major topic finishes with some pointers as to how the subject might be made to interact with contemporary culture or some other current issue in church life. This I hope will help you as your research idea starts to take shape. These concluding sections are signposts to further research rather than items of research in their own right.

Lastly (but not at all least), if you are not in academia but in ministry, and you have heard here and there that the atonement has suddenly—and perhaps for reasons that don't seem clear—become an issue of great controversy, this is for you. This book only very tentatively sketches out what my own conclusions are with regards to what is of merit in atonement theology and what is of rather less merit. Most books on the atonement that are coming out at the moment (thick and fast) are part of the controversy. They are polemical. This book tries to generate light rather than heat. It will equip you for debate and for the pulpit. It will not undermine your faith, it will strengthen it. You will be fed by reading the great thoughts of some great thinkers presented here. If you are in ministry then theology is all for you. We do what we do for you. The Christian academy itself is for your benefit and the benefit of your people. So read and be encouraged.

Now, for the parameters. With such a vast subject stretching out before us it seems especially important for me to point out what this book will not be. It will not, first of all, be a biblical survey of atonement theology. There are biblical metaphors of atonement and there are theological theories of atonement. This book deals with the latter. There are biblical authors who each show a particular emphasis in their treatment of the atonement and there are historical theologians who each had something valuable to say in their time. This book deals with the latter. It will exegete their writings using all the skills of a New Testament critic anxious that an author far removed from us in time and space be allowed to speak on their own terms to our situation. Where I do handle Scripture, it is through the lens of these historical theologians and their writings. In almost every case, I am looking at the way a theologian uses a biblical text, rather than analyzing it myself. For this reason, authors such as Frances Young, Martin Hengel, and John Vincent Taylor, who have all done some superb work on the atonement in Scripture, get barely a mention here. I do, however, harbor a strong ambition to eventually follow this book with one that will attempt a biblical theology of atonement. It is then that I will engage with those authors.

The second thing this book is not is that it is not a history of the doctrine of the atonement, but a history of *theories* of the atonement. Nevertheless, I hope it will be a useful update on the standard histories of the doctrine. It differs from them in that it does not survey all the theologians for what they say about the cross. Instead, it focuses on those theologians (and pastors) that have originated a theory of the atonement. Somebody once said that there are springs and there are lakes. Some theologians merely collect water—they are the lakes. Others have that spark of original-ity, that creative something or other that makes them innovators of new forms of theology—they are springs, and it is springs we are mostly looking at there. Lakes are important too, of course, for the way they make use of what the springs have generated, and these are certainly not ignored. Take Thomas Aquinas for instance. He is certainly a monumental theologian but, when it comes to atonement theory, he is a lake. Whereas John McLeod Campbell, though a much lesser light than Thomas when it comes to the atonement, he's a bit of a genius—and so was Irenaeus, Anselm, Abelard, Luther, Calvin, Grotius, Girard, and so on. What about Augustine? Same again: a giant, probably an even bigger one than Thomas, but not when it came to atonement theology. Now I know the dividing line is difficult, since to a large extent they are all lakes: they are all relying on what has gone before and adapting it. However, in some cases this adaptation led to the creation of a recognized new theory of the atonement, a new species (a newt from a fish); in other cases it only resulted in a new breed (a fancy koi from a dull carp).

So, if you are beginning theology or religious studies, or you are a postgraduate researcher, or you are in ministry, this is for you. May God's Spirit use it to help you in your task.

New Year's Day
2014

PART ONE

Christus Victor

THE FATHERS, FROM ORIGEN ONWARDS, are known for their crude meta-phors of fish-hooks and bait and their ideas about the devil having legal rights and being cheated by God and humankind being ransomed from the devil by the giving of Christ's life. Hand-in-hand with the ransom-to-Satan theory went the recapitulation theory. Briefly, this was the idea that Christ was the Second Adam, the new Head of humanity. He retraced the steps of Adam, successfully resisting sin and evil in all the ways that Adam failed to, culminating in the ultimate act of obedience: death on a cross. These ways of looking at the cross then fell out of vogue as Anselm's satisfaction theory, and various responses to it, took center stage from the medieval period onwards. But in the 1930s, the Swedish theologian Gustav Aulèn became enthralled with a view of Christ triumphant over demonic principalities and powers. Ever since his time, we call these patristic ideas the *Christus Victor* way of seeing the cross. More recently still, the ransom-to-Satan theory has been re-appropriated in differing ways in Word of Faith theol-ogy, in feminist theology, and by the emerging church movement. All these new developments are quite surprising and rather fascinating.

The main appeal of this *Christus Victor* view of Christ triumphant at the cross seems to be the motif of resisting evil, and in particular, the fact that Christ did so in a nonviolent way, not answering violence with violence, but rather disabling it with loving obedience. We have here the picture of a hero who has powerfully overcome humankind's worst enemies in the best possible way, and bids us all share in the spoils of his victory.

1

The ransom-to-Satan theory and the recapitulation theory also carry the kudos that comes from being the first ever reasonably well-developed theories of the atonement. This is massively appealing to those who point to the pre-Constantinian church—the church before Christendom—as the place where we should be learning all the lessons we will need as we try to adapt to post-Christendom. In these new contexts the classic ransom-to-Satan idea is never appropriated wholesale, and neither is the recapitulation idea, but in each case these adaptations seem to be all about a desire to move away from passive, defeatist, or austere ways of being human in favor of something more muscular and less individualistic.

This first chapter will look at the ransom-to-Satan theory specifically. It will examine the context in which the ransom-to-Satan theory first arose, and seek to determine why our contemporary context seems once again to be such a ready receptacle for it.

1

The Ransom to Satan

Origins 1: The Context

THE RANSOM-TO-SATAN THEORY AROSE FROM a profound awareness of evil. Not only were Christians, until 313 CE,[1] being systematically persecuted but, as McDonald observes:

> The condition of the Gentile world made such notions as bondage and release, captivity and ransom, more tragically familiar. . . . Everywhere economic terror and spiritual fear reigned and intertwined to make human life doubly miserable. Many were enduring bondage and slavery physically, but all were caught up in them spiritually.[2]

So conscious were the early Christians of the pervasiveness of Satanically inspired evil (see the book of Revelation) that they developed strong dualistic tendencies: God on one side, the devil on the other, and no neutral ground in between. This dualism in turn was fed by the now-thriving gnostic theories that were proving so popular as to almost swamp

---

1. This was the date of the so-called "Edict of Milan," which, among other things, secured a benevolent attitude towards Christians throughout the two halves of the Roman Empire (West and East).

2. McDonald, *The Atonement of the Death of Christ*, 138. Specifically, he cites "marauding gangs" who roamed about "capturing travelers and demanding payment for their release." McDonald, *The Atonement of the Death of Christ*, 139.

the church.[3] Gnosticism is described aptly by Franks as "like the cuckoo in the sparrow's nest."[4]

Gnosticism, a sprawling aggregate of somewhat extravagant beliefs, is divided into certain distinct groups. Grensted[5] claims two types—Valentinian and Marcionite—as the true source of the ransom-to-Satan theory. These types of Gnosticism tended to teach something like this: humankind is under the Demiurge. Some humans have the spark of a heavenly nature, and the goal is to free this spiritual inner self by means of enlightenment (gnosis). The inner self must be released from its bondage to matter. How? The revelation of the Logos from the heavenly world. The Logos, an important Greek philosophical idea, was the very mind of the supreme God, spoken out into the world. He alone could grant enlightenment to truly spiritual people and free them from their false attachment to all things material. But, even those who come from the heavenly world, such as the Logos, must not ignore the power of the Demiurge. The Demiurge was the evil demi-god that created this stultifying, unspiritual thing called matter in the first place. Further solution: the Logos must conform outwardly to material conditions. He must not reveal who he really is—like a king in disguise. Thus, the Demiurge is deceived by this outward conformity by which a totally cosmic Logos takes on the *appearance* of physical form in order to defeat the Demiurge and free all those that have the inner spark to be able to live a more spiritual existence.

The missing link between these gnostic ideas and the early Christian doctrine of a Ransom to Satan is a very surprising one. It appears that the very person who was one of the most outspoken early critics of Gnosticism actually borrowed quite extensively from their ideas. His name was Irenaeus (130–c.202 CE). Rashdall commented aptly on what was happening here: "Irenaeus simply substituted the devil for the Demiurge."[6] And even before Irenaeus came along, writers such as Justin Martyr were equating Jesus with the Greek Logos. Apart from these two slight changes to the leading characters, the drama remains very similar to the gnostic one. Thus, as the theory developed in Origen and Gregory of Nyssa, Christ is

---

3. Grensted, *A Short History of the Doctrine of the Atonement*, 34–35.

4. Franks, *A History of the Work of Christ* I, 16.

5. Grensted, *A Short History of the Doctrine of the Atonement*, 34–35.

6. Rashdall, *The Idea of Atonement in Christian Theology*, 245. Teselle, likewise is not shy of attributing to anti-heretical writers such as Theophilus, Irenaeus, and Hyppolytus the nasty habit of appropriating the very ideas they were writing against: TeSelle, "The Cross as Ransom," 158.

seen to take the form of a frail human delivered into the hands of the devil without the devil fully understanding that he had bitten off more than he could chew. He is deceived by outward appearances. The result is the devil's defeat and the liberation of Christ's people.

Franks points to the Marcionite gnostics as the first to use 1 Cor 2:8 (that those who crucified the Lord of glory would not have done so had they known who he was) as a New Testament precedent for the concept that the true God misleads the devil, a passage that would later be quoted very freely in patristic writings in support of the idea that God deceived the devil.[7] In fact, all forms of Gnosticism held in common the notion that Christ only *seemed* to be crucified. Basilides, a significant gnostic leader, has the real Christ standing by laughing while Simon of Cyrene is crucified by mistake due to Christ having engineering a deceptive change in Simon's appearance.[8] So the element of deception, of those crucifying Jesus being misled by appearances, is a prominent gnostic teaching that was, it seems, allowed to flow into the mainstream teaching of the church.[9]

Origins 2: Emergence

This way of looking at the atonement was soon favored by most of the Fathers, but in varying forms, some more crude than others. Irenaeus, Origen, Gregory of Nyssa, and Augustine[10] each develop the ransom-to-Satan theory in cruder and cruder forms. Two elements emerged progressively, especially from Origen onwards: one, as we have already seen, was that God deceived the devil and the other was that the devil's rights over humans were legitimate.

Irenaeus only tentatively introduced the idea that the ransom spoken of in the New Testament was in fact paid to the devil, and did not emphasize the idea that the devil had any legitimate rights over humans. Here is the very first suggestion of the theory. "Apostasy" here refers to Satan:

7. Franks, *A History of the Work of Christ* I, 15.

8. According to Irenaeus, *Against Heresies* 1:349.

9. Likewise, TeSelle believes that the ransom motif probably arose from within various heterodox groups that were preoccupied with the idea of Christ in disguise: TeSelle, "The Cross as Ransom," 157.

10. Augustine won't be discussed here, but see his *On the Trinity* 4.14.14; 5.13.19; and 4.14.18–19.

> And since the apostasy held unjust sway over us, and, though naturally we belonged to God Almighty, had estranged us from Him unnaturally, making us his own disciples, the all-powerful Word of God, who lacks not in His own righteousness, justly turned against that same apostasy, redeeming from it His own not by force, after the manner in which the devil had held sway over us at the first, greedily seizing what was not his own, but by persuasion, even as it befitted God to take what He wished by persuading and not by imposing force, so that there should neither be any infringement of justice, nor should God's ancient creation perish utterly.[11]

Irenaeus is clear that the devil is a usurper, having no rights. God must be in total control. Yet even with the usurper, God observes fair play.[12] Also, and crucially for recent feminist re-appropriations, Irenaeus "avoids mere external compulsion or blind force, even where He might legitimately be expected to use it."[13] Origen then takes Irenaeus' idea and adds his own emphasis:

> If then we were "bought with a price," as Paul asserts, we were doubtless bought from one whose servants we were, who also named what price he would for releasing those whom he held from his power. Now it was the devil that held us, to whose side we had been drawn away by our sins. He asked, therefore, as our price the blood of Christ.[14]

Of note is the addition, in Origen's *Commentary on Matthew*, of the notion that the devil was deceived in the transaction:

> The Evil One had been deceived and led to suppose that he was capable of mastering the soul, and did not see that to hold Him involved a trial of strength greater than he could successfully undertake.[15]

---

11. Irenaeus, *Against Heresies* V.1.1. "A certain justice forbade God to employ the methods characteristic of the devil." Grensted, *A Short History of the Doctrine of the Atonement*, 36.

12. Turner, *The Patristic Doctrine of Redemption*, 54.

13. Ibid.

14. Origen, *On Romans* II.13. Cited in Grensted, *A Short History of the Doctrine of the Atonement*, 37.

15. On Matt 25:1, 8. This is the earliest occurrence of the notion, aside from a passing reference in Ignatius' *Letter to the Ephesians*, 19. Turner, *The Patristic Doctrine of Redemption*, 55, n. 3.

In Gregory of Nyssa' *Great Catechetical Oration*, the whole idea of deceiving the devil seems to take over:

> In order to secure that the ransom in our behalf might be easily accepted by him who required it, the Deity was hidden under the veil of our nature, that so, as with ravenous fish, the hook of Deity might be gulped down along with the bait of flesh.[16]

The notion of needing to overtly deceive the devil increases in proportion to the perceived legitimacy of the devil's hold over man. The picture becomes progressively more dualistic: God only finally succeeds because of his superior intellect, and is unable to rightfully use his absolute power.

So, the ransom-to-Satan theory would appear to be the product firstly of the prevalence of gnostic beliefs. This naturally gave rise to the idea of a deception surrounding the death of Christ. Secondly, and rooted in a highly dualistic mindset that accorded considerable power to the devil/ Demiurge, the idea soon took shape that the devil *must* be deceived in this way. His rights were inviolable, even to the supreme God. Freedom for man under Satan's thralldom could only be bought, not taken. Thirdly, the Gospels of Mark (see Mark 10:45) and Matthew (see Matt 20:28) and most of the letters at that time attributed to Paul (see 1 Tim 2:6) were in wide circulation, and these speak of a ransom, though are silent on the matter of to whom the ransom was paid. This silence was doubtless very tempting to fill, though, were it not for the preceding two factors, it is doubtful that such an elaborate and successful theory of the atonement would ever have developed as a result of this temptation alone.

What is for certain is that the ransom-to-Satan way of understanding the atonement became so widespread that, by the time of the medieval period, it was to provoke Anselm into writing his *Cur Deus Homo?* out of sheer irritation with it. The longstanding popularity of the ransom-to-Satan theory is difficult to explain fully. It could be that the theory was needed theologically. The recapitulation theory (which we shall consider in the next chapter) made the death of Jesus climactic but dispensable. Some additional theory was needed that made the death of Jesus actually necessary. It is this theological necessity that possibly explains the survival for 900 years of a theory that seems quite flawed.

Aside from the medieval preoccupation with the harrowing of hell and with all things demonological, there followed, in the wake of Anselm, what

16. Gregory of Nyssa, *Great Catechism*, 24. He defends the divine deception with the claim that the end justifies the means: *Great Catechism* 5:495.

appears to be a great silence about the atonement themes that the Fathers had been so fond of, unless one concedes Aulén's point that Martin Luther principally held to a *Christus Victor* view.[17] At any rate, by the nineteenth century, it seems clear that the battle lines had fallen in a way that divided objective theories from subjective theories, satisfaction-substitution interpretations from morally transformative solutions, and, until Aulén came along, totally ignoring the third option of *Christus Victor*. To him we now turn.

Re-Appropriations 1: Mid-Twentieth-Century Forays

Aulén's Christus Victor

By the 1930s, while Europe was recovering from unprecedented military bloodshed and careering into unknown new worlds fashioned by increasingly powerful dictators and their ideologies, the patristic ways of looking at the cross took on a new value to the Swedish professor and bishop Gustav Aulén (1879–1977).[18] In 1930, he produced a book that was translated into English in 1931 under the title *Christus Victor*.[19] Ever since then, any view of Christ's death that holds it was primarily a victory over spiritual powers has tended to be termed a *Christus Victor* (Victorious Christ) view. Aulén essentially rewrote church history in favor of his view, claiming that it always was the "classic" view of the atonement. To argue that this was the case from the Fathers was straightforward enough. But to get around the overtly penal views of the atonement held during the Reformation, he had to claim that Luther himself held the *Christus Victor* view, and that, beginning with Luther's successor Melanchthon, this had been ignored by subsequent advocates of penal substitution. Aulén, not surprisingly, calls

17. John Calvin's Christology is also said to contain *Christus Victor* elements: Peterson, *Calvin's Doctrine of the Atonement*, 46–54.

18. Postwar too: "In the wake of Auschwitz and Hiroshima the notion that malevolent forces twist and pervert relations among nations and persons, spawning countless forms of sin, began to sound strangely plausible." Finger, "Pilgram Marpeck and the Christus Victor Motif," 54.

19. Originally titled, *Den kristna försoningstanken* (The Christian Idea of the Atonement), this was published in 1930 in the wake his series of lectures that were delivered in Upsala that same year. The English translation appeared in 1931: *Christus Victor: An Historical Study of the Three Main Types of the Idea of Atonement.*

into question all subsequent scholarship, urging a return to the classic view of the Fathers and Luther.

Serious theological reflection on the patristic doctrine of the atonement dates back to the origins of the discipline of historical theology itself, with a number of historical theologians including significant discussion of the origins and development of the ransom to Satan,[20] culminating in 1919 with Hastings Rashdall writing one of the most scathing treatments of the ransom-to-Satan theory that would ever be written.[21] Complementing the offerings of the historical theology tradition came a serious treatment of the patristic theory from the Anglican Nathaniel Dimock.[22] The trio of British historians of the atonement: Franks,[23] Grensted,[24] and (much later) McDonald,[25] summarize helpfully the findings of the earlier Continental historians of dogma, but add nothing new to the discussion. The contributions of the late nineteenth and early twentieth centuries were important in producing a body of critical reflection on the history of the theory sufficient to bring it to the attention of a new generation of theologians at mid century.

Not until Bishop Gustav Aulén's Olaus Petri Lectures of 1930 was there any serious attempt at a contemporary re-appropriation of the doctrine. Until him, the ransom-to-Satan is treated entirely as a historical curio. Further treatments of the doctrine that were of this kind would yet appear,[26] but it seems that there was no going back from this point. Within a few decades, discussions in articles of the *Christus Victor* model from a great

---

20. Seeberg, *Lehrbuch der Dogmengeschichte* Vol. 1 (Originally 1898) English translation: *Text-Book of the History of Dogma*; Harnack, *History of Dogma* Vol. 2, 367–68; Loofs, *Leitfaden zum Studien der Dogmengeschichte*; Riviere, *Le dogme de la Redemption*.

21. Rashdall, *The Christian Idea of Atonement*.

22. Dimock, *The Doctrine of the Death of Christ*.

23. Franks, *A History of the Work of Christ* I.

24. Grensted, *A Short History of the Doctrine of the Atonement*.

25. McDonald, *The Atonement of the Death of Christ*.

26. Most notably, Turner, *Patristic Doctrine of the Atonement*.

variety of perspectives appeared,[27] especially after the American edition of the book went to press in 1951.[28]

In 1953, Dillistone[29] persuasively added his advocacy of a *Christus Victor* approach as the one most in line with the general tenor of salvation history in both Old and New Testaments. John Macquarrie also lent his weight.[30] Volume 2 of Paul Tillich's *Systematic Theology,* appearing in 1957, broke new ground in re-appropriating *Christus Victor* categories in the service of his existentialist vision of the Christian faith.[31] Oscar Cullman also gave some support.[32]

27. Firstly, and not surprisingly given Aulen's radical reinterpretation of Luther, there came a Lutheran response in 1957: Evenson, "A Critique of Aulen's *Christus Victor Concordia Theological* Monthly," (and later, in 1972, Peters, "The Atonement in Anselm and Luther, Second Thoughts about Aulen's *Christus Victor,*"); then, in 1961, from an Anglo-Catholic perspective, came Fairweather, "Incarnation and Atonement: An Anselmian Response to Aulen's *Christus Victor.*" In 1975 there appeared a study around *Christus Victor* and J. S. Bach: Naylor, "Bach's Interpretation of the Cross" (and later, Stapert, "Christus Victor: Bach's *St. John Passion,*"). In 1979, *Christus Victor* and youth work were juxtaposed: Espy, "In Celebration of Amsterdam 1939." In 1982 came a Roman Catholic response: Heath, "Salvation: A Roman Catholic Perspective," and from an Anglican perspective came Loewe, "Irenaeus' Soteriology: *Christus Victor* Revisited" (1985), and more recently, Ovey, "Appropriating Aulén? Employing *Christus Victor* Models of the Atonement" (2010). Colin Gunton engaged with the model in his "*Christus Victor* Revisited: A Study in Metaphor and the Transformation of Meaning" (1985) and in his book *The Actuality of Atonement* (1988), especially 57–58. Rather more recently has come a series of Mennonite responses: Weaver, "*Christus Victor*, Ecclesiology and Christology" (1994), and Weaver, "Some Theological Implications of *Christus Victor*" (1994), and, in response to Weaver, Thomas Finger's, "*Christus Victor* and the Creeds: Some Historical Considerations" (1998), Finger, "Pilgrim Marpek and the *Christus Victor* Motif" (2004), and Finger, *A Contemporary Anabaptist Theology* (2004). From a Nazarene perspective came Greathouse, "Sanctfication and the *Christus Victor* Motif in Wesleyan Theology" (2003). In 2005, Brad Harper explored the potential place of *Christus Victor* within contemporary culture: "*Christus Victor*, Postmodernism and the Shaping of Atonement Theology." Finally, 2008 brought a Brethren response to Weaver's particular version of *Christus Victor*: Eisenbise. "Resurrection as Victory? The eschatological implications of J. Denny Weaver's 'Narrative *Christus Victor*' Model of the Atonement."

28. Aulen, *Christus Victor: A Study of the Three Main Types of the Idea of Atonement.* New York: Macmillan, 1951. Boersma goes as far as to say that the "earlier publication of Aulén's work in 1931 was an isolated occurrence." Boersma, *Violence, Hospitality and the Cross*, 194, n. 52.

29. Dillistone, "A Biblical and Historical Appraisal of Theories of the Atonement," 185–95.

30. Macquarrie, "Demonology and the Classic Idea of the Atonement," 5–6, 60–63.

31. Tillich, *Systematic Theology,* Vol. II, 197–98.

32. Cullman, *Christ and Time*, 193.

Next, in apparent isolation from the still growing *Christus Victor* debate, there arose within the Neo-Pentecostalism of the 1970s, an extraordinarily dramatic and, at times, grotesque view of the atonement that utilized the patristic belief in a descent into Hades as a key component in the defeat of Satan.[33] The *Christus Victor* view was also found to speak to liberation theology better than other models of the atonement.[34] Darby Kathleen Ray,[35] taking her cue from Paul Fiddes,[36] adapted and demythologized the ransom to Satan for the feminist argument. She was followed by J. Denny Weaver, who, during the 1990s, began to recognize the nonviolent appeal of the model. He applied a similar re-appropriation to black and womanist contexts, culminating in his *The Nonviolent Atonement*.[37] Eugene TeSelle, in his short but significant work, also retrieved the model in the interests of social and political justice.[38] More recently still, the emerging church movement favors a transition from penal substitution to *Christus Victor* as the preferred model.[39] Other evangelical responses have also continued to flow steadily.[40] It is to the first appearance of this new paradigm in modern theology that I will now turn in more detail.

Gunton's critique was among the more serious treatments.[41] He saw the following as a passage that captures the heart of Aulén's understanding of the *Christus Victor* view:

> This type of view may be described provisionally as the "dramatic."
> Its central theme is the idea of the Atonement as a Divine conflict
> and victory; Christ—Christus Victor—fights against and triumphs
> over the evil powers of the world, the "tyrants" under which

33. Analyzed most recently by Atkinson, "A Theological Appraisal of the Doctrine that Jesus Died Spiritually, as Taught by Kenyon, Hagin and Copeland."

34. Maimela, "The Atonement in the Context of Liberation Theology," 45–54.

35. Ray, *Deceiving the Devil: Atonement, Abuse and Ransom*. Similarly: Megill-Cobbler, "A Feminist Rethinking of Punishment Imagery in Atonement," 14–20.

36. Fiddes, *Past Event and Present Salvation*.

37. Weaver, *The Nonviolent Atonement*, see also his "Narrative *Christus Victor*: The Answer to Anselmian Atonement Violence."

38. TeSelle, "The Cross as Ransom," 147–70.

39. Greg Boyd, popular within the emerging church movement, is coauthor of Boyd, et al., *The Nature of the Atonement: Four Views*, and *God at War: The Bible and Spiritual Conflict*. He has also named his ministry "Christus Victor Ministries."

40. Dembele, "Salvation as Victory"; Blocher, "Agnus Victor: The Atonement as Victory and Vicarious Punishment."

41. Gunton, *The Actuality of Atonement*, esp. 57–58.

mankind is in bondage and suffering, and in Him reconciles the world to Himself.[42]

Gunton's two main concerns are, firstly, that Aulén's view needs to be extended from a mythology of a past event into something of ongoing significance. Paul speaks of an ongoing life of victory that is available to believers (Rom 8:37). Aulén seems content with a mere "story of the gods."[43] However, in Aulén's defense, he claims in his closing paragraphs that his purpose in writing the book had not been "apologetic" but "historical."[44] He claims that his primary intention was not to advance the theory as something that should ongoingly inform contemporary praxis, though he clearly believed that it should. Aulén concludes thus:

> I am persuaded that no form of Christian teaching has any future before it except such as can keep steadily in view the reality of evil in the world, and go to meet the evil with a battle-song of triumph. Therefore I believe that the classic idea of the Atonement and of Christianity is coming back—that is to say, the genuine, authentic Christian faith.[45]

Secondly, according to Gunton, Aulén is too triumphalistic, not taking into account "the human and even tragic elements in the story."[46] These two observations, namely, that the model is too dualistic and mythological and, arising out of this very other worldliness of the theory, that it fails to acknowledge tragedy and suffering both in the gospel narrative itself and in human life generally, recur in the critiques surrounding *Christus Victor*. The prevalence of human suffering today provokes questions as to the nature of the alleged victory over evil. Yet, despite these obvious difficulties, this

---

42. Aulén, *Christus Victor*, 20.

43. Gunton, *Actuality of Atonement*, 57.

44 Aulén's closing caveat does not appear to have been persuasive for most reviewers however, e.g., Boersma: "It is clear that Aulén feels that we need a return to the Christus Victor theme . . ." Boersma, *Violence, Hospitality and the Cross*, 182, a fact that Boersma clearly agrees with: ibid., 181–82.

45. Aulén, *Christus Victor*, 176.

46. Gunton, *The Actuality of Atonement*, 58. He is similarly accused of being too "monergistic," making salvation into the work of God alone to the point of effectively denying the full humanity of Christ in docetic fashion: Boersma, *Violence, Hospitality and the Cross*, 185, who also cites Fairweather, "Incarnation and Atonement: An Anselmian Response to Aulén's Christus Victor," 161–75, and Dembele, "Salvation as Victory," 65–66 in support. Boersma also calls for a more participatory element to Aulén's model: Boersma, *Violence, Hospitality and the Cross*, 185.

approach is gaining popularity. The decline of Enlightenment naturalism is often named, and very plausibly, as a factor that has allowed a resurgence of interest in, and belief in, the existence of supernatural evil powers at work in the world.[47] This adds greatly to the credibility of a cosmic victory over such powers, however incomplete the mopping up operation.

Tillich's Christus Victor

Paul Tillich also would be among those who, mid-century, made some preliminary forays into a re-appropriation of the patristic model. This was not to say that Tillich was especially favorable to the patristic doctrine in its original forms; he describes Origen's depictions as "almost a comedy."[48] He understood the world of early Christianity to be one that was steeped in fear of demonic powers from which people were in need of liberation. Life was filled with a fear that he describes as existential estrangement: "Without the experience of the conquest of existential estrangement, the *Christus Victor* symbol never could have arisen either in Paul or in Origen."[49]

Tillich's analysis of *Christus Victor* as part of a conversation between the questions of philosophy and the answers of theology anticipate the very recent efforts on the part of emerging church advocates to re-contextualize the model within postmodernity.

Re-Appropriations 2: The Late Twentieth Century

Word of Faith Christus Victor

Fundamental to Word of Faith theology is the belief that man came under the authority of Satan at the fall. Salvation therefore, had to involve a decisive blow to Satan's dominion. The consequent re-titling of man with a renewed authority over creation, and over Satan himself, is commonly

---

47. Boersma, *Violence, Hospitality and the Cross*, 193–94, who cites in support, Aulén, Christus Victor (1951 ed.), 7–15, Boyd, *God at War*, 61–72, and Dembele, "Salvation as Victory," 12. So Weaver, who notes that, "cosmic and demonic imagery" had been, "incompatible with a modern world view." Weaver, "Atonement for the NonConstantinian Church," 307.

48. Tillich, *Systematic Theology* Vol. II, 198.

49. Ibid.

appropriated via various spiritual warfare strategies.[50] However, the Word of Faith theory of the atonement goes significantly beyond this basic understanding and envisages a highly dramatic showdown between Jesus and the devil in hell.

William Atkinson's PhD is the first major analysis of the atonement in Word of Faith teaching.[51] As with all other aspects of Word of Faith teaching,[52] the genealogy of the Word of Faith view of the atonement is traceable to the nineteenth-century New England preacher and prolific writer, E. W. Kenyon.[53] He, in turn, appears to have been influenced at least by Irenaeus, and possibly by other patristic writings.[54] From Kenyon, Kenneth Hagin[55] and then Kenneth Copeland[56] derived all their leading ideas. At the heart of the Word of Faith concept of the atonement is the "Jesus Died Spiritually" (JDS) idea, a doctrine so controversial as to have aroused some opposition from within the Word of Faith movement itself.[57] On this view, the substitutionary nature of Christ's death is taken to dramatic extremes, with the notion being introduced that, if the sin-nature in man is at its core satanic, then Christ must have taken on himself a satanic nature on the cross.[58] This was what caused him to die spiritually, that is, to be cut

50. Scholarly treatments of spiritual warfare include: Carr, *Angels and Principalities*; Wink, *Naming the Powers*; Walker, *Enemy Territory*; Wright, *The Fair Face of Evil*; Guelich, "Spiritual Warfare: Jesus, Paul and Peretti"; Arnold, *Powers of Darkness*; Hiebert, *Anthropological Reflections on Missiological Issues*, 203–15; Walker, "The Devil You Think You Know," *3 Crucial Questions about Spiritual Warfare*; Ellis, *Raising the Devil*.

51. William Atkinson, "Theological Appraisal." It is also available as a book: *The Death of Jesus: A Pentecostal Investigation*. An earlier version of part of the work has also appeared in the *Evangelical Review of Theology*: Atkinson, "The Nature of the Crucified Christ in Word-Faith Teaching."

52. See my "What the Faith Teachers Mean by 'Faith,'" for an analysis of the faith concept.

53. Three books of his are significant: *What Happened from the Cross to the Throne*, *Identification: A Romance in Redemption*, and, *The Wonderful Name of Jesus*.

54. Atkinson, "Theological Appraisal," 227–28.

55. See his, *The Name of Jesus*, *Authority of the Believer*, and his *El Shaddai*.

56. Especially his *Jesus Died Spiritually* and his *Jesus in Hell*.

57. Freeman, *Did Jesus Die Spiritually? Exposing the JDS Heresy*.

58. Man apparently must, "partake either of God's nature or of Satan's nature," Kenyon, *The Bible in the Light of Our Redemption*, 28. See also, Dan McConnell's appraisal: "Spiritual death is thus 'a nature,' leading to a 'new Satanic creation.'" McConnell, *The Promise of Health and Wealth*, 118, citing Kenyon, *The Bible in the Light of Our Redemption*, 28. Likewise Hagin: "Spiritual death means having Satan's nature." Hagin, *Redemption*, 29.

off from God. But not only was he cut off from God, he descended into hell, where, as the bearer now of a satanic nature, he was required to "serve time."[59] Satan mistakenly thought he had the Son of God in his grasp. I will let Hagin tell the rest:

> I'm certain that all the devils of hell raced up and down the back alleys of hell rejoicing, "We've got the Son of God in our hands! We've defeated God's purpose!" But on that third morning, the God who is more than enough said, "It is enough! He has satisfied the claims of justice."[60]

Copeland is still more theatrical as he describes the climactic moment:

> the power of the Almighty God began to stream down from heaven and break the locks off the gates of hell. . . . Jesus began to stir. The power of heaven penetrated and re-created His spirit. He rose up and in a moment of super conquest, He kicked the daylights out of the devil and all those who were doing his work. . . . Then Jesus came up out of that place of torment in triumph, went back through the tomb, into His body, and walked out of there.[61]

This version of events clearly falls within the *Christus Victor* tradition, but the extent to which it resembles the patristic ransom-to-Satan theories has been the subject of some debate.[62] The dissimilarities, according to Atkinson, are these:

1. Nowhere in these writings is the atonement referred to as a ransom. There is no concept that anything was paid to the devil. Instead, as we saw from the extracts, it is God's justice that is satisfied in true penal substitutionary fashion.

59. Fred Price, writing in his *Ever Increasing Faith Messenger*. The most reliable citation of this seems to be that it was June 1980 (page 7), quoted in McConnell, *The Promise of Health and Wealth*, 120. Original source not found. The saying attributed to him is this: "Do you think that the punishment for our sin was to die on a cross? If that were the case, the two thieves could have paid our price. No, the punishment was to go into hell itself and to serve time in hell separated from God." Of some interest on this subject is Grudem, "He Did Not Descend into Hell."

60. Hagin, *El Shaddai*, 7.

61. Copeland, "The Gates of Hell Shall Not Prevail," 4–7. I am indebted to Atkinson for both of these extraordinary extracts.

62. According to Atkinson, those who stress the similarities include: Perriman, *Faith, Health and Prosperity*, 115; McConnell, *The Promise of Health and Wealth*, 119, 125–26; Smail et al., "'Revelation Knowledge' and Knowledge of Revelation"; DeArteaga, *Quenching the Spirit*, 240, 270–71; Spencer, *Heresy Hunters*, 102. Emphasizing the differences there is a mere footnote in Hannegraaff, *Christianity in Crisis*, 395 n. 2.

2. The location of Christ's victory over the devil is hell. In the patristic theories, there is a descent into hell, which is understood to be plundered by Jesus, yet the moment of victory occurs on the cross itself.[63]

Feminist Christus Victor: Darby Kathleen Ray

One of the biggest surprises has been that a view of the cross that is so triumphalistic should make its appeal within the last twenty years to feminism. Darby Kathleen Ray has been the strongest advocate of this feminist re-appropriation of the patristic view of the atonement.[64] Its attraction to her appears to be the fact that, on this view—and this is especially noticeable in Irenaeus, whom she references a lot—God demonstrates for us the ultimate nonviolent resistance of evil. Even though God is almighty, he chooses, Narnia style,[65] to enter into negotiations with the enemy and set humankind free from the power of evil by observing the rights ceded to it by human sin.

Even the later developments of the ransom theory from Origen and Gregory of Nyssa onwards, in which the deception of Satan is overtly included, seem not to present a stumbling block to Ray. It is in such patristic authors that the metaphors so despised by Rashdall appear: Christ is the bait concealing the hook of divinity that catches the satanic fish (Gregory of Nyssa's *Greater Catechism*, 24), or the unjust crucifixion of Christ is bait on a divine mousetrap that snaps shut with Christ's vindication (Augustine's *Sermon*, 263), or the satanic bird is caught in the net of Christ's passion (Gregory the Great's *Commentary on Job*, 33.15).[66] Yet these images seem not to present a stumbling block to Ray. She claims that, "All were metaphorical attempts to express the conviction that the powers of evil were

63. Atkinson, "Theological Appraisal," 225–26.

64. She is at the moderate end of a scale that, at its most radical, despairs of any existing soteriology that is relevant to women: Storkey, "Atonement and Feminism," 227–28. From a similar perspective, see also Houts, "Classical Atonement Imagery," 1–6. Darby Kathleen Ray is given a very positive review by evangelicals Joel Green and Mark Baker, *Recovering the Scandal of the Cross*, 171–83. Much cooler is Boersma's treatment in *Violence, Hospitality and the Cross*, 196–99. Besides feminism, Ray also speaks to Latin American liberation issues with eloquence: "Together [Christ conquering and conquered], these two sides of the same christological coin feed the violence of the few and the passivity of the many." Ray, *Deceiving the Devil*, 88.

65. See Charles Taliaferro, "A Narnian Theory of the Atonement."

66. Rashdall, *The Idea of Atonement in Christian Theology*, 241–310.

defeated at the moment of their apparent victory, and that, paradoxically, Christ was triumphant at the moment of his defeat on the cross."[67]

Ray's crucial move as she attempts to retrieve the patristic theory is to demythologize and broaden the concept of a ransom paid to the devil into a ransom paid to evil. She takes her cue from Paul Fiddes' work, *Past Event and Present Salvation.*[68] Fiddes wrestles with the question of just how, in the face of so much present day evil, we can claim that a comprehensive victory has been won, or even that a turning point in the war has been reached, as had been Aulén's claim. He begins to answer this by more clearly identifying the "tyrants" that held humankind so that we then understand in what realm, from God's viewpoint, that victory is meant to have been won. For Fiddes, there are three tyrants, all taken from Paul's letters: sin, the law, and death. And it is this move away from a victory over demons into a theory resting on a victory over less mythological and more specific evils that seems to have caught Ray's eye.

However, her broadening of the concept into a general evil threatens to lead her into a corner where she could be accused, in an age rampant with evil, of a totally fictitious victory. This she anticipates by emphasizing the volitional element. We have all given evil permission to reign whenever we have failed to resist it. In the case of women, this is the failure to assert oneself, which is understood to be just as serious a sin as the more masculine sin of pride that traditional depictions of the cross are intended to address. It is not want of humility, she argues, that is the thing that needs atoning for in women—at least not typically. It is want of self-assertion. She cites a Methodist set prayer that emphasizes obedience, saying, "Prayers such as this one, though seemingly innocuous, inscribe their petitioners with an ideology of quietude that treats resistance to authority as a shameful transgression."[69] Using this female kind of sin, on the one hand, and the male kind of sin, "the unjust or avaricious use of power,"[70] on the other,

---

67. Ray, *Deceiving the Devil*, 121.

68. Fiddes, *Past Event and Present Salvation*, especially 115–24.

69. Ray, *Deceiving the Devil*, 25. Storkey sums up the view of many feminist theologians in saying that all that is involved with Christ being a sacrificial victim "leaves women anchored in their own victim status which is justified and romanticized as identification with the Savior." Storkey, "Atonement and Feminism," 231. In a similar vein is Rita Nakashima Brock: "The shadow of the punitive father must always lurk behind the atonement. He haunts images of forgiving grace." Brock, "And a Little Child will lead Us," 53.

70. Ray, *Deceiving the Devil*, 121.

as definitive of evil, she is then in a position to disable the main objection to the ransom to Satan theory, namely that it presupposes that the devil has rights. In her version, there is no devil and there are no rights to bestow upon him. Evil, however, has been given great power by both men and women, such that it "seems to take on a life of its own."[71] We have given evil its rights by not resisting it. Evil is thus depersonalized, but then begins to be re-personified as a power that, in citing Irenaeus, "transgresses all boundaries."[72] Her ideas are summed up in the following appraisal of Irenaeus. She agrees with his conviction that:

> in the person of Jesus, God has acted not only to reveal the true nature of evil but also to decenter and delegitimate its authority by luring it into exposing its own moral bankruptcy and thus defeating itself, hence opening up the possibility for human beings to escape enslavement to evil.[73]

She identifies the weaknesses of the patristic view as the following: firstly, it is too dualistic. By this she means that it implies a moral, over-simplistic, self-justifying dualism that demonizes certain groups. Definitions of good and evil are too clear-cut.[74] Secondly, it is too cosmic. Humans are passive and irresponsible. It is susceptible of a comic-book superhero interpretation.[75] Lastly, it is too triumphalistic. The patristic view portrays the victory as a done deal, whereas, "the suggestion that good has defeated evil, even from an eschatological perspective, seems impossible to confirm."[76]

Broadening the Appeal: Wink, Weaver, and Nonviolent Atonement

Pre-dating Ray, but not significantly influencing atonement theory until more recently, has been the celebrated work of Walter Wink. His most influential work was his *The Powers* trilogy,[77] which was a ground-breaking

71. Ray, *Deceiving the Devil*, 122.

72. Ibid., 123, endnote 13, citing *Against Heresies* V 21.2 and V 21.112.

73. Ray, *Deceiving the Devil*, 123. Similarly, TeSelle gives an important insight into what the cross does to the abuse of power. He defines the abuse of power as "overstepping one's authority and consequently being discredited." TeSelle, "The Cross as Ransom," 161.

74. Ray, *Deceiving the Devil*, 126–27.

75. Ibid., 126–28.

76. Ibid., 28.

77. *Naming the Powers* (1984), *Unmasking the Powers* (1986), *Engaging the Powers* (1992).

re-assessment of the Pauline concept of principalities and powers. With Aulén having already used "powers" language in his work, and with New Testament demonology already having received fresh scholarly and popular attention, the stage was set for Wink's work to make a significant and lasting impact. The last book, *Engaging the Powers* (1992), the biggest and best of his trilogy, had an especially lasting impact upon North American theology. In America, the Historic Peace Churches,[78] in particular, have contributed a significant amount of literature that has at its heart a marriage between a Winkian view of satanic evil as systemic (that is, rooted in human systems, e.g., oppressive governments, multinational corporations, some forms of popular culture), and a *Christus Victor* view of atonement. The *Christus Victor* approach has, for Peace Church scholars, the added appeal of being pre-Constantinian in origin, the advent of Christendom being seen as an especially disastrous turn of events by Christians within this tradition.

Wink himself portrayed the *Christus Victor* model as a nonviolent theory of the atonement that unmasks systemic evil:

> They scourged him with whips, but with each stroke of the lash their own legitimacy was laid open. They mocked him with a robe and a crown of thorns, spit on him, struck him on the head with a reed, and ridiculed him with the ironic ovation, "Hail, King of the Jews!"—not knowing that their acclamation would echo down the centuries. They stripped him naked and crucified him in humiliation, all unaware that this very act had stripped them of the last covering that disguised the towering wrongness of the whole way of living that their violence defended.[79]

The cross is thus "the ultimate paradigm of nonviolence."[80] The effect of this unmasking of systemic violence disseminates across the world, re-sensitizing humanity to its own propensities towards this kind of evil: "Killing Jesus was like trying to destroy a dandelion seed-head by blowing on it. It was like shattering a sun into a million fragments of light."[81] Wink is able to harmonize the gospel of the cross with the gospel of the kingdom: "The

---

78. Specifically these are the Mennonites, the Quakers (see Vail, "Theorising a Quaker View of the Atonement." George Fox is thought to have held to a *Christus Victor* view: 113; see also Freiday, "'Atonement' in Historical Perspective"), and the Church of the Brethren.

79. Walter Wink, *Engaging the Powers*, 139.

80. Ibid., 141.

81. Ibid., 143.

reign of God means the complete and definitive elimination of every form of violence between individuals and nations."[82] Here is how it works:

> Only by being driven out by violence could God signal to humanity that the divine is nonviolent and is antithetical to the Kingdom of Violence.[83]

And further:

> And because he was not only innocent, but the very embodiment of true religion, true law, and true order, this victim exposed their violence for what it was: not the defense of society, but an attack against God.[84]

Another writer who is attracted to the notion of nonviolent resistance in the patristic models is the Mennonite J. Denny Weaver.[85] In his work he takes up the cause not only of feminists but also of black[86] and womanist theologians. He also sides clearly with the primitivism of Anabaptist churchmanship by drawing parallels between the post-Christian West and the pre-Constantine church in which *Christus Victor* views of atonement held sway.[87]

His particular theory is, "narrative Christus Victor," by which he means, "Christus Victor depicted in the realm of history."[88] Reflecting on the book of Revelation, he explains that narrative Christus Victor is, "The historical framework of emperors and the construct of church confronting

---

82. Ibid., 149.

83. Ibid., referencing Réné Girard, *Things Hidden from the Foundation of the World*, 129.

84. Wink, *Engaging the Powers*, 140.

85. Weaver, *The Nonviolent Atonement*. This book is most rigorously critiqued from within the Mennonite movement by Peter Martens, "The Quest for an Anabaptist Atonement," 281–311.

86. See also James Cone, *God of the Oppressed*, 131–32. Black liberation theology seemingly frowns upon all models of the atonement, but least so when it comes to the patristic ransom approach: Maimela, "Atonement in the Context of Liberation Theology," 50. For an interesting discussion of the cross and African-American Christians from the lynching period onwards see Yong and Alexander, eds., *Afro-Pentecostalism*, chapter 6.

87. "It is the modern 'post-Christian generation' which has rediscovered Christus Victor. That is, the renewal of attention to this view of atonement has come at a time when the western world is starting to be aware of the disintegration of the Constantinian synthesis." Weaver, "Atonement for the NonConstantinian Church," 316.

88. Weaver, *Nonviolent Atonement*, 25.

empire."[89] He further claims that the Gospels fit Revelation in this regard, reinforcing this "universal and cosmic story of the confrontation of reign of God and rule of Satan."[90]

> Narrative Christus Victor is indeed atonement if one means a story in which the death and resurrection of Jesus definitively reveal the basis of power in the universe, so that the invitation from God to participate in God's rule . . . overcomes the forces of sin and reconciles sinners to God.[91]

Weaver understands the devil to be not a literal person but an accumulation of evil within human institutions, organizations, and cultures. These are the "principalities and powers" that Paul speaks of. Chief of these was the accumulation of evils that conspired to kill Jesus. Christ's nonviolent resistance towards such abusive powers is good news for victims of abuse today:

> When Jesus confronts the rule of evil . . . there is no longer the difficulty of a problematic image for victims of abuse. Jesus depicted in narrative Christus Victor is no passive victim. He is an active participant in confronting evil.[92]

Re-Appropriations 3: The Present Time

Emerging Christus Victor

Though anticipated by earlier movements elsewhere in the English-speaking world,[93] from the late 1990s in America there arose a scattered movement that sought to deconstruct modernist ways of being church in favor of a wholesale adoption of postmodernism by the church.[94] A leading

89. Ibid., 27.

90. Ibid., 34.

91. Ibid., 45–46.

92. Ibid., 211–12.

93. For instance, the now discredited "Nine O'Clock Service" in the UK.

94. The earliest significant work was Robert Webber's, *Ancient-Future Faith* (1999). He recommends a return to the *Christus Victor* approach on pages 43–61. Attracting far more attention, however, was Brian McLaren's, *A New Kind of Christian* of 2001. A fairly reactionary appraisal of the movement has come from Don Carson: *Becoming Conversant with the Emerging Church*. The most recent assessment of it is Bielo, *Emerging Evangelicals* (2011).

light has been Brian McLaren, whose interest mostly lies in deconstructing North American evangelical churchmanship. A typical result of this style of deconstruction on atonement theology has been what has recently been termed the kaleidoscopic view of the atonement[95]—a commitment-free embrace of all ways of looking at the atonement.[96]

Leading the way in theological reflection on behalf of the emerging church movement has been Greg Boyd. He is distinct in his attempt to offer some positive alternatives to traditional evangelicalism. While McLaren is known more for his relentless and provocative criticism of evangelical orthodoxy, Boyd attempts something more constructive. He is insistent that, while diversity in atonement theology should be celebrated, there is an underlying and unified reality to it that repays careful study.[97] He presents a convincing case for the fundamentally cosmic and demonological context in which salvation in both Testaments is understood.[98] In a nuanced way, he is even able to support from Scripture the patristic notions of God deceiving the devil, and successfully retrieves the notion from its notorious crudity.[99] He does this by ingeniously appealing to the fact that, while demons crying out clearly understood who Jesus was, they were seemingly not aware (as in 1 Cor 2:8) of why he came since their evil blinded them to the sacrificial love that had sent the Son into their realm.

Via the emerging church, the *Christus Victor* approach promises to speak to a new generation of churchgoers who are conscious as never before of pernicious global evils to which more individualistic versions of the gospel message seem to have few answers. However, it is significant that the leaders of the emerging church movement are classic "Gen-Xers," characterized by distrust of authority and established social structures. The

95. Boyd et al., *The Nature of the Atonement*, chapter 4. Rob Bell's *Love Wins*, 121–57, is a typical example. See also Schmiechen, *Saving Power*, and Burnhope's critique of this approach: "Beyond the Kaleidoscope."

96. Boyd, "Christus Victor View," in Boyd et al., *The Nature of the Atonement: Four Views*, 24.

97. "[T]he biblical narrative could in fact be accurately described as a story of God's ongoing conflict with and ultimate victory over cosmic and human agents who oppose him and who threaten his creation." Boyd, "Christus Victor View," 25. Also, "Everything the New Testament says about the soteriological significance of Christ's work is predicated on the cosmic significance of his work." Boyd, "Christus Victor View," 34.

98. "[H]e truth embodied in the most ancient ways of thinking about the atonement was that God did, in a sense, deceive Satan and the powers, and that Jesus was, in a sense, bait."

99. Boyd, "Christus Victor View," 36–38.

generation succeeding them, often termed the "Millennials" (because they were born within the two decades or so before the year 2000), are much less prone to deconstruction and much more concerned with connectedness.[100] It remains to be seen whether the other major facet to patristic atonement theology—the participation in Christ—will prove popular amongst them.

Summary and Evaluation

All of the views considered in this chapter can be summed up by saying that the cross is here seen as a victory over evil, often either personified as the devil or as other equally personal powers that are in perpetual antipathy towards God and his rule.

This evil is dealt with either by:

1. Undoing its basis. The patristic theories understand man as having come under the authority of the devil or under the thralldom of corruptibility. A ransom is paid to buy off the devil's claims. The emerging church retrieval makes use of this original patristic understanding that evil somehow implodes and defeats itself at the cross. Evil, through its ignorance of the Son's mission, oversteps the mark and is forced to relinquish its claims.

2. Nonviolently resisting it. This is the feminist take on the patristic theory that takes note of the way in which the devil is overcome in the ransom theory. He is not overcome by force, even though it lies within God's power to do so. God instead stoops to overcome the devil's hold on humankind in a nonviolent way that honors claims made by the devil however legitimate or otherwise these are. This amplifies the element identified above of evil defeating itself.

3. Taking power from it. This is the Word of Faith understanding, which shares the fundamental patristic starting point, namely, that humans surrendered their authority to the devil at the fall. From that time the devil has held a legal right over humanity and over what was intended as humanity's domain: creation. With this understanding of the

---

100. The classic text so far on Millennials is Howe and Strauss, *Millennials Rising*. See also a Christian take on the subject: Rainer and Rainer, *The Millennials*. For a critique of generational approaches in popular Christian writings see Hilborn and Bird, *God and the Generations*.

problem, the cross and resurrection are construed as a dethroning of the devil and an enthronement of born-again man.

A number of things may be seen as having conspired to bring the victory motif in from the cold within Christian reflection, both at an academic and a practitioner level. Firstly, the existence of systemic evil attaching itself to ideologies and governments to the point of bringing about two world wars has made a cosmic understanding of evil much more imaginable than it could have been before the twentieth century. Secondly, advances in biblical theology have allowed us to see that the Bible itself was all along infused with this kind of a worldview, so that whatever we understand salvation by the cross to be, it must fit in with this framework in order to be exegetically credible, before we even begin to apply such insights to the church or the life of faith. Thirdly, the retreat of Christianity from public life and sociopolitical privilege has inevitably spawned religious radicalism, such as that found within the Word of Faith movement. A gospel that aligns itself with the victory of Christ over evil powers finds a ready audience amongst those whose faith claims are newly marginalized by a pluralist, relativist, and radically secular society.

By way of evaluation, the least credible of the various attempts at retrieving the ransom theory would seem to be the Word of Faith version. It misunderstands the crucial inner logic of the theory. In the context of the systemic evil of Rome, the persecuted church of Irenaeus' era was comforted by the idea of a God who did not stoop to the level of the brutally oppressive, satanic methods of the empire, but subverted and dismantled their power in a nonviolent way.[101] Seizing upon the dramatic flavor of *Christus Victor*, Hagin and Copeland (however they came by this model) instead end up distorting the model into something intensely violent in which Christ "kicks the living daylights out of the devil." For similar reasons, the strongest of the retrievals would be that of Darby Kathleen Ray. She depersonalizes Irenaeus' devil and pictures humankind as needing liberation from the power of systemic evil, to which humans have ceded their authority. This hubristic evil is made to implode by Christ drawing its sting, concentrating all its powers on achieving the death of the Son of God, only to find that death could not hold him. This retains the spirit of Irenaeus'

101. This critique of empire is, for Wink, definitive of the shape that pre-Constantinian atonement theology took, in contrast to the later legal, punitive approaches more acceptable to a church that was now part of the empire: Walter Wink, *Engaging the Powers*, 150.

original view, dominated as it was by the notes of divine cleverness proving more powerful than brute force, at the same time as bringing us back to what Boyd correctly observed was a biblical as well as an early church worldview of a cosmos locked in combat.[102] But what of application? What are we to do in light of this victory if it is to amount to more than a mythic fiction? Darby's outcomes are highly exemplarist, though surely worth reproducing here: "His [Christ's] use of courage, creativity, and the power of truth to uncover and disrupt the hegemony of power-as-control becomes a prototype for further strategies and action."[103] Thus, at the cross, we are shown what it looks like for "power-as-control" to be replaced by "power-as-compassion."[104] To be true to Irenaeus (and the Bible), something more than this is needed, and Irenaeus supplies it. The other half of Irenaeus' theory was his "recapitulation" model: Christ's participation in every aspect of the human, which was always coupled with what would later be called *theosis:* our partaking of the divine nature: "[Christ became] what we are, that He might bring us to be even what He is Himself."[105] Our actual participation by faith in the risen life of the victorious Christ empowers us to live in the good of that victory as part of the answer to, no longer part of the problem of, satanically-inspired human evil.

This model of the work of Christ seems worthy of continued attention from those who seek culturally relevant ways of communicating the Christian gospel. There remain untapped riches within the many facets of this model that might be retrieved by ministers and third-sector Christian workers as they serve people caught at a personal, social, or political level, in the terrible power of evil.

---

102. And the New Testament belief in a personal devil who orchestrates systemic evil need not be abandoned, of course.

103. Ray, *Deceiving the Devil*, 144.

104. Ibid.

105. Irenaeus, *Against Heresies* V, Preface.

2

Recapitulation and *Theosis*

THERE IS A THREAD OF thought that begins with Irenaeus and the doctrines of recapitulation and *theosis,* and continues through diverse aspects of Christian tradition, both academic and popular, that is concerned with Christ's union with humanity, on the one hand, and with humanity's union with Christ, on the other. I shall analyze this thread with a view to offering some suggestions as to a salvation message that might resonate with a generation that, like no other before it, values connectedness and participation: the Millennial generation.

The Origins of Recapitulation

The recapitulation theory takes its bearings from the incarnation rather than the death of Christ. It is a way of looking at the work of Christ that asserts that everything Adam did, Jesus undid. Everything Adam failed to do, the Second Adam did. Jesus, as it were, retraces the steps of Adam obediently, instead of disobediently. He is the new *capita,* or new *head* of humanity. He recapitulated the human race. But only as both God and man could he do this. Jesus, on the cross, dies as our representative in ultimate obedience to God. The death of Jesus here becomes a symbol of what human obedience to God looks like in the face of totally overwhelming reasons not to obey. It is a theology of Gethsemane. It is the benchmark of faithfulness to God. All those incorporated into Christ, who claim him as their federal head, are implicated in this new achievement, and can tap into the power of the one who achieved it.

It is, therefore, not only a new head of a new humanity that Christ becomes, according to this model. Franks described the fundamental idea of the "new ferment in human nature . . . renewing it to holiness and immortality."[1] This thought of a new life principle now coursing through humanity as a result of the union of the divine and human in Jesus is prominent in Irenaeus, and points to a closely related doctrine, that of the *theosis* or deification.

We will look first of all at some of the key texts in Irenaeus, the originator of both recapitulation and *theosis*. Looking at the structure of his thought, it is clear that, in a way evocative of the ransom theory and anticipatory of the Latin legal theories, an exchange, or interchange of equivalents, is understood to have taken place:

> For as the disobedience of one man, who was originally moulded from virgin soil, the many were made sinners, and forfeited life, so it was necessary, that by the obedience of one man, who was originally born of a virgin, many should be justified and receive salvation.[2]

The incarnational side of the interchange is balanced by the edificatory side; the objective is balanced by the subjective. Drawing further parallels in a somewhat poetic or even fanciful way, Irenaeus describes the incarnational side by saying that Christ undid "that disobedience which took place at the tree by that obedience which was accomplished on a tree."[3]

In doing what he did, Jesus was, to quote Irenaeus, "summing up universal man in himself even to the end, summing up also his death."[4] He was consummating in himself what man ought to be. McDonald summarizes: "He kept fully the commands of God; he lived entirely the life of a man of God; he resisted completely the temptations if the devil; and he accepted finally death at the hands of wicked men. Thus has he made good Adam's fall."[5]

The origins of the concept appear to be Pauline (Rom 5:12–21; 1 Cor 15:45–50), with the term itself arising as a translation into Latin theology of

1. Franks, *The Atonement*, 80–81.
2. Irenaeus, *Against Heresies* 3, 18.7.
3. Ibid., V, 29.1.
4. Ibid., V, 1.
5. McDonald, *The Atonement of the Death of Christ*, 129.

the Greek *anakephalaitōsis* found in Ephesians 1:10, which speaks of Christ summing up all things in himself. Justin Martyr was the first to begin to make use of the concept, though Irenaeus was the first to fully develop it.[6]

Re-Appropriations of Recapitulation

Adam Christology

In biblical studies a recent resurgence of interest in the recapitulation theory has come in the form of Adam Christology. Leading thinkers in this area are James Dunn and N. T. Wright.[7] A central passage in the discussion is Philippians 2:5–11. Dunn makes the point that the passage is about obedience versus disobedience. It is not about Jesus' heavenly position and then his earthly one. It is a reversal—what Adam has: an opportunity to be one with God—and what he became: a slave—is contrasted with Christ. To a significant extent, it can be said that Jesus was not raised from the dead because he was the Son of God but because he was the obedient human being. Obedience is crucial to the relationship that God wants with man. Our problem is our disobedience. Yet Jesus is the only human being who has been totally obedient to God, therefore he was raised from the dead.

Wright points out that for people of New Testament times Adam was a corporate concept. Using the language of Adam rather than Abraham extended the claims about Israel as the people of God to include all nations. Jesus as the Second Adam is intended to involve us all in a corporate likeness. All those who are in Christ move from being like Adam to being like Christ. They are born again into a new community, the New Adam, the New Israel—and this is what the church is. The emphasis is a corporate one. It is about corporate participation in Christ as head of a new humanity.

Slightly more recently, Morna Hooker also offered some reflections upon this theme within Paul,[8] highlighting the importance of the restoration of the image of God in humankind. This is the logic: Christ the image of God takes on the image of humans so that the divine image in humans

6. Irenaeus cites Justin here: *Against Heresies* IV, 6.1.

7. Dunn, *Christology in the Making*, 14–15; Wright, "Adam in Pauline Christology," 359–89 (see also his adaptation of the same material in *The Climax of the Covenant: Christ and the Law in Pauline Theology*, 18–40). Also N. T. Wright, "Jesus and the Identity of God."

8. Hooker, *From Adam to Christ*, and *Not Ashamed of the Gospel*.

may be restored. This happens as each individual makes their own personal identification with Christ.[9] In her *Not Ashamed of the Gospel* of 1995, she highlights a further important truth about the way in which this whole system works in Paul's thinking:

> Paul's understanding of how Christ's death "works" depends on the notion of human solidarity. Just as we are united in our common humanity by our weakness and sin and subjection to death, so now we can be united in a new humanity—one that is marked by power, by righteousness and by life.[10]

Thomas Smail

Not long after this, this time from outside of the discipline of New Testament studies, there came a contribution from a charismatic theologian influenced by Karl Barth: Thomas Smail, whom we'll be hearing from again later on in this book. Having, in a number of his works, made it clear that he was repulsed by penal substitution,[11] Smail introduces his restatement of recapitulation by starting with the New Testament metaphor upon which penal substitution most depends: the metaphor of sacrifice. He begins with the observation that in the transition from the Old Covenant sacrificial system to the New Testament interpretation of the death of Jesus as sacrifice in Hebrews 10:8–10, "Sacrifice is re-defined as obedient self-offering."[12] It is thus, "obedience expressed in the self-offering of the whole person."[13] Logically, this works well as the foundation for his argument since it stands to reason that the offering up of an animal and the voluntary self-offering of a human being are so qualitatively different as to transform the whole notion of sacrifice. He then builds upon this in a way that clearly has echoes of Barth:

---

9. Hooker, *From Adam to Christ,* 18–19. See also Burnhope, "Beyond the Kaleidoscope: Towards a Synthesis of Views on the Atonement," 363–64.

10. Hooker, *Not Ashamed of the Gospel,* 37.

11. Smail, *Forgotten Father,* 129, *Windows on the Cross,* 39–51. Also, "Can One Man Die for the People?" Here he first begins to introduce his advocacy of a representative obedient man, rather than a punished substitute.

12. Smail, *Once and for All,* 111.

13. Ibid.

> The suffering of Jesus in the place of abandonment, where God seems to be absent, is not simply the consequence of other people's sins but becomes in him the enactment of that trustful surrender to the Father's will with which he emerged from the agonising wrestling of Gethsemane: "*Abba,* Father, not my will but yours be done." Where that is not only said but done from the midst of the human mess the new man is born.[14]

Scot McKnight

Most recently of all, emerging church advocate Scot McKnight chooses a confusing array of starting points from which to arrive at his destination, though a leading one of these is, as with Hooker, the need to restore the cracked *eikon* or image of God in humankind: "The atonement is designed by God to restore cracked Eikons into glory-producing Eikons by participation in the perfect Eikon, Jesus Christ."[15] He defines the crackedness of the human Eikon with the help of Pennenberg: it is, "the universal failure to achieve our human destiny."[16] Significantly, he also moves atonement theology out of soteriology and into ecclesiology, highlighting the "ecclesial focus of redemption."[17] This ecclesial focus in turn is indebted to a social model of the Trinity expressing itself in community. He is doing here for atonement theology the same thing that John Zizioulas did for the doctrine of the Trinity itself: moving everything into an ecclesial, communitarian sphere, outside of which salvation simply does not work and the Trinity cannot be truly understood.[18] Weaknesses emerge as a result of McKnight's search for a golf bag into which, as he puts it, "all the clubs can fit."[19] His work is part of a search that attempts to move beyond the easy-going "kaleidoscopic" approach mentioned earlier, which prefers not to seek a synthesis but holds all views of the atonement in tension. He prefers to seek after a unified theory that subsumes the best in all models but inevitably accents one particular viewpoint as the unifying agent. His argument is mostly too

14. Ibid.

15. McKnight, *A Community Called Atonement,* 21.

16. Pannenberg, *Systematic Theology,* Vol. 2, 252; McKnight, *A Community Called Atonement,* 23.

17. McKnight, *A Community Called Atonement,* 27.

18. Zizioulas, *Being as Communion,* passim.

19. McKnight, *A Community Called Atonement,* 35.

diffuse to easily follow since much of what he discusses along the way has no direct bearing on atonement theories at all. Eventually, however, he arrives at his bag that holds all the clubs: "identification for incorporation."[20] He defines it thus:

> He *identifies* with us all the way down to death in order that we might be *incorporated* into him. To be incorporated "in Christ" is not only a personal relationship with Jesus Christ but also a personal relationship with his people.[21]

He emphasizes: "In this scoping out of atonement we find its centrality in relationship: in being connected to Christ."[22] Not an especially profound end point to reach after such a lengthy argument, though this language of connectedness is clearly significant to this study.

It is evident from the foregoing that the recapitulation cannot be discussed without reference to individual and corporate union or solidarity with Christ and with his people. This being the case, a discussion of recapitulation is not complete without some exploration also of its companion concept, which also has its origins with Irenaeus, the doctrine of *theosis,* to which we now turn.

Theosis: Recapitulation's Companion Doctrine

The doctrine of *theosis* took some time to be named as that but the ideas behind it are traceable to Greek philosophical ideas about being assimilated into God, which originate with Plato,[23] and the idea was common in the pagan philosophy and religion of the patristic period.[24] The Christian use of the term *theosis* appears to have begun with Gregory of Nazianzus,[25] towards the end of the fourth century, one hundred and fifty years after Irenaeus first hinted at it as the corollary of the recapitulation. Biblically, the concept relies rather heavily on 2 Peter 1:4 and the phrase, "partakers of the divine nature." This was understood, not to involve actually becoming

---

20. Ibid., 107.
21. Ibid.
22. Ibid., 108.
23. Louth, "Holiness and the Vision of God in the Eastern Fathers," 221.
24. Norris, "Deification: Consensual and Cogent," 415.
25. Gregory of Nazianzus *Theological Orations.*

in essence divine, but to be permitted to share in the divine "energies."[26] Nevertheless the actual appropriation, however partial, of divine attributes is clearly in view.

Gregory of Nazianzus is especially lyrical in his exposition of the concept: "God came forth with the assumed, one out of two opposites, flesh and spirit, the one deifying, the other deified. O new mixing! O paradoxical blending!"[27] This aspect of the new arrangement would involve a radical and volitional participation of human nature with the divine nature of Christ. By becoming one with humanity, God opens the way for humanity to become one with God in Christ. The former does not appear to be the cause of the latter in any quasi-scientific sense, despite one study that sought to explain it in terms of quantum physics.[28] It is simply a meeting between divinity and humanity that happens by means of divine initiative on the one side and human response on the other. This results in Gregory's "paradoxical blending."

There was clearly a need, however, to explore further the question: If God became human via the incarnation, and the goal is for humankind in some way to become god-like again, then how might humankind make use of the breathtaking new potential now being held out? How does *theosis* actually happen? Some answers are sketched out by Athanasius.

In Athanasius, the recapitulation is more or less taken over by *theosis*, though he does not yet use the term. He is slightly bolder than Irenaeus, stating, "He [Christ] became man that we might be made god."[29] Because of the prominence of the subjective salvific effect of the work of Christ, there is much more emphasis on the Spirit in Athanasius, the one who applies to us the benefits of the incarnation of the Son of God. For Athanasius, the Spirit is the "Spirit of the Son."[30] The Spirit belongs to the Son and "is from him given to the disciples."[31] Likewise, Shapland has well said

26. Norris, "Deification: Consensual and Cogent," 417.

27. Gregory of Nazianzus, *Theological Orations*, 38:13 and 45:9.

28. Norris, "Deification: Consensual and Cogent," 426–28.

29. Athanasius, *On the Incarnation* 54:3.

30. *To Serapion* 1.2. All citations from *To Serapion* are from Shapland's translation.

31. *To Serapion* 1.2. See Shapland, *The Letters of Saint Athanasius concerning the Holy Spirit*, 65 n. 14: "The Spirit derives His existence from the Father and receives His mission from the Son." Campbell makes it clear that much of this aspect of Athanasius' pneumatology is a development on his earlier *Against the Arians*. In *Against the Arians* I:47–48, the Son is clearly the one dispensing the Spirit. Campbell, "The Doctrine of the Holy Spirit in the Theology of Athanasius," 414.

of Athanasius that "Behind his concept of the Spirit stands Christ."[32] This is further brought out as Athanasius contemplates the work of the Spirit: "The Seal [the Spirit] gives the impress of the Son, so that he who is sealed has the form of Christ."[33] So, in Athanasius the issue of exactly how human nature is divinized is given very definite form as the work of the Holy Spirit who, as image-bearer of the Son, applies that likeness to the inner life of a believer. Basil of Caesarea agreed on the centrality of the Holy Spirit's role in *theosis*: "[the Holy Spirit] being God by nature deifies by grace those who still belong to a nature subject to change."[34]

So then, Christ travels the path of the first Adam, with whom all humankind has been walking in inescapable solidarity. But Christ's solidarity with Adam is transformative. By being obedient where Adam was disobedient, Christ opens up a new kind of solidarity, releases a "new ferment" into human nature. This new solidarity is forged by the Spirit through whom, out of their union with the new head of the new humanity, Christ's image is imprinted on his people so that they begin to live his resurrected life.

Re-Appropriations of *Theosis*

The doctrine of *theosis* remained central to the soteriology of Eastern Orthodoxy. In the West very different terminology was used, though it seems likely that something very like *theosis* was held to by a number of Western thinkers using different designations for it. Not until the mid-twentieth-century re-flowering of Eastern Orthodoxy were Westerners brought into fresh contact with the Eastern Orthodox concept—and we have been making intriguing and useful comparisons ever since. At a practitioner level, something very like *theosis*, began to emerge in the West in the early 1970s.

---

32. Shapland, *Letters*, 35. Also: "by insisting that it is from our knowledge of the Son that we must derive our knowledge of the Spirit, Athanasius reveals . . . a vigorous and profound apprehension of his subject." Compare Dunn and his understanding of Pauline Pneumatology: "In Paul then the distinctive mark of the Spirit becomes his Christness. . . . The touch of the Spirit becomes finally and definitively the touch of Christ." Dunn, *Jesus and the Spirit*, 325.

33. *To Serapion* III, 3.

34. Basil of Caesarea, *On the Holy Spirit* 1:2

Word of Faith

The Word of Faith movement, which we met earlier, espoused a doctrine that it called "identification." As with all the leading ideas of the Word of Faith movement, this doctrine originates with the little-known nineteenth-century preacher E. W. Kenyon. Kenyon unpacks his concept of identification in ways such as the following: "The New Creation is a God-man, born of heaven. He is like the sample, Jesus. He is God's superman. He is to walk in the realm of the supernatural."[35] It is believed that Kenyon was acquainted with the writings of Irenaeus[36] but likely drew his most formative influences from New Thought Philosophy, a branch of New England transcendentalism that had strong affinities with Christian Science.[37] Like all forms of transcendentalism, New Thought espoused a very high anthropology in which, via the power of Mind, human beings could create their own reality. In the hands of Kenneth Hagin and Kenneth Copeland, the creative power of Mind over matter transmuted into claims concerning the creative power of spoken words over matter. Mark 11:22–25 was then used as the basis for teaching that, "you can have whatever you say."

Based on a rendering of Mark 11:22 as saying, "Have the faith of God," it was understood that God himself has faith, and that this faith is the power that created the universe and was activated by words "Let there be . . ." In the same way, when a born again believer receives a new nature he or she also receives the "God-kind of faith." They too may now speak things into being. This new nature that includes divine faith is understood to be nothing less than the divine nature itself. Earl Paulk notoriously claimed that Christians are "little gods,"[38] an idea that would have been quite at home in the writings of some of the Eastern Fathers who freely appealed to the phrase, "I said you are gods," as discussed by Jesus in John 10:34. Basing themselves strongly on Calvary, Word of Faith advocates teach that on the

35. Kenyon, *The Two Kinds of Life*, 29.

36. Atkinson, "A Theological Appraisal of the Doctrine that Jesus Died Spiritually, as Taught by Kenyon, Hagin and Copeland," 227–28.

37. McConnell, *A Different Gospel*, passim, and Neuman, "Cultic Origins of the Word-Faith Theology within the Charismatic Movement," 32–55. Countered by DeArteaga, *Quenching the Spirit* and McIntyre, *E. W. Kenyon and His Message of Faith*.

38. This belief was evaluated quite extensively in the literature surrounding the faith controversy. Among the more thoughtful are: Bowman, "'Ye Are Gods?' Orthodox and Heretical Views on the Deification of Man," and Perriman, *Faith, Health and Prosperity*, 26–29.

cross Jesus received a satanic nature so that born again humans can receive a divine nature. It is an exact exchange between two profound opposites with Jesus facilitating it. This he does both on the cross and in a descent into hell while dead, during which Satan's power is defeated and resurrection ensues. So, in Word of Faith teaching there is no recapitulation corollary to *theosis*. There is instead a substitutionary corollary. All is made possible by Christ taking the believer's place on the cross.

Luther Studies

More recently, this time amongst academics, a very fruitful dialogue has been underway between Luther studies and Eastern Orthodox theology. Luther scholarship, especially of the Finnish school, has highlighted an overlooked element in Luther's theology that serves to helpfully correct theological grotesques of him as infatuated with purely judicial, extrinsic concepts of justification. To the contrary, it has been noted that there is in Luther a strong notion, not only of mystical union with Christ, but of transforming deification in Christ in which believers are frequently described as gods. The German word *vergöttlichung*, together with its Latin translation, *deificatio,* is more frequent in Luther's writings than the Latin term *theologia crucis.*[39] There is an especially remarkable passage in Luther in which he states:

> Just as the word of God became flesh, so it is certainly also necessary that the flesh become word. For the word becomes flesh precisely so that the flesh may become word. In other words: God becomes man so that man may become God.[40]

And further:

> For it is true that a man helped by grace is more than a man; indeed, the grace of God gives him the form of God and deifies him, so that even the scriptures call him "God" and "God's son."[41]

Perhaps most shocking of all, Luther claims, "we become completely divine, not having a piece or even a few pieces of God, but all abundance."[42]

39. Mannermaa, "Theosis as a Subject of Finnish Luther Research."
40. Luther, *D. Martin Luthers Werke* Vol. 1, 28, 25–32.
41. WA 2 I, 28, 25–32.
42. WA 17 I, 438, 14–28.

This is perhaps clarified by the following: "Christ remains in me, and that life through which I live is Christ."[43]

Echoing Morna Hooker and Scot McKnight, Luther's understanding of 2 Peter 1:4 was that the divine life permeates the believer like leaven, with the aim of restoring the image of God.[44] Not only is *theosis* a notable concept in Luther but there is also something very like recapitulation to act as its prior corollary. It is based on the Golden Rule. Christ does unto others what he would have them do to him. Christ enters into the human situation, doing for humankind what he would have wanted doing for him had he been in the same situation.[45] This note of identification with a view to restoration is a bridge to the recapitulation concept.

The Contemporary Context

Business leaders, marketing experts, and Christian leaders in the United States have been focusing their energies on how to reach and/or how to work with the Millennial generation.[46] Often also referred to as Generation Y (the preferred term in the UK), and sometimes as the Echo Boomers,[47] the Net Generation,[48] the Boomerang Generation,[49] the Peter Pan Generation,[50] Generation We,[51] and Generation Me,[52] their own preferred epithet is Millennials.[53] This is the Generation succeeding Generation X, but which was mostly reared by a combination of early Xers and late Boomers, whose parenting style was considerably more attentive than was the experience of Gen X "latchkey" children. Experts differ on

---

43. WA 40 I, 283, 7–9.

44. Mannermaa, "Theosis as a Subject of Finnish Luther Research," 42.

45. Ibid., 44.

46. Serious empirical studies include: Pirie and Worcester, *The Millennial Generation*, Collins-Mayo et al., *The Faith of Generation Y*, Smith et al., *Lost in Translation*, Twenge et al., "Generational Differences in Young Adults' Life Goals, Concern for Others and Civic Orientation, 1966–2009."

47. Because of the comparable size of the cohort in America, estimated at 80 million.

48. Most recently, Mesch and Talmud, *Wired Youth*, 45.

49. Because they go back to live with their parents after college.

50. Because they never grow up.

51. Because of their supposed civic and community engagement.

52. Because of the lack of concrete evidence for the above.

53. Howe and Strauss, *Millennials Rising*, 6.

the details, but, broadly, Millennials are construed as having been born towards the beginning of the last two decades of the twentieth century. Howe and Strauss date the end of this birth cohort at 2003, and its beginning in 1982.[54] The oldest of them are currently in their early thirties. The most unique thing about them is that they are the first generation of people to have been born into the internet age. They are "Digital Natives."[55] They are the most digitally connected generation ever to have been born. This is the most compelling fact that makes the awarding of a distinct category to them seem credible.

Given their online connectedness, it is not surprising to find that the chief Millennial characteristic that is reported in the literature is that they value social connectedness more highly than anything else.[56] They continually narrate their lives to one another on social networking sites. They have a need to journey together, to rise and fall together with other fellow travelers. One youth work expert observes, "For generation Y relationships are the key to a happy life."[57] In fact, the more negative appraisals rate them as being potentially the most high maintenance workforce ever due to their inability to work independently.[58] And some Christian appraisals are apocalyptic.[59] The most glowing appraisals, by contrast, predict that these are a new hero generation that have given up the rebellion of the Boomers

---

54. How and Strauss, *Millennials Rising*, 41; Strauss and Howe, *Generations*, 84–87.

55. Prensky, "Digital Natives, Digital Immigrants."

56. There are contradictions in the literature, however. One Christian leader describes them as living in a "bubble" of painful isolation: Nydam, "The Relational Theology of Generation Y," 324, 328–29, arguing that this is the reason for their hunger for connectedness.

57. Collins-Mayo et al., *Faith of Gen Y*, 124. I have found only found one book that definitely does not characterize Millennials as relational: McAllister states that, in his view, "The lack of trust is the salient issue of this generation." McAllister, *Saving the Millennial Generation*, 8.

58. E.g., Kiisel. "Gimme, Gimme, Gimme." Some of the reasons are explored by Lawrence, *Engaging Gen Y*, 5–10.

59. Elmore, *Generation iY*; Stanton, "Fact Checker: Are Millennials More Self-Sacrificing and Community-Minded Than Previous Generations?"

and the deconstruction of the Xers and wish to rebuild society.[60] Very little published comment has so far emerged from Millennials themselves.[61]

In the UK a voice of extreme caution resounded at the very early stages of Millennial fever, pointing out that the generational stratification of society is a mostly North American phenomenon,[62] and that, even given an American context, the fourfold division of generations into idealists, reactives, civics, and adaptives that Howe and Strauss were proposing, was historiographically far too simplistic.[63]

However, even if the assigning of certain characteristics to certain birth cohorts was found to be a completely worthless exercise—and it does appear to have some value—there is another cultural factor that is nudging this generation in a communitarian direction: postmodernity. It could be argued that there are only two positive outcomes for an episode so self-defeating as the postmodern turn and its attendant collapse of consensus about what is true and real—pragmatism: what works is true, and communitarianism: what we agree on is true. Even the earlier postmodernist literature kept coming back to community as definitive of what postmodern society ought to look like, even if it had not yet taken that form,[64] the

---

60. Howe and Strauss, *Millennials Rising*, passim. Byassee notes in young ministers an "almost total lack of cynicism," and feels sure that their defining quality is "hope," and that "everything they touch will turn to gold." Byassee, "Abounding in Hope," 411, 414. In the UK, the very early findings of a 1998 report were perhaps prematurely negative, the "civic" mood of American Millennials having not materialized in the UK: Pirie and Worcester, *Millennial Generation*, 21. See also Furlong and Cartmel, *Young People and Social Change*, 96–108. A recent American study is nuanced: "It is clear that many young citizens of this digital and global age have demonstrated interest in making contributions to society," and, "there are impressive signs of youth civic engagement," and yet, "younger generations have disconnected from conventional politics and government in alarming numbers." Bennett, "Changing Citizenship in the 'Digital Age,'" 1–2.

61. A particularly interesting blog post titled "In Defense of Millennials." *Letters from Home*, October 21, 2012, http://bethanyslettersfromhome.blogspot.co.uk/2012/10/in-defense-of-millennials.html.

62. "[W]e [the UK] simply do not define ourselves, or segment out culture, so ostensibly in generational terms." Hilborn and Bird, *God and the Generations*, 88. See also a recent *Financial Times Lexicon* article http://lexicon.ft.com/Term?term=generation-Y [accessed online 26/03/2013].

63. Hilborn and Bird, *God and the Generations*, 88–94. The generational stratification of culture is a trend that started as early as 1967 when the term "generation gap" was first coined. Ibid., 3.

64. "[C]ommunity has in fact become a key concern of the more recent postmodernist approaches." Delanty, *Modernity and Postmodernity*, 114.

quest for community having already begun in late modernity.[65] As early as the mid-1990s, rave culture grew around a "sense of community and sociability."[66] Millennials, at the very least, may be characterized as those that have intensified the quest for community, making full use of the new potentialities of social media in pursuit of that. Though they probably attain their ideal only rarely, their commitment to it marks them out as those that are piloting a new phase in postmodernity's quest for a new kind of consensus.

So it seems plausible that Gen X postmodernity differs from Millennial postmodernity, Millennials having seemingly moved beyond the negativity and cynicism of Gen X. Few of the Christian responses, however, have so far addressed the subject of what kind of gospel should be preached to Millennials, or what kind of atonement theory would be intelligible to them. McAllister testifies of the impact that simply telling the story of the cross has: "When we talk about the Cross, we can address the point where they are aching, and the love of Christ can meet them there."[67] Also at the cross, Nydam offers the cry of dereliction as a message that will resonate with Gen Y's feelings of emptiness and suggests that the abundance of life promised in John 10:10 will be far more appealing than the offer of forgiveness.[68] "The primary spiritual struggle of Generation Y," he says, "is about mattering to someone and about meaning something to self and to others and, ultimately, to God."[69] Hill identifies the things that will not work with Gen Y: "They are intensely relational but impervious to anything they see as a sales pitch."[70] He offers an anecdote about young people being invited to events that discuss big issues such as, "peace, sex, anxiety, politics, the environment." This approach proved successful.[71]

Accepting that the gospel does not equal a theory of the atonement, it is the case that atonement theology is an exceedingly rich seam of

65. The modernist philosophies of Marxism and socialism, and even fascism and anarchism, also aspired to the communitarian ideal. In fact, aspects of modernity were characterized by a reactive quest for "community"—characterized by solidarity, trust and autonomy—as an antidote for "society," which was characterized more by, "rationalisation, individualisation, industrialisation, disenchantment." Delanty, *Modernity and Postmodernity*, 117–18.

66. France, *Understanding Youth in Late Modernity*, 134.

67. McAllister, *Saving the Millennial Generation*, 118.

68. Nydam, "Relational Theology," 329.

69. Ibid., 328.

70. Hill, "The Church and Gen Y: Missing the Signs," 29.

71. Ibid., 30.

theological reflection, offering insights that are of crucial importance to every generation. In most of the portraits of Millennials, one characteristic emerges as dominant: they are communal, they are participatory, they are relational. To say that this ends 1,500 years of Augustinian and Cartesian inward-looking selves might be premature. What is happening is that we are witnessing the "death of the subject,"[72] the subject being seen now to have "created the havoc of science and technology."[73] We are, perhaps, on the way to becoming post-individualists.

A theory of atonement that has human solidarity at its heart is one that already speaks the language of a generation that has only partly reached its longed-for utopia. Mesch and Talmud make clear how many young people are "socially anxious" and so tend to form vast "bridging" networks of loose, highly heterogeneous connections. These bring just enough in the way of "shared sentiments" and "mutual support," but will not bring the unwelcome peer pressure and social selection of more closely knit "bonding" networks, which tend to be offline as well as online.[74]

In the right direction seems to be McKnight's attempted union between soteriology and ecclesiology. Orthodox theologian John Zizioulas reflected, in a way that now has fresh relevance, upon how each of us is a "being in relationship," and how important the "corporate personality" of Christ is.[75]

It should go without saying that Irenaeus and Athanasius were not referring to a union between "me" and Christ. Rather such a union inevitably involves a person in a union with all those that are also in a living and vital union with Christ. It is a "bonding" social network, the small and intimate kind, yet on the vast scale of a "bridging" social network. And all is infused with the divine "energies" that Gregory of Nazianzus spoke of. If we retain in the church the emphasis on the Holy Spirit that Athanasius understood to be pivotal, then we have a society of the "new mixing" and the "paradoxical blending," a supernatural society of energized connectedness.

When we speak of Christ's work to eighteen- to thirty-year-olds, it seems we should accent the representative corporate Christ as the hero of the piece and, perhaps, soft-pedal the substitutionary sin-bearer. We should probably emphasize the partaking of abundant divine life, and not, in the

72. Heller, *Can Modernity Survive?* 63.

73. Ibid.

74. Mesch and Talmud, *Wired Youth*, 115–17.

75. Zizioulas, *Being as Communion*, 130.

first instance, the bestowing of God's free forgiveness. We should talk of the bigger picture of a new people of God reflecting his image into the world, and not harp on about the fulfillment of individual needs that we all once found so compelling. Simply telling the story of the cross is as appealing to this generation as to the previous one, but when we come to interpret and apply the story, it seems we should un-learn some of the familiar language and try a different emphasis. As is hopefully clear, the fresh influences of Eastern Orthodox theology that have now flowed into the West are extremely timely. Their doctrines of recapitulation and *theosis* are a deep and refreshing well from which we can all abundantly draw.

PART TWO

Objective Theories

IN THIS SECTION WE WILL continue to travel through the history of Christian thought, focusing now on all those theories that begin to emerge in the Middle Ages. These theories tend to understand the death of Christ as having to do with justice and substitution. Justice is the key concept here and the question of how divine justice can be satisfied is what the cross answers. Some views within this category lean more towards the satisfaction of justice and picture Christ as representative rather than substitute (e.g., Anselm), while others lean more towards substitution while down-playing the need to bear a penalty or meet the demands of justice (e.g., charismatic views that are oriented around healing and release). Rather than evil powers, the orientation of the work of Christ here is the Father—the atonement was meant to have an effect upon the Father, often portrayed as being propitiated by the perfect self-offering of Christ. And, rather than the kingly office, this view corresponds to the priestly office of Christ in which he is priest and sacrificial victim and focuses our attention upon the first person of the Trinity. He is the person we are brought to in reconciliation.

3

Satisfaction Guaranteed

Anselm

"It has seldom been given to any writer to work such a change in the history of thought as that wrought by Anselm's short treatise, *Cur Deus Homo*."[1] James Denney described the work as "the truest and greatest book on the Atonement that has ever been written."[2] Darby recoils at Anselm's God, who is a "status-paranoid power-monger who deliberately humiliates and infantilizes human beings under the guise of justice."[3] Love him or hate him, Anselm is a contributor to atonement theory who is impossible to ignore. If Athanasius can be credited with the first ever treatise on the Holy Spirit,[4] then it is to Anselm's little book of 1099 that we look for the first ever sustained treatment of the subject of the atonement and the first ever attempt to articulate the work of Christ in a rational and comprehensive way. Apart from the *Christus Victor* approaches that we have just explored, all theories of the atonement, properly so called, have their roots here. All are either developments of, or reactions against, Anselm's *Cur Deus Homo*.

---

1. Grensted, *A Short History of the Doctrine of the Atonement*, 120. "Philosophers and theologians have continued to wrestle with his arguments not for their antiquarian interest but for their intrinsic value and importance until the present moment." Evans, "Anselm of Canterbury," in Evans, ed., *The Medieval Theologians*, 101.

2. Denney, *The Atonement and the Modern Mind*, 84.

3. Ray, *Deceiving the Devil*, 51.

4. Athanasius, *Letters to Serapion*.

Of course, as I hope my previous two chapters have shown, this does not mean that all prior *ad hoc* attempts to articulate here and there the purpose of the death of Christ ought to be ignored. To the contrary, Anselm's raw materials are the patristic writings. In fact, it is my conviction that we should view the satisfaction theory more as a development of earlier thought than as a precursor to Calvin's penal substitution.[5]

Studies of *Cur Deus Homo*: The Story So Far

There did not appear a substantial critical work on Anselm's theory of satisfaction until George Foley's book of 1909,[6] though a number of critiques (mostly unfavorable) had appeared as chapters within larger works on the history of doctrine.[7] It is surprising that Foley's monumental work is very seldom referred to in recent literature. A uniquely thorough survey of patristic writings is undertaken, which notes interesting points of comparison, or possible influences and points of origin.[8] This is useful in itself, however, the point of all that scholarship appears to be merely to prove that the satisfaction theory is a late-comer and found only incipiently in the classical authors. For Foley there is some sort of ill-defined time limit, of say 500 CE, beyond which foundational definitions of Christian belief, even if they are credible, are to be ignored.[9] He also helped to popularize the ever popular notion that Anselm was influenced by medieval feudalism,[10] on which more later.

Discussion does not progress much until when, in 1930, Aulén draws attention to the satisfaction theory's central place within objective ways of looking at the atonement.[11]

---

5. "Penal substitution," of course, being a phrase that Calvin himself would not have been familiar with (or any French equivalent). The term is generally attributed to Princeton professor Charles Hodge.

6. Foley, *Anselm's Theory of the Atonement*.

7. E.g., Harnack, *The History of Dogma*, Vol. 6, 41–57.

8. Despite his claim to be searching "in the patristic ideas for any possible antecedents and anticipations." Foley, *Anselm's Theory of the Atonement*, 10.

9. Ibid., 9.

10. Prior to him see also Cremer, "Die Wurzeln des Anselm'schen Satisfactionsbegriffes," and "Der germanische Satisfactionsbegriff in der Versöhnungslehre." Also, Harnack, *The History of Dogma*, Vol. 6, 54–83.

11. Though see Rivière, *Le dogme de la Redemption*, 291–324, of 1914, and his, "Sur la Satisfaction du Christ."

The publication in America of the English translation of Aulén's *Christus Victor* in 1951 was soon followed by the first significant volume to deal exclusively with the satisfaction theory since Foley: John McIntyre's *St. Anselm and His Critics*, which is still cited today. This work draws attention to Anselm's theological method, which was about "faith seeking understanding," and then goes on to defend the theology of *Cur Deus Homo* by noting how Anselm's prior theological commitment (even clearer in his *Proslogion*) to the divine attribute of "aseity" shines through everywhere. Aseity is self-existence, self-origination, self-sufficiency, independence. For Anselm, it seems, this was definitive of the being of God from which every other attribute logically flowed. He uses it in *Cur Deus Homo* as a rather excellent way of countering the patristic ideas that God might have been under some sort of obligation, even to the devil. For Anselm the notion that the devil's originator, his creator, could ever be in his debt was absurd. The absolute freedom of the divine being is recovered because, for Anselm, God has the right to act in his own creation just as he pleases.

The 1980s saw the emergence of a significant study by the Swiss Catholic theologian Hans Urs von Balthasar, which drew attention to how "radiant and perfectly balanced" the whole Anselmian corpus is. Balthasar was more interested in the aesthetic of Anselm's reasoning—the beauty of his logic—than in any particular aspect of the things Anselm tried to argue for.[12] And ever since Balthasar, this note of "fittingness," that seems so important to Anselm, has been noted a few times, most recently in Hogg's *The Beauty of Theology*.[13] Chapter 3 of Book I is especially notable. It also has very strong resonances with Irenaeus' *Against Heresies* 5:19:[14]

> For it was appropriate that, just as death entered the human race
> through a man's disobedience, so life should be restored through
> man's obedience; and that, just as the sin which was the cause of
> our damnation originated from a woman, similarly the originator
> of our justification and salvation should be born of a woman. Also
> that the devil, who defeated the man whom he beguiled through
> the taste of a tree, should himself similarly be defeated by a man

12. Balthasar, "Anselm," 211–57.

13. E.g., Hogg, *Anselm of Canterbury*, 168, where Hogg records that the Latin *oportet*, "fitting," "appropriate," occurs seventy-six times in CDH. Against this perspective on Anselm is Gorringe, *God's Just Vengeance*, 91, 94. McGrath saw rectitude as the underlying principle of CDH: McGrath, "Rectitude."

14. Though Hogg wisely cautions: "To make the case that Anselm was drawing on Irenaeus directly would be hard to prove." Hogg, *Anselm of Canterbury*, 10.

> through a tree-induced suffering which he, the devil, inflicted. There are many other things, too, which, if carefully considered, display the indescribable beauty of the fact that our redemption was procured in this way.[15]

We might be forgiven for thinking that we are not to lean too much weight on the aesthetic, or pretty, bits, such as the extract above. We might think these are not meant to be weight-bearing, but merely poetic. But we would, I think, be mistaken. Central, after all, to Anselm's whole concept of sin is "the order and beauty of the universe"[16] that has been disrupted by human sin.[17] There is, however, a variation in the weight that Anselm's arguments are intended to bear, though this is not connected to aesthetics, but to overall trajectory. McIntyre[18] describes how Anselm always "leaves the best wine until last." His weakest replies to Boso tend to appear first, building up to much stronger reasoning as he goes along.

Interest continued to increase, both immediately before and after 1999,[19] the year that the 900th anniversary of the publication of *Cur Deus Homo* (CDH) was marked.[20] In 2009 the *Epworth Review* marked the 900th anniversary of Anselm's death with a volume dedicated to this subject.

Interestingly, most of the studies since McIntyre's have, like his, been aimed at a retrieval of Anselm from his detractors, while most of the detractors have been anti-penal substitutionists writing a few pages of invective against him as part of a usually rather cursory "history of atonement theories" chapter.[21] The retrievers of CDH have mostly been a lot more artful in their task than the denouncers,[22] though this is changing. The last decade

---

15. CDH I:3.

16. *Cur Deus Homo* I:15.

17. Salai, "Anselm, Girard, and Sacramental Theology," 95.

18. McIntyre, *St. Anselm and His Critics*.

19. Brown, "Anselm's *Cur Deus Homo* Revisited," 189–204; Campbell, "The Conceptual Roots of Anselm's Soteriology"; Gilbert et al., *Cur Deus Homo*; Gomocz, "Anselm von Aosta als Schecken der 'europäischen' Anthropologie?"; Asiedu, "Anselm and the Unbelievers."

20. The year itself was marked by a significant collection of essays in: Gilbert, *Cur Deus Homo*.

21. E.g., Finlan, *Problems with Atonement*, 71–75; Ray, *Deceiving the Devil*, 8–13, 49–52; Flood, *Healing the Gospel*, 33–35; Shelton, *Cross and Covenant*, 175–80; Green and Baker make some effort to be fair to Anselm: *Recovering the Scandal of the Cross*, 128–38.

22. E.g., Bell, "God Does Not Demand Blood," 39–61, 152–53. Two exceptions being Weaver, "Atonement and (Non) Violence," 29–46, and Cross, "Atonement without

has seen a succession of Girardian (followers of René Girard) authors take up strongly argued positions that sometimes analyze Anselm quite fairly, yet are able to take up a position diametrically opposed to him.[23] Mark Heim is especially penetrating in his deconstruction of CDH. However, he wrongly takes as Anselm's starting point the injustice of the crucifixion. As a way of explaining and defending the death of the innocent Jesus, Anselm, so Heim avers, ends up twisting the human wrongness of the scapegoating of Jesus into something divinely approved and right, and causing untold damage in the process. In other words, if God is now on the side of the abusers of Jesus, how are victims of abuse to understand God's posture towards them in their plight?[24] However, as I will argue, a starting point that is more true to Anselm is the Chalcedonian Christ, the God-Man, and the need to explain this in a way that preserves God's freedom to act how he chooses, instead of in the way that the ransom theory implied. Heim's issue is a legitimate one to explore, yet the human crime of crucifying the innocent Jesus is not the thing that Anselm is trying to explain, still less defend.

Retrieval often takes place by juxtaposing him with another author who is seen as rather less of a bogeyman than poor old Anselm, such as Athanasius,[25] Thomas Aquinas,[26] Richard Hooker,[27] John McLeod Campbell,[28] Karl Barth,[29] or even René Girard.[30] Some, however, prefer to

Satisfaction," 397–416.

23. Most notably and persuasively, Heim, *Saved from Sacrifice*, 292–302, but also Milavec, "Is God Arbitrary and Sadistic?" 45–94, and his more recent *Salvation is of the Jews*, 72–76.

24. Heim, *Saved from Sacrifice*, 297–99: "He assumes, as scripture does, the injustice of the crucifixion. . . . Anselm's departure is to insist with a new systematic rigor that it is actually coming from God."

25. Gasper, "Anselm's *Cur Deus Homo* and Athanaius's *De Incarnatione*," 147–64.

26. Bracken, "Thomas Aquinas and Anselm's Satisfaction Theory," 501–30; Nieuwenhove, "St. Anselm and St. Thomas on 'Satisfaction,'" 159–76.

27. Neelands, "Crime, Guilt, and the Punishment of Christ," 197–213.

28. Hart, "Anselm of Canterbury and John McLeod Campbell: Where Opposites Meet?" 311–33. Hefling seems also to speak very Campbellian language, saying that satisfaction in the penitential system, "is appropriate to the extent that detestation of the offense and sorrow over it are manifested." Hefling, "A Perhaps Permanently Valid Achievement," 64, and, echoing him, LaChance, "Understanding Christ's Satisfaction Today," 60–66.

29. Jones, "Barth and Anselm," 257–82; Watson, "A Study in St. Anselm's Soteriology and Karl Barth's Theological Method," 493–512.

30. Salai, "Anselm, Girard, and Sacramental Theology."

place Anselm next to a still more notorious fiend for contemporary theology, such as John Calvin[31] or Martin Luther:[32] blood-curdling stuff. There is even one attempt to place CDH in the context of Mormonism,[33] as well as one study that discusses it in the context of Islam,[34] and one that covers, "pagans, Jews and Christians."[35]

Many studies have been entirely non-polemical and have, like Balthasar and Hogg, shown a huge delectation for the structural qualities of the little book itself: drawing attention either to its aesthetics[36] or its logic.[37] Others attempt to shed more light on Anselm's own historical context,[38] or set him within ours.[39] Others still are more interested in the philosophical merits of Anselm's work,[40] or the relation of his atonement theology to the Eucharist.[41]

Of particular interest are recent studies that give an Eastern Orthodox slant on CDH[42] and, related to that, those that attempt to compare Anselm

31. Strimple, "St. Anselm's *Cur Deus Homo* and John Calvin's Doctrine of the Atonement."

32. Eckhart, *Anselm and Luther on the Atonement?*; Visser, "St. Anselm's *Cur Deus Homo* and the *Heidelberg Catechism* (1563)," 607–34.

33. Payne, "Alma and Anselm: Satisfaction Theory in the *Book of Mormon*," http://www.mormonstudies.net/html/payne/alma.html#_ftn8 [accessed 5 Jun 2013]

34. Bebawi, "Atonement and Mercy."

35. Asiedu, "Anselm and the Unbelievers," 530–48.

36. Holmes, "The Upholding of Beauty," 189–203; Leftow, "Anselm on the Beauty of the Incarnation," 109–24.

37. Evans, "*Cur Deus Homo*: The Nature of Anselm's Appeal to Reason," 33–50; Root, "Necessity and Unfittingness in Anselm's *Cur Deus Homo*," 211–30.

38. Fortin, "*Satisfactio* in St. Benedict's *Regula* and St. Anselm's *Cur Deus Homo*," 305–11; Deem, "A Christological Renaissance," 42–51; Whidden, "The Alleged Feudalism of Anselm's *Cur Deus Homo* and the Benedictine Concepts of Obedience, Honor, and Order," 1055–87; Barnes, "Necessary, Fitting, or Possible," 657–88; Langston, "Scotus' Departure from Anselm's Theory of the Atonement," 227–41; Robson, "The Impact of *Cur Deus Homo* on the Early Franciscan School."

39. Holmes, "Cur Deus Pomo?"; Culleton, "Punishment and Human Dignity in the *Cur Deus Homo* by Anselm of Canterbury (1033–1109)"; Sumner, "Why Anselm Still Matters," 25–36.

40. Houston, "Was the Anselm of *Cur Deus Homo* a Retributivist?"; Hopkins, "God's Sacrifice of Himself as a Man"; Leftow, "Anselm on the Necessity of the Incarnation," 167–85; Leftow, "Anselm on the Cost of Salvation," 73–92; Rogers, "A Defense of Anselm's *Cur Deus Homo* Argument," 187–200; Rogers, "Christ our Brother," 223–36.

41. Williams, *Anselm: Communion and Atonement.*

42. Hart, "A Gift Exceeding Every Debt"; Nellas, "Redemption or Deification?"

to one or more of the patristic writers.[43] In effect, such work takes us full circle to Foley, who clearly intuited the significance of patristic thought to any right understanding of CDH but perhaps was too driven by the polemics of his own particular argument. Any studies that attempt to deliver Anselm from associations with Reformation theology and that juxtapose him with patristic thinkers are, I think, pointing in the right direction.

The remarkable similarities between CDH I, 3 and Irenaeus' *Against Heresies* 5,19 have already been noted above and are discussed by Hogg.[44] The penitential theologies of Tertullian and Cyprian have also been noted as concepts that Anselm uses and critiques.[45] It is clear also that typically Anselmian concepts, such as satisfaction and a concept of sin as debt, were already well developed in Athanasius,[46] and had, since as early as the seventh century, been "embedded in the liturgy."[47] Gasper,[48] Hart,[49] and McMahon[50] each make extensive comparisons with Athanasius' *De Incarnatione Verbi Dei* (The Incarnation of the Word of God). Hart asserts: "the closer the attention one pays Anselm's argument, the harder it becomes to locate a point at which he actually breaks from patristic theology,"[51] and, with regards to Athanasius in particular: "Already present in Athanasius's account is the very story whose inner shape Anselm will, in a moment of intense critical reflection, attempt to grasp as necessary."[52] Foley picks up on the theme in Clement of Alexandria.[53] Gregory the Great would appear to be the first to link Christ's work to the idea of merit.[54] Rivière dated the linking of Christ's work with the concept of satisfaction to an obscure writer by the name

---

43. McMahon,"The Cross and the Pearl"; Rodger, "The Soteriology of Anselm of Canterbury," 19–43.

44. Hogg, *Anselm of Canterbury,* 10, 12, 161.

45. Hart, "Where Opposites Meet?" 319.

46. E.g., *On the Incarnation of the Word* xx:2.

47. Neelands, "Substitution and the Biblical Background to *Cur Deus Homo*," 80, who cites the Easter Proclamation *Exultet*—"Jesus Christ, our Lord and Saviour who paid for us to the eternal Father the debt of Adam's transgression"—as an example.

48. Gasper, "Anselm's *Cur Deus Homo* and Athanasius's *De Incarnatione Verbi*."

49. Hart, "A Gift Exceeding Every Debt," 342–47.

50. McMahon, "The Cross and the Pearl."

51. Hart, "A Gift Exceeding Every Debt," 342.

52. Ibid., 347.

53. *Quis dives Salvetur,* 23, 49. Foley, *Anselm's Theory of the Atonement,* 38.

54. *Moral.,* xxiv.2, 4; 3, 5; 17, 30. Foley, *Anselm's Theory of the Atonement,* 94.

of Radulphus Ardeus.[55] The importance of Augustine,[56] especially his very strong concept of the seriousness of sin,[57] and Chalcedonian doctrine as mediated via Leo I are highlighted by Deem: "The ontological [focused on the being or person of Christ] Christology of Chalcedon is pressed into the service of a functional Christology."[58]

In every case, direct dependencies cannot be demonstrated for the simple reason that Anselm has deliberately stripped his work of references to the Bible and Christian tradition so as to demonstrate by logic and aesthetics alone the unassailable reasonableness of what is already revealed to faith. There appears, nonetheless, to be a case to be made that Anselm's concepts of justice and the payment of human debt had "deep patristic roots,"[59] despite his most distinctive concept, that of honor, being apparently without precedent in the patristic writings.

Anselm's Context: Theological and Cultural

Gunton offers a refreshing defense of Anselm, praising him especially for his battle against what was for Gunton an important issue: the misuse of a metaphor: "In face of a tendency to mythologise the metaphor of ransom, Anselm's achievement is immense."[60]

Here is Anselm himself on the matter of the ransom-to-Satan theory that was so prevalent in his day:

> The devil and man belong to God alone, and neither one stands outside God's power, what case, then, did God have to plead with his own creature, concerning his own creature, in his own affair?[61]

---

55. Rivière, *Le dogme de la Redemption*, 289.

56. See especially Augustine's concept that Christ was both priest and victim. As God, Jesus *received* a true and worthy sacrifice. As man, he *offered* a true and worthy sacrifice: *City of God* 10:3–6; 18–20. Compare CDH II, 18, in which Christ offers his humanity to his divinity.

57. Foley, *Anselm's Theory of the Atonement*, 99: "Augustin [sic] certainly had laid the foundation by a new and vigorous apprehension of the significance of Christ's work, by emphasising so strongly the gravity of sin, and by representing the relation between God and man under the scheme of sin and grace. At this point Anselm came in."

58. Deem, "A Christological Renaissance," 50.

59. McMahon, "The Cross and the Pearl," 57.

60. Gunton, *Actuality of Atonement*, 87.

61. CDH I:7. See also Anselm's *A Meditation on Human Redemption*: "Did the Devil justly have against God or against man some claim which obliged God to act against him

Anselm's task was to seek some other way of accounting for the necessity of the atonement. When he arrives at it he is careful to hide it within what seems to be a discussion solely about the incarnation: *Why did God Become Man?* He is also careful to put all of his most provocative questions into the mouth of "Boso,"[62] who is the devil's advocate in the conversation.[63]

The thing that has been one of the strongest bases for the summary dismissal of CDH is the alleged feudal or Teutonic cultural setting that Anselm engages with. A very small but increasing number of voices are dissenting from this view, however.[64] According to the received wisdom, the world he spoke to was the world in which moral order was maintained, not by a remote imperial sovereign, as during the patristic and Carolingian periods, but by overlords or vassals—the knights and earls—who, in turn, owed allegiance to a regional sovereign who was understood to own all the land. The age of chivalry is the assumed setting here. It was an age of instability in which a power vacuum had been created by the collapse of Charlemagne's dynasty. The genius of the feudal system was that, when yet another war broke out, a king could call his barons to arms, and these in turn could expect to very quickly summon the loyal military service of everyone in the hierarchy, down to the serfs that worked the land. In return for such loyalty, the serfs could depend upon the overlord's protection, and profit from the produce of his land. Any infringement was a personal infringement of this relationship, rather than a breaking of a law. Reparation had to be made of a kind that showed due regard for the personal honor and dignity of the person offended, rather than for any strict legalities. Basically, the more noble the person offended, the higher the price needed to be if their wrath was to be appeased.

---

on man's behalf in this manner rather than by open force? No, for surely God did not owe the Devil anything except punishment." Hopkins and Richardson (eds) *Anselm of Canterbury,* Vol. 1, 138.

62. He was a real person, who succeeded Anselm as Abbot of Bec, but whose dialogue is certainly fictitious.

63. Grensted is very perceptive of these political dynamics: Grensted, *A Short History of the Doctrine of the Atonement,* 124, 126.

64. Whiddon, "The Alleged Feudalism of Anselm's *Cur Deus Homo* and the Benedictine Concepts of Obedience, Honor, and Order," 1055–87; Fortin, "*Satisfactio* in St. Benedict's *Regula* and St. Anselm's *Cur Deus* Homo," 305–11; Fortin, "The Influence of Benedict's *Regula* on Anselm's Concept of Justice"; Cohen, "Feudal Imagery or Christian Tradition?" 154–71; Mansini, "St. Anselm, 'satisfactio,' and the 'Rule' of St. Benedict," 101–21.

The main problem that Whidden[65] highlighted seems to be a lack of cross-disciplinary communication between theology and history. The situation has not been helped by writers within Anselm studies who likewise do not seem to have paid enough visits to the medieval history department.[66] It is the theologians writing about atonement theories who are mainly to blame, however. They have been endlessly carbon-copying one another, trotting out the feudal background to Anselm because it sounds plausible, without seemingly even being aware that, as early as 1974, historians have been querying whether feudalism *ever* really existed[67] and, if it did, whether there is any evidence for its appearance any earlier than 1100.[68] Whidden suspects quite rightly, that, "the real function of the feudal charge may somehow be to delegitimize Anselm's argument."[69] Further, Whidden claims, even if we allow a feudal context, there is almost no evidence at all in *Cur Deus Homo* that Anselm is making use of feudal concepts. Almost none of the Latin terms normally associated with feudalism appear anywhere in the book,[70] despite Green and Baker, who wrongly cite *vassal* as a term that Anselm actually used.[71] However, a decent explanation for the prominence of Anselm's concept of honor, if not within feudalism, is yet to appear. Whidden's claim of strong Benedictine influence upon Anselm's thought, owing to his thirty-three-year stint in a Benedictine monastery, holds good for most of the concepts in *Cur Deus Homo,* but, even by Whidden's own admission, honor is not exactly the most prominent feature of the *Rule of St. Benedict.*[72] I tried out Whidden's recommendation

---

65. Whidden "The Alleged Feudalism of Anselm's *Cur Deus Homo*," 1055–87

66. Whidden highlights Richard Southern's *Saint Anselm: A Portrait in a Landscape.*

67. Brown, "The Tyranny of a Construct." It is believed that feudalism is in fact an eighteenth-century construct imposed retrospectively upon historical data that simply was not that simple: Brown, "The Tyranny of a Construct," 1086. In modern times, Bloch and Gansholf contributed significantly towards making the feudal concept paradigmatic: Bloch and Gansholf, *Feudal Society* (original French edition, 1939); Gansholf, *Feudalism* (original Belgian edition, 1944). Doubts first began to be voiced in Richardson and Sayles, *The Governance of Medieval England from the Conquest to Magna Carta.*

68. Reynolds, *Fiefs and Vassals*, 59, 70. So Tabluteau, "Definitions of Feudal Military Obligations in Eleventh-Century Normandy," 19.

69. Whidden "The Alleged Feudalism of Anselm's *Cur Deus Homo*," 1059.

70. Specifically: *vassi, vassalli, feodum, casamentum, milites* and *homagium*. Whidden "The Alleged Feudalism of Anselm's *Cur Deus Homo*," 1066.

71. Green and Baker, *Recovering the Scandal of the Cross*, 132.

72. Whidden "The Alleged Feudalism of Anselm's *Cur Deus Homo*," 1078.

that we read CDH in one hand with the *Rule* open in the other. The concept of honor did not exactly jump out at me from the latter.[73]

The Man and His Message

In 1093, Anselm became Archbishop of Canterbury and, after a few years arguing with the king, resulting in an exile from 1097–1100, took the time to write *Cur Deus Homo,* completing it in 1099. The argument went as follows: We have all robbed God of the honor that is due to him. In order for that honor to be fully repaid, something greater than all creation needs to be offered to God in compensation—our situation is that serious.

> Anyone who does not give this honour to God steals from God what belongs to him, and dishonours God, and this is sin. What is more, as long as he does not repay what he stole, he remains guilty. And it is not enough simply to repay what he stole. Because he insulted God, he must give back something more than what he took.[74]

This compensation must only be made by man. No one must pay it for him—that would be unjust.[75] But only God has the power to make such a payment. Only he could offer something so valuable that it is the equivalent to everything in creation. The debt is total, the obligation to pay it, total, the power to pay it, zero. What better solution then, that God, who alone has the means to pay it, should become man and in man pay that debt?

> Anselm: So no one except God can make the satisfaction.
>
> Boso: That follows.
>
> Anselm: But no one except humanity ought to do it—otherwise, humanity has not made satisfaction.
>
> Boso: Nothing could be more just.
>
> Anselm: . . . So if no one except God can make it and no one except man ought to make it, there must be a God-Man to make it.

73. Yet Foley lists the motif of honor as first and foremost in his reasons for identifying a feudal background to the concept: Foley, *Anselm's Theory of the Atonement*, 114.

74. CDH I, 11.

75. See a more recent reflection along similar lines, but more decidedly penal: "Hence, we as his people do indeed receive our just deserts for our misdemeanours inasmuch as Christ, having united himself to us in his incarnation, fully discharges the debt we owe." Letham, *The Work of Christ*, 136.

Boso: Blessed be God.[76]

That the Son should offer himself is more than enough to satisfy divine justice, so, in fact, merits a reward. The Son has no need of such a reward, so freely bestows his merit, his reward, on all those who believe in him:

> Anselm: No member of the human race except Christ ever gave to God, by dying, anything which that person was not at some time going to lose as a matter of necessity. Nor did anyone ever pay a debt to God which he did not owe. But Christ of his own accord gave to his Father what he was never going to lose as a matter of necessity, and he paid, on behalf of sinners, a debt which he did not owe.[77]

Boso ends up in raptures of delight at the outcome of his discussion with the learned Anselm:

> Boso: There can be nothing more logical, nothing sweeter, nothing more desirable that the world can hear. I indeed derive such confidence from this that I cannot now express in words with what joy my heart is rejoicing.[78]

It is important to note at this point the main thing that distinguishes this theory from penal substitution, which was a development of this theory. In this theory, punishment is *averted*. In penal substitution, punishment is *absorbed*: "Satisfaction is . . . according to Anselm the way by which God is enabled *not* to exact a tribute of compensatory penalty from the sinner."[79]

> In the order of things, there is nothing less to be endured than that the creature should take away the honour due the Creator, and not restore what he has taken away. . . . Therefore the honour taken away must be repaid or punishment must follow; otherwise, either God will not be just to himself, or he will be weak in respect to both parties.[80]

So, on this point, Anselm's engagement with patristic theology is negative, and reflects it by way of contrast with the patristic view that Anselm

---

76. CDH II, 6.

77. CDH II, 18.

78. CDH II, 19.

79. Gunton, *The Actuality of Atonement*, 90, italics original. So McIntyre, *St. Anselm and his Critics*, 86ff. See also Balthasar, *The Glory of the Lord: A Theological Aesthetics II*, 249.

80. CDH I, 13. This translation is by Deane in *St. Anselm Basic Writings*, 220–21.

inherited. Instead of God owing something to the devil, it is the outraged honor of God that is demanding the payment, and that payment is now conceived of as a debt, a due, rather than a ransom. Anselm has a clear vision of the seriousness of sin in the eyes of God, that it robs God of honor in a way that is more intolerable for God than anything our finite minds can conceive. In return man owes everything.[81] Only man ought to make this satisfaction, but only God can. The answer is the God-Man. In true Athanasian style, the salvation of man must all be of God or man is not saved. The insight that is added is that it must also be truly man that brings the component of satisfaction to the saving action: "Otherwise it would not be man making the satisfaction."[82]

There is no concept of a transfer of guilt magically from us to Christ. Christ is us paying what we owe, and Christ is God receiving the payment. And all of this merits an overflow of unwanted reward, a reward that arises from the fact that, though he is us, yet he is not us in one very important respect. In the film *The Green Mile,* is the unforgettable line: "We each owe a death."[83] Not so with this man. He, uniquely, was not obligated to die, and in doing so went beyond the recapitulating obedience of life that Irenaeus and Athanasius saw. To go as far as dying was to go as far as paying what he did not owe. In a sense, this is the very opposite of the concerns that nonviolent atonement critics raise, namely, that God is vengefully and inflexibly demanding this payment. Within Anselm's logic, it is the very fact that God is *not* demanding this self-giving death from his Son that makes it meritorious.[84] It merits an overflow of reward and blessing which he, having no need of, distributes to his people.

In Anselm's thinking, Christ offers himself to God as *an equivalent to* the punishment of sinners. In the penal substitutionary model, Christ himself *is punished* for sinners. In the satisfaction theory, the action is from Christ to God. In the penal substitutionary theory the action is from God to Christ.

Perhaps of greatest significance is that Anselm answers the significant question of "why?" Why was it necessary for Christ to die? God is understood to be both loving and just, and both to an infinite degree. God must maintain who he is in the face of human sin. His love for the sinner and his

---

81. See Stott's dense but informative review of Anselm in *Cross of Christ*, 118–20.

82. CDH II, 6.

83. Warner Bros., 1999.

84. So Hart, "Where Opposites Meet?" 319–20.

righteous hatred of sin must both be maintained, so that God is "just and the justifier of the one who has faith in Jesus" (Rom 3:26). Anselm is probably right in saying that we do not fully understand how serious an issue sin is to a holy God.[85] Neither do we fully understand the full extent of his love for us. But whatever theory we adopt, we must always ask, does this theory make Christ's death absolutely necessary?

Reflections

In defense of Anselm, I would recommend that, in our evaluation of his theory of the atonement, we make the following shifts of emphasis so as to allow him to speak on his own terms and not be drowned out by the voices of his many critics:

Content

CUR DEUS HOMO SHOULD BE VIEWED AS MORE CHRISTOLOGICAL THAN THEOLOGICAL

It is unfortunate that one of Anselm's staunchest defenders, John McIntyre, actually plays into the hands of some of Anselm's bitterest critics by interpreting *Cur Deus Homo* as though it was all about God. The emphasis on divine aseity that McIntyre notes in an effort to save the work gives the impression that this is a contribution to the doctrine of God, yet it is patently intended to be a contribution to Christology. It is all about the *Deus-Homo*, the God-Man of Chalcedon. Anselm is taking this divine man of the Chalcedonian definition and animating the otherwise static figure that it presents us with. He is asking what it means for our salvation that Jesus of Nazareth was both fully God and fully man. This balance is not always maintained, yet the intentions are plain: to answer the question, why, in terms of the work of Christ, was it so essential that the person of Christ is all that we affirm him to be?

A genealogy of interdependent ideas could be conjectured that would place the recapitulation theory first, then Chalcedon, then the satisfaction theory, though I have so far found just one ally in my personal hunch that Anselm's thought can be seen as a development of the recapitulation

85. Anselm's "most famous sentence" in CDH: Whale, *Victor and Victim*, 75.

theory.[86] The trajectory begins with the affirmation that God becoming man achieved something divine in man, proceeds with a further refinement of who the God-Man is, thus shifting attention away from man to Christ. Then, it goes back in the direction of recapitulation to consider again what the incarnation achieved, but without returning to the emphasis on human subjectivity. During this process, Athanasius' assertion that "what is not assumed cannot be healed," becomes something more like, "what is not assumed cannot be forgiven." Perhaps Anselmian theory could be creatively enhanced by joining it back up to recapitulation.

I say that to shift the emphasis away from the *Cur Deus Homo*'s Christology to its implied theology proper is to play into the hands of Anselm's opponents, because, almost without exception, all of the critics who seem to be the most squeamish about Anselm's theory are so, not on the basis of the logic of his Christology, but on the basis of what his scheme implies about God the Father.[87] All the emphasis is placed on the issue of how God could be so inflexible and vindictive as to require this, and, perhaps more seriously, whether God really forgives anything at all, if in fact he has not cancelled the debt but simply been "reimbursed," so to speak, or compensated, via the violent sacrifice of his own Son?

In reply to these, it could be said that there is no such thing as a nonviolent atonement theory. Every theory of the atonement, even nonviolent ones, involve God in redemptive violence. The only way that this could not be the case would be if what we are dealing with is simply a martyrdom. In which case, there would be no "theology" or "theory" of the death of Christ at all; there would instead be a theodicy of the cross: a way of explaining why God "allowed" such a tragedy, and other suffering like it, rather than explaining why God apparently required or planned it. Nonviolent theories of the atonement succeed only because, in the portrayals given, the emphasis is shifted away from the God who requires or orchestrates or uses the events of the crucifixion to an almost total emphasis on the human beings that perpetrated it. Yet a different portrayal might quite easily transform a nonviolent theory into something very different if the accent was altered slightly. If the emphasis was placed upon a God looking on from heaven insisting that this vicious scapegoating of his Son at the hands of evil people

---

86. Sowle Cahill, "*Quaesti Disputata:* The Atonement Paradigm," 423.

87. The term *Pater* ("Father") appears no more than twenty-five times throughout the work, and almost every occurrence is part of an attempt to tackle head-on the kinds of criticisms that are levelled at him today.

was the only cure for mimetic violence then the theory could become every bit as cruel as the worst distortions of objective theories. Likewise, objective theories—including Anselm's—can be nuanced in directions that place the emphasis on a voluntary Christ and a united Trinity, as indeed Anselm does repeatedly throughout his work.

CUR DEUS HOMO SHOULD BE VIEWED AS MORE POST-PATRISTIC THAN PROTO-REFORMED

There is a tendency to read Anselm through Reformation-shaped spectacles and subsume his theory within the grander narrative of penal theories, yet, as mentioned earlier, *Cur Deus Homo* is categorically not a penal theory. It is an exploration of the logic of penalty-avoidance through the God-Man's representative self-donation. It is also important to remember that all of Anselm's sources were the patristic authors or sources immediately following the patristic era. Attention has already been drawn to Irenaeus and Athanasius. Equally plain is his adherence to Chalcedon and Leo I's interpretations of it, as well as his attachment to the *Rule of St. Benedict*. It is with these spectacles on that Anselm must be read.

Anselm's Context

MORE MONASTIC THAN FEUDAL

Despite the repetition of Anselm's supposed feudal context, there is less than adequate evidence that feudalism was the true shape of society at the time that Anselm wrote this treatise. Knowing references to the darkly primitive ideas that most authors imply by referring to this are intended to reinforce our, to quote C. S. Lewis, "chronological snobbery,"[88] as a way of writing off Anselm's theory for today. A convincing case has been made for a significant level of Benedictine influence, and the whole of CDH is an implied correction to the excesses of the penitential system inspired by Cyprian. However, a fully satisfying explanation for the origins of the concept of "honor" that dominates CDH is yet to appear. It is clear that, by the Reformation, a shift in criminal law away from various reparations made towards offended parties and back to the old Roman way of upholding law

---

88. Lewis, *Surprised by Joy*, 207–8.

as an impersonal principle of justice, had begun to take place.[89] It does appear then that, although feudalism is probably not the right term for it, a highly relational judicial system was in existence at the time of Anselm, living as he did between the Roman and Reformation ages. This must account for his highly personal descriptions of what criminality looked like to him, and these portrayals are not a million miles away from what it did in fact look like in the so-called feudal era. Caution is needed, however, and more place needs to be given to his very long stint in the Benedictine monastery at Bec where the *Rule of St. Benedict* would have been memorized and quoted from frequently. To this at least we owe his strong concept of the value of obedience.

Our Context

At this point the wise words of Christian psychologist Paul Tournier seem pertinent: "it is inscribed in the human heart: everything must be paid for!"[90] Tournier here is sounding rather like Anselm. It is probably to Anselm that we owe the use of "debt" as a way of referring to the work of Christ. In the Gospels, the concept of debt is used in the context of human forgiveness, but it is Anselm, probably inspired by Athanasius, that develops this concept fully as a cross-concept. It speaks to us today in two fairly obvious ways:

THE BURDEN OF FINANCIAL INDEBTEDNESS

Despite the rather frequent bursting of financial bubbles, our society has been enslaved to debt, to false wealth, for a long time. Consumerism seems to be the engine that drives us there by its constant appeal to what we are told we lack. Our spiritual bankruptcy is described back to us in terms of a material insufficiently, albeit with often very spiritual overtones. This leads to the creation of false needs that lead to over-spending to meet these needs. This in turn results in material indebtedness. Consumerism thus produces what it offers to cure. This state of affairs at least offers a point of recognition. Despite denunciations of transactional mercantile atonement motifs, we can at least say that these concepts do resonate with people today.

89. E.g., Lenman and Parker, "The State, the Community and the Criminal Law in Early Modern Europe," 23.

90. Tournier, *Guilt and Grace*, 175–76.

THE BURDEN OF GUILT

Here we come to the heart of Tournier's critique of the human condition. Psychologists seem fairly unanimous that human guilt is a pervasive problem that, if dealt with, could cure a whole host of mental health problems that are linked to it. Using the logic that "everything must be paid for," which, according to Tournier, is a human logic, we could even leave the question of God requiring payment to one side at this point. The really important thing, it could be said, is that *we* require payment. We need to see our sin, in the words of Packer, to be "not simply disregarded, but judged, judged to the full and paid for to the full."[91] And it is Anselm's joyful news at the very end of his treatise, that draws from Boso an uncharacteristic paean of praise, that our debts have been *more* than paid for. The incalculable merits that overflow from Christ having paid a debt he did not owe are freely transferred from the all-sufficient Christ who has no possible use for his reward to you and I, whose need is so acute. This description of a super-abundance of blessing is not to be missed. Among those today who are able to register a sense of spiritual debt, this truth could easily be appreciated.

91. Packer, *Celebrating the Saving Work of God* Vol. 1., 135. See also Atkinson: "For guilt to be handled, there must be reparation. The demands of right and wrong must be satisfied. Only then can life goon creatively. . . . In Christ, God makes the costly reparation; in Christ, we are liberated to live creatively again." Atkinson, "What Difference Does the Cross Make to Life?" 267.

4

Luther and Calvin

WE LOOK NOW AT THE time-honored and venerable evangelical doctrine of penal substitution. The term is attributed to nineteenth-century Princeton theologian, Charles Hodge,[1] though the concept was birthed during the Reformation. It has become the most widely held doctrine amongst evangelicals. Penal substitution simply means that Jesus died to bear the penalty for my sins, hence "penal," and that he did this in my place, hence "substitution." The bearing of penalty implies that God needed to punish sin and that something actually happened to Jesus on the cross that constituted a punishment of the innocent Christ and which was accepted by the Father as a satisfactory equivalent to the punishment that was due to the human race as a whole.

Substitution is a stronger word than representation. Representation is what Jesus does with our implicit participation. He can go to the Father as one of us, in a way that includes all of us and affects all of us, like the high priest of the tabernacle ministry. Substitution implies that there were

---

1. Something very like the phrase is used in Hodge, *Systematic Theology* Vol II, 488: "If, however, sin be pardoned it can be pardoned in consistency with the divine justice only on the ground of a forensic penal satisfaction." This idea is couched in substitutionary terms, e.g., ibid., 494: "by his obedience and suffering, by his whole righteousness, active and passive, he, as our representative and substitute, did and endured all that the law demands," so it is easy to see how the phrase then transmutes into "penal substitution," and this indeed is true to his intentions. Green and Baker devote considerable space to Hodge's treatment of the atonement: *Recovering the Scandal*, 146–50.

certain things that only Jesus could do for us. He did these things alone, without us, and, indeed, to spare us. In this sense, he suffered instead of us, so that we would not have to. As our representative, he suffers with us. As our substitute, he suffers instead of us, and it is this latter note that penal substitution emphasizes. Hence it is a radicalization of Anselm's theory.

My purpose here in this first section on Luther will be to try to discover the reasons for this radicalization of the Anselmian model: why did representation become substitution; and what added the penal, punitive element? Secondly, what aspects of the totality of Luther's *theological crucis* could be re-appropriated for a postmodern world?

Setting the Scene 1: Late Medieval Spirituality

To set the scene, a brief glance at medieval crucicentrism will be of benefit before we come to examine Martin Luther's distinctive theology of the cross, his *theologia crucis*. Crucicentrism, or cross-centeredness, though it found a congenial home in evangelical spirituality, was originally a product of medieval sacramental spirituality.[2] By AD 1000 the idea of transubstantiation was widely held, and was officially recognized at the Fourth Lateran Council of 1215, then reaffirmed at the Council of Trent.[3] This belief, entailing as it did the repeated offering of the Lord's body and blood,[4] led to the multiplication of Masses,[5] as well as to the creation of a new feast, the feast of Corpus Christi. "Awe and veneration"[6] surrounded such symbols of sacrifice, as these had become the only way of salvation. Consequently, the cross, the central feature of the sacramental system, became the rallying point for monastic and lay worshippers alike. Besides these developments, the medieval period also witnessed growing devotion to the Sacred Heart in France, as well as to the Five Sacred Wounds in Portugal, and the creation of "Calvaries": life-size sculptures of scenes depicting the final hours of

---

2. Gillett points out that crucicentrism has always been a feature of Western Christianity (as opposed to Eastern Orthodox). Evangelicalism simply "held more tenaciously to what has always been the heart of Western Catholicism." Gillett, *Trust and Obey*, 66.

3. McBrien, ed., *The Harper Collins Encyclopedia of Catholicism*, 1264.

4. The idea of the Eucharist as a sacrifice presented to God by the worshipping church goes back at least as far as Irenaeus *Against Heresies* IV:18, 4–6.

5. Dillistone, *Christianity and Symbolism*, 249–50.

6. Ibid., 250.

Jesus' life on earth, not to mention the appearance of countless splinters of the cross, and the dissemination of various Holy Grail myths.[7]

The factors that gave rise to passion mysticism in the medieval period would appear to be a shift of emphasis taking place throughout the medieval and Renaissance periods. This was a shift in popular devotion from a kingly, exalted Christ in heaven to a very human Jesus, suffering and dying on a cross.[8] After such emphasis on the divinity of Christ as had been seen in late antiquity, perhaps it was inevitable that the pendulum would eventually swing the other way. The trigger for this swing of the pendulum seems to have been the growing misery of ordinary people as the Middle Ages reached their height. Until the first bubonic plague of 1349–51, population growth meant that people began to outstrip the natural resources available to sustain them. There was widespread rural poverty and a massive immigration to the cities where sanitation was poor and life expectancies short. A suffering human Christ could transfigure the deprivations of churchgoers as they beheld the various pictorial sermons of a Christ who suffered yet overcame death.

The Emergence of Martin Luther's *Theologia Crucis*

By the time of Martin Luther, passion meditation was widespread, being espoused by Thomas à Kempis, the most widely read of the medieval mystics,[9] Johannes von Paltz (a close friend of Luther's), and Johannes von Staupitz (Luther's superior at Erfurt). Meditation on the wounds of Jesus was recommended by Saupitz as a way out of temptation and anxiety.[10]

---

7. Three studies of the body and blood of Christ in medieval spirituality are noteworthy: Beckwith, *Christ's Body*; Camporesi, *Juice of Life*; and Bynum, "The Blood of Christ in the Later Middle Ages."

8. Medieval spirituality focused, according to Beckwith, on "Christ the incarnate God, and more specifically Christ both as infant and as crucified, the two moments of birth and death, which insist on the claims of the body most emphatically and obviously." Beckwith, *Christ's Body*, 17.

9. "If you cannot contemplate high and heavenly things take refuge in the Passion of Christ and love to dwell within his sacred wounds. For if you devoutly seek the wounds of Jesus and the precious marks of his passion you will find great strength in all troubles." Kempis, *The Imitation of Christ*, 68.

10. Tomlin, *The Power of the Cross*, 138. "By pointing Luther to the cross, Staupitz had 'started the doctrine,' as Luther put it, that would eventually lead to his Reformation breakthrough." George, "The Atonement in Martin Luther's Theology," 265.

Luther himself recommended it as a route to conviction of sin. This would be followed by a profound transformation that is like a new birth.[11]

The passion mysticism with which Luther was acquainted included various different styles of meditation on the cross. One style that the early Luther practiced, based on *humilitas* theology,[12] was to meditate in detail on each of the wounds of Jesus. This was designed to reveal to oneself the true awfulness of one's sin, inspiring true penitence. Such moments afforded Luther some comfort as his mind was lifted from himself altogether.[13] Luther insists:

> Faith must spring up and flow from the blood and wounds and death of Christ. If you see in these that God is so kindly disposed toward you that he even gives his own Son for you, then your heart in turn must grow sweet and disposed toward God.[14]

Ultimately, it is probably not possible to understand Luther without recognizing the very high value he placed upon experience, and in particular, the defining experience of finding peace with God that he himself enjoyed. This breakthrough, though not unrelated to the passion, did not come from passion meditation, but from meditation on the book of Romans. It is Luther's "tower experience"[15]:

> I meditated night and day on those words until at last, by the mercy of God, I noticed their context: "The righteousness of God is revealed in it, as it is written, 'The righteous person lives by faith.'" I began to understand that in this verse the "righteousness of God" means the way in which a righteous person lives through a gift of God—that is, by faith. I began to understand that this verse means that the righteousness of God is revealed through the Gospel, but it is a passive righteousness—that is, it is that by which the merciful God makes us righteous by faith, as it is written, "The righteous person lives by faith." All at once I felt that I had been born again and entered into paradise itself through open gates. Immediately I saw the whole of scripture in a different light.

---

11. *LW* 42.11, Luther's *Meditation on Christ's Passion*, dating from 1519.

12. Ngien, *The Suffering of God according to Martin Luther's "Theologia Crucis,"* 29.

13. Tomlin, *Luther and His World*, 42–44.

14. Martin Luther, *Good Works* (1520) in *LW* 44, 38.

15. Because it occurred in the tower of the Black Cloister at the monastery in Wittenberg.

This breakthrough is thought to have occurred sometime around 1515, while Luther was giving lectures in Wittenberg University on the book of Romans, though this fragment was actually written towards the end of his life as he reflected upon this life changing moment. It seems that by the time Johann Tetzel came on the scene selling indulgences in 1517 (the year of the famous *Ninety-Five Theses*), Luther's theological perspective had radically changed. The ultimate origins of the breakthrough may even be datable to an earlier point than the lectures on Romans. In 1513, a year after he was appointed to the university at Wittenberg, we find him lecturing on the Psalms. A key verse for him was Psalm 71:2: "In your righteousness deliver me."[16] This verse may well have begun to point the way to an interpretation of divine righteousness as a way of salvation rather than a means of judgment against human unrighteousness.[17]

Outline of Luther's *Theologia Crucis*

In giving the foregoing account of the influences flowing into Luther's view of the cross I have, following Tomlin,[18] majored on the elements already there in the young Luther and his early milieu, and circumvented, for now, the wider discussion about what Luther was reacting against. This too is of interest, but I think rather less so, and such negative influences, where relevant, will be highlighted as we go along.

The Importance of Humility and the Exclusion of Works

As with Paul, scholars are not completely unanimous about what is the "center" of Luther's theology: is it his *theologia crucis?* Is it "law and gospel"? Is it justification by faith? Is it Christology?[19] There is such a lot of overlap

16. McGrath, *Luther's Theology of the Cross*, 156–57.

17. So Bainton, *Here I Stand*, 51. Strangely, it seems that Luther was not exactly going against the tide of scholarly opinion as to the righteousness of God in Romans. The view that this was indeed a justifying rather than condemning justice was already widely held. It seems clear, however, that Luther had not truly understood this until his Tower Experience.

18. Tomlin, *Power of the Cross*, 111–95.

19. The origins of this discussion are largely traceable to the translation into English of Loewenich's seminal work: *Luther's Theology of the Cross* (1976; original: *Luthers Theologia Crucis*, München: Kaiser, 1929). In the context of global warfare and the miseries caused by human sin that were particularly apparent in the twentieth century,

between these concepts that one cannot go too far wrong by choosing any of these four, or a combination of them, at least as a starting point. A helpful observation, however, has been Luther's fixation with methodology. In other words, Luther is less interested in the content of any particular doctrine (after all, he was not a systematic theologian but a lecturer in biblical studies), but much more interested in the way theology should be done. He was interested in great big schemes of interpretation that could make the whole of the Bible—not to mention life as we know it—make sense.[20] This is what the *theologia crucis* actually is. It is anything but a theory of the atonement. Rather, it is a way of speaking about how God reveals himself and what humanity really is: "A theologian of the cross calls things what they actually are."[21] It was an antidote to the speculations of medieval scholasticism and the vainglory of those who supposed that a person could do the best they could and God would do the rest. Luther insisted on a path to justification that every true believer must take, and it was the path of self-humbling: "Luther had experienced the enormity of Sin in all its destructive fury, as few others have done. This consciousness of the reality of evil in the world becomes the centre of his thinking."[22]

Loewenich's book sparked renewed interest in Luther's theology of the cross: Aulén, *Christus Victor,* 117–44; Watson, *Let God Be God!* (1947); Rupp, *The Righteousness of God* (1953); Bornkamm, *Luther's World of Thought* (1958); McDonough, *The Law and the Gospel in Luther* (1963); Ebeling, *Luther: Einführung in sein Denken* (1964), later as *Luther: An Introduction to His Thought* (1970); Althaus, *The Theology of Martin Luther* (1966); Iwand, "Theologia crucis," in Iwand, *Nachgelassene Werke* II (1966); Prenter, *Luther's Theology of the Cross* (1966); Moltmann, *The Crucified God* (1974); McGrath, *Luther's Theology of the Cross* (1985); Ngien, *The Suffering of God according to Martin Luther's* Theologia Crucis (1995); Forde, *On Being a Theologian of the Cross* (1997); Solberg, *Compelling Knowledge* (1997); Tomlin, *The Power of the Cross* (1999), 111–95; Lohse, *Martin Luther's Theology* (1999); Ngien, "Ultimate Reality and Meaning in Luther's Theology of the Cross" (2004). In Luther's own writings, the term "*theologia crucis*" is extremely rare. It appears twice in the *Heidelberg Disputation* (*LW* 31, 40), once in a dispute with Johann Eck (*LW* 31, 309), once in his *Lectures on Hebrews* (*LW* 29), and once in his *Explanations of the Ninety-Five Theses* (*LW* 31, 225–26).

20. So Holl: "This was more than a new exposition of Rom 1:17, this was the fountain of a new doctrine of God." Holl, *Gesammelte Aufsätze zur Kirchengeschichte,* Vol. 3, 188. (Translation courtesy of Rupp, *The Righteousness of God,* 128). Yet, even so, he has been accused of not being consistent with his own system, e.g., Gritsch, *Martin Luther's Anti-Semitism,* 140–41.

21. Martin Luther, *Heidelberg Disputation* (1518), Thesis 21.

22. Lortz, *Die Reformation in Deutschand,* Vol. 1, 192. Quoted in English by Rupp, *Righteousness of God,* 27.

This is where his law-gospel dichotomy comes into play. The law of Moses condemns us all as sinful beyond remedy. Only as we realize our complete helplessness against sin, only as we understand the bondage of our will that renders us all the wretched captives of sin, death, and the devil, and only as we realize the perilous state that this leaves us in as we contemplate eternity, only then is there any hope for us:[23] "The proper subject of theology is the man accursed for his sin and lost, and the God who justifies and saves the sinner."[24]

Law and gospel thus produce in man a "dualistic struggle" that resolves in "despairing utterly in self and believing absolutely in Christ."[25] Only as we are humbled by God beneath the law's terrible demands does the gospel become gospel to us. It is good news, but only to those who have been through this process—as Luther himself had by the time he wrote the *Heidelberg Disputations* in 1518, the classic expression of his *theologia crucis*. It is a "despair-faith experience."[26] It is at that point that we enter upon our lifelong state of repentance, and it is only then that the sight of Christ crucified on the cross becomes precious to us, a good thing: a God moment. And this paradox illuminates all the rest of his thinking so that, as far as Luther is concerned, everything we may know about God is paradoxical, dialectical: "When God brings to life, he does so by killing; when he justifies, then he does so by accusing us; when he brings us into heaven, he does so by leading us to hell."[27]

Other paradoxes are his well-known attachment, on the basis of Isaiah 45:15 and Exodus 33:23,[28] to the concept of God being a hidden God, a *Deus Absconditus*, whose most important and truest qualities are always hidden beneath their opposite and are only visible to faith.[29] This concept also clearly has echoes of Paul's paradoxes in relation to the cross in 1 Corinthians 1:21 and 2:2. Ngien says it well: "To grasp God aright is to grasp him as he wills to be grasped, that is, not in power but in weakness, not

23. See Luther's *The Bondage of the Will* of 1525 for elaborations on this.

24. *WA* 40/2, 328. From his commentary on Galatians.

25. McDonough, *The Law and the Gospel in Luther*, 1

26. Ibid., 146.

27. *WA* 18, 633. This is Section 24 of his *The Bondage of the Will* of 1525.

28. His use of Exod 33:22–23, where God allows only a view of his back, was probably inspired by Bernard of Clairvaux. Tomlin, *The Power of the Cross*, 132.

29. McGrath, *Luther's Theology of the Cross*, 150. Yet all the various paradoxical permutations date to his one initial revelation of the true meaning of the "righteousness of God" in Rom 1:17. McGrath, *Luther's Theology of the Cross*, 152.

in majesty but in lowliness, not in glory but in the shame of the cross of Christ."[30]

God's Mercy Concealed beneath His Justice

And so the law brings us to the gospel via humility and repentance, then what? Then we see God. But God is not to be found where we expect him. He is certainly not in the lofty speculations of the schoolmen; quite the reverse. As a conflicted monk, so disillusioned that, before his flash of insight, he felt that he hated God, the great question that burned in Luther's heart was "how can I find a gracious God?" More specifically, "How may I know that I have been justified?" And it is there, in the wrath poured out on the cross, that the mercy of God is most truly and definitively to be found. It is when we see God's wrath that was upon us, now concentrated at the cross, that our afflicted consciences find sweet relief. In his larger commentary on Galatians of 1525, we find these ideas most strikingly expressed. To this we now turn.

Penal Substitution in Luther

It is Luther's exposition of Galatians 3:13 that is often, and with good reason, cited to illustrate how Luther's thought had gone one step beyond Anselm to something much more radical. What I find interesting, especially as we hold before us Luther's big question, "how may I be sure that I am justified?" is the following extract. It pictures Christ on the cross having taken up the position of everyman, having agreed to "be the person who has committed the sins of all men":

> Now the law comes and says: "I find him a sinner, who takes upon Himself the sins of all men. I do not see any other sins than those in Him. Therefore let Him die on the cross!"[31]

Luther presents a profound image here in which Christ so fully absorbs the sins of everyman that none are visible outside of him. In Christ alone, therefore, is the judgment of God completely and exhaustively concentrated,

---

30. Ngien, *Luther as a Spiritual Adviser*, 161.

31. *LW* 26, 280.

so that all who put their faith in him are completely free of judgment. This is a clear break with Anselm's *either* punishment *or* satisfaction.[32]

And so it now becomes clear how both of the main elements of Luther's *theologia crucis* went on to shape atonement theology in the direction of penal substitution. The cross becomes radically substitutionary in Luther because there must be no risk of a synergistic cooperation between God and man. Man, whose righteousness is filthy rags, must play no part. The crucified God must completely take over the work of redemption, must absolutely take man's place. And the cross becomes penal because there is no escaping the judgment and wrath of God. Luther, however, never understands wrath to have the last word.[33] He does not seem to attach the eschatological hell-bound significance to it that later Protestantism did. The situation is redeemable. If we will first be humbled beneath his wrath we will then see how God, at the cross, has revealed his justifying mercy beneath its opposite. On the cross we see all judgment absorbed and our sentence of condemnation passed, and all is horror and darkness and God-forsakenness. But in that very moment is to be found the justifying mercy of God. Hence the cross works for those who have humbled themselves beneath the awful awareness of what their sins deserve, and it works for them because there they see Christ taking their judgment. There they see the Judge exhausting all judgment.

God of the Addicted? Luther's Theology and Addictionology

Much of Luther's theology seems rather negative to those who cannot identify with the profound sense of sin that it demands and assumes. There is one group, however, whose ethos chimes exactly with Luther's: Alcoholics Anonymous. Step One of the famous twelve steps is described by AA's founder, Bill W. thus: "We admitted we were powerless over alcohol—that our lives had become unmanageable."[34] In his *Lectures on Romans*, Luther

32. George, "Atonement in Martin Luther's Theology," 274. This is not to say that Luther was especially well acquainted with Anselm, but the satisfaction theory, especially as mediated via Thomas Aquinas, was clearly the theological context in which Luther forged his own atonement theology.

33. "God's wrath is his penultimate and not his final, word." McGrath, *Luther's Theology of the Cross*, 155.

34. Anon., *Alcoholics Anonymous: The Story of How Many Thousands of Men and Women Have Recovered from Alcoholism*, 59. Much research has been done in

similarly speaks of faith being more or less identical with a humility in which one "justifies," or agrees with, God.[35] The faith that lays hold of God's deliverance is synonymous with a deep-seated and repentant honesty.[36] "It therefore behooves us to be very certain about the distinction between God's power and our own, God's work and our own, if we want to live a godly life."[37] And it is precisely this level of complete emotional honesty that AA and other twelve-step fellowships insist on as the starting point. The volunteers are all recovering alcoholics themselves and know only too well how the addict's inability to be honest about the true extent of the addiction is their Achilles heel. There is, quite literally, no hope without getting past this first step. And the Lutheran faith is a faith of those humiliating first steps towards being honest with ourselves about the full extent of our difficulties and how these things are too strong for us.

The idea of an addicted society, in which almost everyone is addicted to something, is perhaps exaggerated, though there have been some worthwhile reflections on addiction,[38] and there is clearly room for further reflection using the rich theological resources that Luther bequeathed.

Hyperreality, Image, and the Crucified God

Theologians have flirted with postmodern philosophers very tentatively when it comes to atonement theory,[39] though one philosopher who has been flagged as a potential conversation partner is Jean Baudrillard. Just

addictionology to try to determine the relative sobriety rates of the various styles of twelve-step fellowship, as well as their effectiveness as a group over against alternatives such as cognitive-behavioral coping skills training or Motivational Enhancement Therapy. The results so far appear to be inconclusive. A considerable literature is introduced by Ferri and Davoli, "Alcoholics Anonymous and other 12-step programmes for alcohol dependence (Review)," *The Cochrane Library*.

35. *WA* 56, 220, 9–11.

36. "[T]he word makes one 'become a sinner,' by a radical *metanoia* of self-assessment," Wicks, "Justification and Faith in Luther's Theology," 5.

37. *LW* 33, 35.

38. Schaef, *When Society Becomes an Addict*; Martin, *Regaining Control*; Schaef, *Escape From Intimacy*; Royce, "Alcohol and Other Drugs in Spiritual Formation"; Stibbe, *O Brave New Church*.

39. But see Tomlin, "'The Theology of the Cross," 59–73; Brown, "The Atonement"; Boersma, "Irenaeus, Derrida and Hospitality"; Vanhoozer, "The Atonement in Postmodernity"; Harper, "Christus Victor, Postmodernism, and the Shaping of Atonement Theology."

such a dialogue took place at the 2005 atonement symposium in London. An effort was made to forge a link between his thought and penal substitution.[40] Baudrillard's despair at the way our culture replicates itself, televises itself, comments upon itself, watches itself to the point where reality itself seems in some ways to have been replaced by one great big simulation, is easy to identify with.[41] Yet, a "theologian of the cross," Luther says, "sees things as they really are." In Baudrillard's world, reconciliation between the empty image of the thing and the thing itself is no longer possible because the thing itself, real life, has long gone. We can no longer even say that we are alienated from the real when the real exists only as faded fragments. Robbins naturally sees a link between his thought and humankind's loss of the image of God.[42] In celebrities, we are even encouraged to worship the image-bearer rather than the original image—and these image-bearers are usually pastiches of other previous celebrities, and so it goes on. At Calvary, we are confronted with the way God really is and the way we really are: "The atonement makes real alienation and its resolution possible."[43] A connection with reality can finally be restored.

Like the theologians of glory in Luther's day, theology today can likewise become a simulation of theology. As I hinted at earlier, critiques of Anselm, for instance, are endlessly reproduced copies of other critiques to the point where Anselm himself has been lost. Theology gets lost in secondary sources. "The cross is all our theology," said Luther. It is the primary source for theology.

Setting the Scene 2: The Criminal Justice System during the Reformation

Before we go on to consider Calvin, and his still more developed penal substitutionary theory, it seems good at this point to do some more scene setting. This time, we consider the criminal justice system current at the time of the Reformation.

40. Robbins, "Atonement in Contemporary Culture."

41. See especially Baudrillard, *Simulations*. For an excellent introduction see Richard Lane, *Jean Baudrillard*. See also Baudrillard's penetrating critique of the media coverage of the Gulf War: *The Gulf War Did Not Take Place*, which illustrates what he means by hyper-reality.

42. Robbins, "Atonement in Contemporary Culture," 334.

43. Ibid., 337.

Despite Durkheim's original hypothesis, which was based on criminal records from the fourteenth century, that criminal justice progressed in early modernity from the barbaric to the more humane, and from the punitive to the restitutive, it is now widely accepted that almost the reverse was the case. Beginning in the tenth century and continuing until the nineteenth century, but especially notable during the sixteenth century, criminal justice throughout most of Europe made the transition from the private to the public, from what we would call settlements "out-of-court" that involved compensating victims, to prosecutions under the auspices of the state that led to various capital and corporal punishments.

Quite a range of crimes became capital offenses—there were no prisons as we know them today. Though successful prosecutions were not common in Geneva, records exist that are contemporaneous with Calvin's latter years there that innumerate fourteen executions for the year of 1562. The crimes include homicide, the rape of children, serious theft, sodomy, and witchcraft.[44] This was part and parcel of a judicial revolution, which in turn reflected a new social reality across Europe. Small rural communities in which a community justice system could operate were disrupted by mass migration into ever-growing urban centers where sections of a new lower class took to crime as a way of life and threatened the social order. Crime rates soared. This new situation fully emerged between around 1450 and 1600. During the Reformation and the emergence of the penal substitution doctrine, comprehensive criminal codes were being developed at a national level and new judicial bodies were being formed for their execution: "statute replaced tradition."[45] This was the way the fledgling nation states of Europe dealt with an era of social unrest.

Naturally, a direct link is often made between the thought of someone like Calvin and the changes to the judicial system that were happening all around him. It is assumed that Luther and Calvin alike imbibed the judicial revolution by osmosis and deployed its new paradigms in their preaching

44. Lenman and Parker, "The State, the Community and the Criminal Law in Early Modern Europe," 14. In addition to these, a number of executions were, at least tacitly, authorized by Calvin himself. Two fairly recent accounts of his difficult time in Geneva before things finally settled down in 1555 are: Ganoczy, "Calvin's Life" and Greef, *The Writings of John Calvin*, 17–81. Interestingly, Gorringe overtly links the judicial revolution with Calvinism: "Wherever Calvinism spread, punitive sentencing followed," though it is difficult to see how a causal link could be proven: Gorringe, *God's Just Vengeance*, 140.

45. Weisser, *Crime and Punishment in Early Modern Europe*, 94.

and writing without feeling the need to explain or defend it. Green and Baker, in particular, rely so heavily on the plausibility of such an argument that no evidence is presented. And this is the main problem historiographically. There does not appear to be a single shred of evidence that Luther or Calvin were either consciously or subconsciously making use of contemporary legal categories. This is more problematic when we consider how very new and how very current the judicial revolution was. It was in process all around them. It had not yet settled into the new unquestioned reality—that would not happen for another two hundred years. So if, by intruding the ideas of law and vicarious punishment into the satisfaction theory, they were intending a nodding reference to the emerging new realities of the criminal justice system, one would expect some explanation or discussion. By no means all of the people were happy with the new system and they would have needed some winning over.

Secondly, summary dismissals of Luther and Calvin on the basis of criminal law fail to take account of the very obvious fact that, in context, both writers were dealing with the "law" in Paul's thought. This is especially the case with Luther's all-important New Testament letter: Galatians. In Galatians 3:13 Christ bears the curse of the law—the law of Moses. Luther is attempting to expound the hugely dominant concept of law in Galatians, a letter in which it has such prominence as an actor in salvation that Luther goes as far as to personify it: "The law comes along and says . . ."

The most that could be said about the judicial revolution is that it contributed to making penal substitution conceivable. We can say further, that with the normalizing of the new criminal justice system in subsequent generations, the propagation of penal substitutionary atonement as "gospel" also became possible. The real driver behind a legal interpretation of the cross, however, would appear to be the need to find a basis for a forensic definition of justification. Contemporary understandings of the possibility of earning, by self-effort, just enough merit to be justified by God were a significant problem to the Reformers, and it was these popular notions that forced the issue. The pastoral and ethical implications of this *via moderna,* this modern way, were seen by Luther as disastrous. The trivialization of personal sin by the selling of indulgences had been a case in point. No, a person's status before God needed to be taken out of his or her hands altogether and made into a declaration of God on the basis of a work of God, the cross.

In an atmosphere of widespread crucicentrism, justification would not survive unless systematically linked to the cross in some way. The result is a new angle on the cross that gives the sinner no escape from the wrath of God except by way of seeing that wrath being expunged at the cross. The inflexibility of God's law—a concept rooted in his perfect immutability—is linked to God's wrath and serves to stop the faithful from casting around for half-measures such as indulgences, penances, and pilgrimages. The result is a solid logical footing for the simple but profound assertion that humans can do nothing to justify themselves. Only faith in a work carried out for them and without their help could justify them in the sight of God.

Penal substitution then, is really a justification-eye-view of the atonement. The real roots of it are justification by faith. The legal color of it is really only the glow of its parent doctrine: justification by faith. This is why theologians have found it so limiting as a complete explanation of the cross. The truth is that it is not an explanation of the cross but an explanation of justification. Penal substitution is, in effect, a justification for justification.

John Calvin (1509–64)

The French reformer John Calvin is commonly acknowledged to be the one who organized and systematized Lutheran ideas. In contrast to Luther he was "shy and bookish."[46] His writing style is very different to Luther's. It is much more ponderous and thorough. In a way that has now become familiar in evangelical scholasticism, but which must have been fairly novel at the time, his writings are a forest of biblical citations.[47] An army of biblical texts assaults the eyes whenever a major point is being made. The system he bequeathed, Calvinism, went on to become the most widely exported theological product of the Reformation, becoming the dominant form of Christianity among such diverse cultures as the Scots, the Dutch, and the Puritan settlers of New England.

Like all the Reformers, he sounded the doctrine of sin loud and clear. This had the effect of maximizing the place of the atonement as the only answer to the rampant and pernicious evil that sin was understood to be:

46. Steinmetz, *Calvin in Context*, 3.

47. Indeed, he has been described as a true biblical theologian: Lane, "The Quest for the Historical Calvin," 113.

"He offered in sacrifice the flesh which he took from us, that by expiation wrought He might destroy our guilt and might appease the Father's just anger."[48]

In light of our terrible predicament, the substitution of Christ, as in Luther, is set forth in stark terms, though note the strongly incarnational element evocative of recapitulation: "Our Lord came forth as true man and took the person and name of Adam in order to take Adam's place in obeying the Father, to present our flesh as the price of satisfaction to God's righteous judgment, and, in the same flesh, to pay the penalty that we had deserved."[49]

The main reason for holding that Christ was actually punished at the cross was the relief this gives to the guilt-stricken conscience:

> This is our absolution, that the guilt, which held us liable to pun-
> ishment, was transferred to the head of the Son of God. For we
> must hold above all to this compensation, that we may not be
> frightened and anxious all our life, as though there still remained
> upon us that just vengeance of God which the Son of God trans-
> ferred to Himself.[50]

Some Misunderstandings

By way of balancing these stark categories, something that is often absent from Calvinism but which is a dominant thought in Calvin himself is the mystical union with Christ.[51] This is the control that prevents his system from becoming a cold and abstract transaction. He is clear that everything that Christ has done for us would remain forever shut up within himself unless faith possesses them. The benefits of the cross are apprehended by way of a faith-union with Christ, the representative second Adam:

---

48. Calvin, *Institutes of the Christian Religion* II.12.3. *Institutes* II.12–17 is a sustained treatment of the atonement.

49. Ibid., II.12.3.

50. Ibid., II.16.5. This is an important key to the overlooked ethical implications of Calvin's atonement theology. See also *Institutes* III.3.2: "no man will ever reverence God who does not trust that God is propitious to him, no man will ever willingly set himself to observe the Law who is not persuaded that his services are pleasing to God[;] . . . the hope of pardon is employed as a stimulus to prevent us from being reckless to sin."

51. This is brought out by Tamburello, *Union with Christ,* and Billings, *Calvin, Participation, and the Gift*. See also Billings, *Union with Christ*.

> This conjunction therefore of Head and members, the dwelling of Christ in our hearts, in a word, the mystical union, are accounted by us of the highest value, so that Christ being ours makes us partakers of the gifts wherewith He is endowed. We do not therefore behold Him without us from afar, so that His righteousness may be imputed to us, but because we have put Him on and are implanted in His body, and He, in short, has deigned to make us one with Himself, therefore do we boast that we have fellowship in righteousness with Him.[52]

In Calvin's doctrine of participation in Christ, there are two blessings that result: justification and sanctification.

> I trust I have now sufficiently shown how man's only resource for escaping from the curse of the law, and recovering salvation, lies in faith. . . . The whole may thus be summed up: Christ given to us by the kindness of God is apprehended and possessed by faith, by means of which we obtain in particular a twofold benefit: first being reconciled by the righteousness of Christ, God, becomes, instead of a judge, an indulgent Father; and, secondly, being sanctified by his Spirit, we aspire to integrity and purity of life.[53]

Note also the element of God's prior love for us that is the moving cause of our redemption, as opposed to caricatures that picture the cross as procuring God's love:

> First by His love God the Father prevents [prévient, that is, prepares the way for] and anticipates our reconciliation in Christ. In short, because He first loves us, he afterwards reconciles us to himself. But since in us, until Christ rescues us by His death, there remains iniquity which merits the wrath of God, and is cursed and condemned before Him, we have no full and firm union with God until Christ joins us to Him. And so of we would find God appeased and propitious towards us, we ought to fix our eyes and minds on Christ alone.[54]

---

52. Calvin, *Institutes* IV.17.2.

53. Ibid. III.11.1.

54. Ibid. II.16.3. See also ibid., II.16.4 for a lengthy quote from Augustine: "For it was not after we were reconciled to him by the blood of his Son that he began to love us, but he loved us before the foundation of the world, that with his only-begotten Son we too might be sons of God before we were anything at all."

Here too, is an important nuance to note over against those who are quick to caricature Calvinistic views of the atonement as involving a rift between Father and Son:

> But we do not suggest that God was ever hostile to Him or angry with Him. For how could He be angry with the beloved Son, in whom His soul was pleased? Or how could Christ placate by His intercession for others a Father who was hostile to Himself? But we say this, that He bore the weight of the Divine severity, in that, being stricken and afflicted by God's hand, he experienced all the signs of an angry and punishing God.[55]

Finally, it is also worth noting that, though Calvin placed "expiating crime"[56] as a central cipher for interpreting what was going on during those hours on the cross, he also made very free use of other images, such as the obedient Second Adam, *Christus Victor,* and Christ as sacrifice and example.[57] There is a blending together of many differing pictures.[58]

Limited or "Definite" Atonement

A recurring theme in Calvin studies is "how Calvinist was Calvin?"[59] This persistent question arises from the fact that the Five Points of Calvinism[60] were developed polemically, in response to the Five Articles of the Remonstrants,[61] the Arminian position. So there was always going to be the danger that Calvin himself would get lost somewhere amid the Calvinist-

---

55. Ibid. II.16.11.

56. Blocher, "The Atonement in John Calvin's Theology," 283.

57. Petersen, *Calvin and the Atonement,* chapters 4–9. Together with Petersen's earlier work, *Calvin's Doctrine of the Atonement,* the only other book dedicated to the subject of Calvin's doctrine of the atonement would appear to be Buren, *Christ in Our Place.* All other works on the subject tend to be part of the "limited atonement" debate.

58. Petersen, *Calvin and the Atonement,* 126.

59. For example, Hall, "Calvin against the Calvinists"; Armstrong, *Calvinism and the Amyraut Heresy,* xvi–xx; Djaballah, "Calvin and the Calvinists"; Bell, "Was Calvin a Calvinist?"; Muller, "Calvin and the 'Calvinists.'"

60. 1) Total depravity, 2) unconditional election, 3) limited atonement, 4) irresistible grace, 5) perseverance of the saints.

61. Which could summarized as something like: 1) Election conditional upon foreseen faith, 2) unlimited atonement, 3) total depravity, 4) grace essential but resistible, 5) falling from grace unlikely but possible. For ease, consult Henry Bettenson's *Documents of the Christian Church* for extracts of all the important confessions.

Arminian debates. This is especially the case with the third point of Calvinism, the doctrine of a "limited" atonement.[62] In fact, there does not appear to be anywhere in Calvin's writings where the atonement is clearly said to be applied only to the elect,[63] though such an idea clearly fits with his ideas about predestination. Logically, with sovereign divine agency playing such a prominent role in his thought, the atonement could not be otherwise than limited to or efficacious for only those for whom it was intended: the elect, those predestined for salvation. Calvin, in any case, was drawing from an Augustinian tradition already rich in notions of particular redemption.[64] Calvinist scholars, such as Roger Nicole (and Helm, Muller, Rainbow, Leahy, Cunningham, Godfrey) that continue to defend this belief as true to Calvin prefer to use the words "definite," or "particular." Such words more accurately depict a Christ who really did obtain redemption for his elect. It definitely worked. There was nothing hit and miss about it. Thus, while the proclamation is rightly addressed to all, it is intended for, and works only for, the elect. They also downplay the view that Calvin's successor, Theodor Beza, who overtly taught limited atonement, brought about a sharp and

62. An extremely thorough introduction to the literature, to which I am indebted here, is Harog, *A Word for the World*. Important contributions to the debate about limited atonement within Calvin studies seem to reach their peak in the early 1980s, an entire edition of the *Evangelical Quarterly* having been devoted to the subject in 1983. The modern debate begins in the late 1960s: Cunningham, *The Reformers and the Theology of the Reformation* (1967), 396–97; Armstrong, *Calvinism and the Amyraut Heresy* (1969); Godfrey, "Reformed Thought on the Extent of the Atonement to 1618" (1975); Kendall, *Calvin and English Calvinism to 1649* (1979); Helm, *Calvin and the Calvinists* (1982); Helm, "Calvin and the Covenant: Unity and Continuity" (1983); Torrance, "The Incarnation and 'Limited Atonement'" (1983); Bell, "Calvin and the Extent of the Atonement" (1983); Bell, "Was Calvin a Calvinist?" (1983); Nicole, "John Calvin's View of the Extent of the Atonement" (1985); Helm, "The Logic of Limited Atonement" (1985); Strehle, "Universal Grace and Amyraldianism" (1989); Rainbow, *The Will of God and the Cross* (1990); Boersma, "Calvin and the Extent of the Atonement" (1992); Leahy, "Calvin and the Extent of the Atonement" (1992); Nicole, "Covenant, Universal Call and Definite Atonement" (1995); Thomas, *The Extent of the Atonement* (1997); Thomas, *The Atonement Controversy in Welsh Theological Literature and Debate, 1707–1841* (2002); Clifford, *Amyraut Affirmed, or "Owenism a Caricature of Calvinism"* (2004); Blacketer, "Definite Atonement in Historical Perspective"; Bond, "Amyraldianism and Assurance" (2007); Rouwendal, "Calvin's Forgotten Classical Position on the Extent of the Atonement" (2008).

63. The two best fits are generally thought to be his comments on 1 John 2:2 in *CO* 55:310 and his discussion of the Eucharist addressed to Heshusius in *CO* 9:484. See Blacketer, "Definite Atonement in Historical Perspective," 314–15.

64. A point very ably made by Blacketer, "Definite Atonement in Historical Perspective," 307–13.

unwelcome departure from the thought of Calvin into the cold rationalism of the later Reformation. They insist there is more continuity with Calvin than this view suggests.

Calvinists who can no longer support this doctrine from Calvin, such as Alan Clifford (and Hall, Armstrong, Kendall, Bond, Thomas, Bell, Boersma, Petersen, Torrance), but who still wish to be identified as Calvinist in outlook, sometimes call themselves Amyraldian Calvinists, naming themselves after the Frenchman Moïse (or Moses) Amyraud (1596–1664), who created a ruckus in 1634[65] for calling limited atonement into question. Amyraldians are, effectively, four-point Calvinists, and tend to emphasize the discontinuity between Calvin and Calvinism. Even these, however, will not go as far as to say that Calvin taught universal redemption, but rather that he did not clearly teach limited atonement, however inconsistent this may make Calvin seem. Some, such as Peterson[66] wish to continue to maintain a belief in limited atonement, but not on the basis of Calvin's writings.

Torrance[67] has wisely pointed out that Calvin does not start with predestination in the same way that Calvinism does. In fact, Calvin does not discuss predestination until Book III of his *Institutes* where it takes its place as part of the end, rather than the beginning. Calvin's *Institutes,* like his soteriology, has a Trinitarian structure. This means that salvation begins with the love of God the Father towards his creatures (Book I), proceeds with the redemption wrought by Christ (Book II), and ends with the application by the Spirit of the benefits of the work of Christ (Book III). Election appears as part of an explanation of how a redemption that was accomplished by Christ and all-sufficient, only ends up being applied by the Spirit to some, not all, people, and this despite the obvious fact that those that do receive it are no more deserving than those who don't. The doctrine of a limited atonement seems only to have become fully developed and defended in John Owen's *The Death of Death in the Death of Christ.* Torrance argues that this development only became possible once Calvin's theology was tidied up so that election was put where it logically belongs: in the eternal decrees of God before time.[68] Sadly, in tidying up Calvin, such Calvinists ended up subordinating the free love of God to the sovereign will of God, something that Calvin did not do.

65. With the publication of his *Traité de la Predestination.*

66. Peterson, *Calvin and the Atonement,* 118.

67. Torrance, "The Incarnation and 'Limited Atonement,'" 83–84.

68. Ibid., 87.

Given that almost all studies of Calvin's doctrine of the atonement focus on the idea of a limited atonement, rather than any other aspect of the atonement in his thought,[69] this subject cannot be passed over without at least a mention. However, it needs to be stressed that the embarrassingly voluminous discussions surrounding this subject are, primarily, not discussions of any given theory of the atonement since all contributors to this debate assume a penal substutionary standpoint. Rather, the discussion is really part of a wider treatment of the role of determinism in Calvin's thought.

A Theological Center?

There is no consensus about whether anything can qualify as the main principle or organizing idea within Calvin's thought. One interesting observation, however, is made by R. Ward Holder.[70] He points out that, when Calvin set out to write his commentaries, it was the Pauline Corpus that he went to first. It was these that he cut his teeth on, and, of these, the book of Romans very deliberately takes first and highest place, a letter that Calvin understands to be principally about justification. Calvin himself introduces it thus: "if we have gained a true understanding of this Epistle, we have an open door to all the most profound treasures of Scripture."[71] And so Holder says, "For any who wish to find Calvin's canon of the canon, either to admire or to castigate, he himself provides enough evidence in this letter."[72] So it is that, as with so much else in Reformation theology, it is the primacy of justification as the chief weapon against the worst contemporary evils that also provides us with our best interpretational key to Luther and Calvin's thinking.

69. Something that Petersen discovered: Petersen, *Calvin and the Atonement*, 115.

70. Holder, "Calvin as Commentator on the Pauline Epistles," 224–25.

71. Calvin, John, *Commentary on Romans* CNTC VIII:5.

72. Holder, "Calvin as Commentator on the Pauline Epistles," 225.

5

The Nineteenth Century

By the late Reformation, the doctrine of penal substitution had become codified in all the Protestant confessions of faith, especially those undergirding the faith of the Puritans, the Calvinists, and the Lutherans. All three faiths soon coalesced (though in an uneasy peace) in the eighteenth-century revivals under the preaching of Calvinists Jonathan Edwards and George Whitefield, Arminians John and Charles Wesley, and Lutheran-influenced Moravian pietists led by Count Zinzendorf. The revivals have been described as the coming of the Spirit upon the doctrines of the Reformation to form a "vital orthodoxy."[1] The revivals were thus a heady mixture of a compelling biblical-theological account of the work of Christ that focused on the plight of the sinner and the abundance of God's grace, combined with supernatural manifestations of the Spirit. As the Enlightenment approached, this warmed up version of Reformation ideas, which we now call evangelicalism, helped to insulate the faithful against the onslaughts of rationalism and empiricism. Revivalism itself became an anti-rational revolt against the penetrating queries of advancing scientific method.

However, the challenges to faith, especially for the evangelicalism that had been born in the revivals, continued to intensify. Everything was changing. It has been noted, for instance, that, for as long as the criminal justice system did not change, the way the atonement was preached among

1. Piggin, *Firestorm of the Lord*, 45–49.

evangelicals did not change either.[2] During the nineteenth century, however, there was a drive towards the reform of criminals and not simply their punishment. Influenced by the epoch-making *On Crimes and Punishments* of 1764, prisons were built in the nineteenth century that were intended for the rehabilitation of offenders, as well as serving the function of removing dangerous people from society.

This period also coincided with the beginnings of a full-scale attack upon penal substitution by theologians influenced by the increasingly powerful German liberal Protestant tradition. The advocating by liberals such as Albrecht Ritschl of exemplarist views of the cross, and the attendant denunciations of penal views, became quite persistent. Even within Anglicanism there came, in 1889, Charles Gore's highly influential book, *Lux Mundi*. This work emphasized the incarnation rather than the atonement as the true heart of Christian faith. The insights of Darwin were conceded and the Spirit's role in the inspiration of Scripture was relativized.[3]

Further, religion itself was now under sustained intellectual attack. By the time of Samuel Butler's 1903 novel, *The Way of all Flesh*,[4] an autobiographical snipe at Victorian religion and family life, the honest doubts of "High-minded Victorian agnosticism had given way to the brasher notes of self-confident progressivism."[5] The age of faith in scientific progress and Darwinian explanations of the world had fully dawned.[6] It was an age in which God was fast becoming nothing more than a "grand Perhaps."[7]

All Christians in the West faced a choice. Either they could accommodate themselves to the prevailing cultural and intellectual mood, which

2. Holmes, *The Wondrous Cross*, 114.

3. Gore, ed., *Lux Mundi*, esp. 247–66, which discusses inspiration. The chapter on the atonement itself (201–29) says little that would have been controversial.

4. Bulter, *The Way of all Flesh*.

5. Jay, *Faith and Doubt in Victorian Britain*, 125.

6. McDonald provides an illuminating anthology of contemporary comment, e.g., "The scientific interpretation of natural phenomena has made the interest of God more remote, God's existence more problematical, and the idea of God unnecessary"; "[T]he Doctrine of Evolution has once and for all deprived natural theology of the materials upon which until lately it subsisted." McDonald, *Ideas of Revelation*, 8.

7. Browning, "Bishop Bougram's Apology" (verse 190). Speaking of the late Victorian crisis of faith and its popularization via the press, Gilbert comments: "the fact remains that doubt and theological uncertainty percolated downwards into the ranks of ordinary believers to an extent unprecedented." Gilbert, *Religion and Society in Industrial England*, 177. The period of this age of doubt is identified as "the last forty years of the century" in Jay, *Faith and Doubt*, 99.

rejected the perceived barbarism of transactional ideas of the atonement, or they could radicalize their Christianity. This radicalization process spawned the first Vatican Council of 1869–70, as well as a number of new dimensions to evangelicalism, including the American holiness movement, the Salvation Army, the Keswick Convention and its spin-offs, and, indirectly, Pentecostalism. Some of these movements were more sectarian than others.[8]

Interestingly, those who gathered in these new movements tended to sing and preach about the "blood" of Jesus more than the "cross" or "Calvary." This was possibly because of the need for an antidote to, or a rebalancing of, the highly objective, transactional ideas that were being promulgated in the penal substitution model. This model logically resulted in an objective change of status from condemned to justified. The result was that, when it came to living a victorious Christian life, penal substitution was, frankly, failing them. In a world so full of temptations, the devout could no longer cope with a gradualist sanctification that was a constant battle and that, thanks to the Reformers, had been abstracted completely from justification. They were not content with a life of inertia—forgiven but not free from the power of sin, and freedom from sin was not systematically linked to the atonement message. To this the blood of Jesus—a concept that pictured the benefits of the cross as fluid, and capable of being applied, sprinkled, or even bathed in—was the answer. And so holiness adherents sang of the "wonder-working power" of the blood and, "nothing but the blood of Jesus."[9] This would increasingly be complemented by a correlative emphasis on the subjective working of the Holy Spirit in sanctification.

Among academics, Princeton became a bastion of religious conservatism which, under the professorships first of Charles Hodge (b. 1797– d. 1878),[10] and then of his son Archibald Alexander Hodge, and B. B. Warfield after him, solidified Reformed doctrine yet further into what would soon be specifically termed "penal substitution."[11] The note of the Father punishing the Son on the cross, which we first met in Luther's comment on Galatians

8. Kent highlights the dimension of protest that contributed to the late Victorian proliferation of sects. It was a protest as much against the older churches as to the growing secularism of the world. Kent, *Holding the Fort*, 301.

9. For more on this theme see my "A Brief History of the Blood."

10. Described as the "most influential American Presbyterian theologian of the nineteenth century." Noll, "Charles Hodge," 561.

11. "Penal satisfaction" is Hodge's preferred phrase, a term he inherits from Turretin, e.g., Turretin's *Institutes of Elenctic Theology* 2:14.XI.ii–iv.

3:13, is sustained in Hodge and his exposition of the same passage: "They were divine inflictions. It pleased the Lord to bruise him. He was smitten of God and afflicted."[12] Under the influence of Calvinist Reformer Francis Turretin (1623–87), Charles Hodge also accented the Aristotelian notes of divine immutability, reinforcing the absolute impossibility that God could ever compromise his law in the slightest, and that punishment must follow its infringement:

> The law of God is immutable. It can neither be abrogated nor dispensed with. . . . Throughout the Scriptures, the immutability of the divine law; the necessity of its demand being satisfied; the impossibility of sinners making satisfaction for themselves; the possibility of it being rendered by substitution; and that a wonderfully constituted person, could and would, and in fact has, accomplished this work on our behalf, are the great constituent principles of the religion of the Bible.[13]

In an important insight, evocative of Anselm's thought, the atonement had to be "consonant with his [God's] perfections and character, which is the highest conceivable kind of necessity."[14] A. A. Hodge wrote in similar terms, further propagating his father's theology: "The justice of God must be an ultimate and unchangeable principle of his nature, determining him to punish sin because of its intrinsic ill desert"[15]

These kinds of assertions may have helped to shape popular gospel preaching around the central pivot of divine inflexibility, the proclamation of what God the Father cannot do, but which the Son has made possible. Predictably enough, and with some plausibility, Green and Baker assert that Charles Hodge, "read the Bible through the lens of the criminal justice system of his era."[16] Hodge does make references to commonly accepted legal processes, though the main burden of his theology, as we saw, is that God must act in accordance with his unchanging attributes, especially that of justice.[17]

12. Charles Hodge, *Systematic Theology,* Vol. 2, 517.

13. Ibid., 493–94.

14. Ibid., 488.

15. A. A. Hodge, *Outlines of Theology,* 155.

16. Green and Baker, *Recovering the Scandal of the Cross,* 146.

17. Contra Green and Baker: "Hodge explains the penal substitutionary model in a way that makes it appear self-evident that God must behave according to late-nineteenth century American notions of justice." Ibid., 147.

Hodge's rendering makes the atonement so objective that it appears to be more about God being true to himself than about the people it was intended to save. Green and Baker lament: "it is so outside of us . . . that what changes through the cross is a legal ruling. According to the logic of the model, an individual could be saved through penal substitution without experiencing a fundamental reorientation of his or her life."[18]

This was exactly what the originators of events such as the Keswick Convention, which was launched in 1875, were trying to address. They saw no fault, however, in their atonement theology, simply the need to subjectivize the language and pursue a more aspirational approach to sanctification.

In Britain, two major theological volleys were launched in defense of penal substitution, the first by George Smeaton,[19] and the second by the Keswick sympathizer, R. W. Dale.[20] Dale's work, in particular, is credited with having lifted the discussion "to a different plane."[21] Refreshingly, he reminded everyone that humans are not saved by a theory of the atonement but by the fact of the atonement. Nevertheless, by 1897, at the annual Fernley Lecture in Leeds, Methodist John Scott-Lidgett was, in spite of his high regard for Dale's work, lamenting the fact that the atonement had been:

> taken out of the hands of the living God and committed to certain of His attributes, especially justice and mercy, which, at least in popular usage, have been almost personified and set bargaining one with the other as to what should be demanded and offered as a satisfaction for sin.[22]

This transactional approach, whether such a view was framed in the language of the law court or of the market place was alienating, he felt, not only the theologians but was "remote from . . . distasteful to the common mind, carrying us into a sphere which is felt to be foreign and even antagonistic to both the simple life of faith and the graciousness of the gospel."[23]

18. Ibid., 149.

19. *The Apostles' Doctrine of the Atonement*, first published in 1870

20 *The Atonement: The Congregational Union Lecture for 1875*.

21. Paul, *The Atonement and the Sacraments*, 163. Moberly said of his work that it "has stood, and will stand, as a real and solid contribution to the faith and goodness of his own generation." Moberly, *Atonement and Personality*, 396.

22. Scott-Lidgett, *The Spiritual Principle of the Atonement*, 3.

23. Ibid., 2.

We pause here to examine one very interesting dissenting voice from within nineteenth-century Scottish Presbyterianism, who tries to address many of these concerns, John McLeod Campbell.

Christ the Perfect Penitent: John McLeod Campbell (1800–1872)

Raised in a devout Presbyterian home on the West Coast of Scotland, the saintly John McLeod Campbell showed particular interest in Scottish philosophy during his time at Glasgow University and went on to develop interests in both science and religion.[24] He had early received a call to the ministry and was given charge of a congregation in Rhu, Dumbartonshire in 1825 where, for five years, he flourished as a preacher and pastor.[25]

John McLeod Campbell's book, *The Nature of the Atonement*,[26] sold slowly at first due to what appeared to be a very parochial focus to the work: it deliberately set out to address issues within Scottish Calvinism.[27] It was also very hard work to read. Even his father had once remarked, "Man, you have a queer way of putting things."[28] His work has to be read ponderously, meditatively, in order to be appreciated. But appreciate it people did. Over a hundred years after the publication of *The Nature of the Atonement,* Torrance would compare Campbell in stature to Athanasius and Anselm,[29] and a galaxy of theological luminaries would likewise go on to voice varying degrees of indebtedness to Campbell and his book: John Caird, R. W. Dale, B. F. Westcott, R. C. Moberly, John Scott Lidgett, P. T. Forsyth, James Denney, Vincent Taylor, not to mention the direction that Scottish Calvinism went on to take towards a softer theology.[30] One was to comment: "Campbell has done more than any other to emancipate his countrymen from the

---

24. Tuttle, *So Rich a Soil*, 12–13.

25. The best rendering of his life is in the short Introduction to the 1959 edition, written by Edgar Dickie: McLeod Campbell, *The Nature of the Atonement* (1959), xiii–xx, but see also Tuttle, *So Rich a Soil*, 11–17, and Torrance, "The Contribution of McLeod Campbell to Scottish Theology."

26. McLeod Campbell, *The Nature of the Atonement* (1865).

27. Tuttle, *So Rich a Soil*, 99.

28. Ibid.

29. Torrance, "The Contribution of McLeod Campbell to Scottish Theology," 295.

30. Tuttle, *So Rich a Soil*, 99–115; Paul, *The Atonement and the Sacraments*, 162–67.

harsher elements of Calvinism."[31] Speaking at the turn of the century, at a time when the atonement was as hotly debated as today, Scott Lidgett said that Campbell's book "puts us on the high road to a true conception of the matter."[32]

In a nutshell, Campbell's theory was a theory of vicarious repentance, which would later be the one adopted by C. S. Lewis as erroneously representing "almost all Christians everywhere."[33] Campbell was reacting against the staunch Calvinism of his Scottish upbringing, and was repulsed by the idea suggested in Calvinistic preaching that the cross made God become gracious towards sinners. The death of God's Son was, in this way, being pictured as twisting the arm of God, wresting forgiveness from him. More importantly for Campbell, however, were the devastating effects that the doctrine of limited atonement was having upon his parishioners. He kept coming across individuals who were wracked with guilt and anxiety, unable to be sure that they were one of the elect and that the atonement had been effective for them. They had been encouraged by other teachings to look for evidences and to be patient with the process of coming to a full assurance of faith. Campbell's main goal, therefore, was to preach an atonement that seemed to him to be capable of producing assurance: an atonement that was for all. Though these efforts were greatly appreciated by his kirk, his departure from Calvinist orthodoxy got him excommunicated and stripped of his position in 1831. Living alone in Glasgow (don't worry, he later married and had four kids), he had the chance to formulate more carefully his arguments.

Campbell points out that the atonement originates in the forgiving grace of God and is the definitive revelation of it: "If God provides the atonement then forgiveness must precede atonement; and the atonement must be the form of the manifestation of the forgiving love of God, not its cause."[34] God is thus pictured as being fatherly and kind. Added to this basic idea is a high Chalcedonian view of Christ as both fully God and fully man: "my attempt to understand and illustrate the nature of the atonement has been made in the way of taking the subject to the light of the incarnation."[35]

---

31. Alexander, *The Shaping Forces of Religious Thought*, 366, cited in Tuttle, *So Rich a Soil*, 59.

32. Scott Lidgett, *The Spiritual Principle of the Atonement*, 175.

33. Lewis, *Mere Christianity*, 6.

34. Campbell, *Nature of the Atonement*, 20.

35. Ibid., xxv, where he also references Anselm.

Despite Campbell's acknowledged lack of expertise in patristics, Tuttle cannot resist comparing his incarnational approach to that of Irenaeus and Athanasius.[36] Nimmo points out how right it is of Campbell to emphasize the "*identity* of the One who suffers and His relation to those for whose sins He suffers."[37] In Campbell's thought, the incarnation never replaces the atonement. Rather, as God, Christ alone could know the true seriousness of sin. As man, he alone could combine in his person this knowledge of its utter culpability with a real experience of its horrors and sorrows for man: "The *sufferer suffers* what he suffers *just through seeing sin and sinners with God's eyes, and feeling in reference to them with God's heart.*"[38]

It is the combination of the "perfect Amen"[39] from his divine nature to the damnable nature of sin, on the one hand, and the human sorrow for sin, on the other, that is the key to Campbell's theory. These combine to bring forth from Christ on the cross a penitence for sin on behalf of mankind that was of necessity far more real and deep than any breast-beating penitence that could be mustered by you or I. A mere human could not know the full extent of sin's seriousness for God. The sufferings of Christ are therefore, "the sorrows of holy love endured in realising our sin and misery."[40] This bridges the gulf between God and humankind: "the love of God has not only desired to bridge over this gulf, but has actually bridged over it, and the atonement is presented to us as that in which this is accomplished."[41]

And the acceptance of the divine sentence on sin inevitably meant the acceptance of death. Here, he starts to move towards penal language in affirming that death is the divine sentence. Indeed, T. F. Torrance claimed that Campbell's theory was in fact a penal theory but of a "fuller and profounder kind."[42] In one sermon, Campbell expounds Galatians 3:13 to the effect that the curse was "exhausted in Christ."[43] He avoids penal language

---

36. Tuttle, *So Rich a Soil*, 83.

37. Nimmo, "A Necessary Suffering?" 64.

38. Campbell, *Nature of the Atonement*, 101, italics original.

39. "This confession, as to its own nature, must have been *a perfect Amen in humanity to the judgment of God on the sin of man.*" Campbell, *Nature of the Atonement*, 135–36 italics original.

40. Ibid., 133.

41. Ibid., 25–26.

42. Torrance, *Scottish Theology from John Knox to John McLeod Campbell*, 308–9.

43. Campbell, *Sermons and Lectures*, 13, cited by Hart, "Anselm of Canterbury and John McLeod Campbell," 323. Hart does not indicate which volume. Three volumes of hand written notes of Campbell's sermons are viewable online:

by insisting that, for a God who is already gracious towards sinners, no punishment was required as a precondition to forgiveness.[44] All that was needed was the upholding of the divine verdict, a full acknowledgement of it, and because divine and human natures converged in the acknowledging of it there was no sense in which one aspect of the divine being was punishing another. The full implications of sin were, in the manner of Athanasius, being "assumed," or in Campbell's wording, "absorbed." They were taken up by Christ in a Godwards direction. There was nothing punitive coming from God towards Christ. To the contrary, at the heart of Campbell's thought is the oneness of mind between the two of them as to the true awfulness of sin. And Christ's oneness with humanity, on the other hand, allowed his confession of sin on their behalf to be more than a fiction.

The human response of faith then is now a response to the offer of a bridge across the gulf. Stepping onto that bridge in faith (my phrase not his) results in the assurance of knowing God's fatherhood, his sentence on sin having been already acknowledged. The forgiving grace that was within him from the start is now released.

Having said this, it is, paradoxically precisely in this area of the subjective appropriation of the atonement, where Campbell has been criticized. Moberly noticed the, "more complete success" with which Campbell discerned "the nature of the relation of Christ to God, than that of the relation of men to Christ."[45] R. S. Paul agrees: "for all the apparent objectivity of Christ's vicarious work, the effective operation of grace depends upon our own effort."[46] Bewkes wondered whether the whole thing is nothing more than a "contortion" of language,[47] and Hughes looked in vain in Campbell's theory for anything in it that really addresses the power of sin.[48]

These and other criticisms of Campbell seem to be largely to do with incompleteness, but for this incompleteness to lie in precisely the area that he was most concerned to address, namely the assurance and well-being of

---

https://archive.org/details/notesofsermonso1camp   https://archive.org/details/notesofsermonso2camp https://archive.org/details/notesofsermonso3camp.

44. This logical ordering of forgiveness as really and actually prior to atonement, rather than merely the desire to forgive being prior to it, has attracted the criticism that he almost makes the cross itself pointless: Macquarrie, "John McLeod Campbell 1800–72," 268: Nimmo, "A Necessary Suffering?" 67.

45. Moberly, *Atonement and Personality*, 402.

46. Paul, *The Atonement and the Sacraments*, 149.

47. Bewkes, *Legacy of a Christian Mind*, 206.

48. Hughes, *The Atonement*, 145–46.

the faithful, seems a bit awkward. There are also some unwise expressions of thought (though, let us not forget that he was not a trained theologian, and made no claims to being one). For instance, there is his idea that God already forgives before the cross, which possibly is not what he really meant. Campbell's greatest achievement is undoubtedly in the way he reintegrated atonement with incarnation, without the one obliterating the other. That we have to do with, to quote the Apostle, "Jesus Christ and him crucified" (1 Cor 2:2), rather than simply "him crucified," is a right intuition. Time and again, the identity of the man on the cross shines through his work in a most profound way, anticipating later developments.

6

Twentieth- and Twenty-First-Century Developments

The Rise of Fundamentalism

EVANGELICALISM WAS FIGHTING A BATTLE on two fronts: renewed Roman Catholicism inspired by Cardinal Newman and the Oxford Movement, on the one hand, and virile German liberalism, on the other. Evangelical resistance to all things liberal, especially liberalism's revulsion at a penal sacrificial concept of the atonement, became a major identity marker.

On both sides of the Atlantic, the Fundamentalist movement was in full swing by the 1920s and 30s. It held to penal substitutionary atonement as the only orthodox way of looking at the cross. "Fear of liberalism," and "fear of resurgent Catholicism" were formative of Anglican evangelicalism as early as the 1820s,[1] and, against the tide of liberal scholarship, Charles Spurgeon had once declared that he would rather have his tongue cut out than ever agree to stop preaching about the blood.[2] Now, preaching the once-for-all atoning blood was a way of opposing the perceived watering-down of the gospel that the liberals had brought with their penchant for

1. Rennie, "Fundamentalism and the Varieties of North Atlantic Evangelicalism," 333.

2. Spurgeon, *The Metropolitan Tabernacle* Vol. 32, 129.

the life and teachings of Jesus; it was also a way of countering the perceived displacement of the preached gospel that the revival in Catholic sacramentalism had brought in the wake of the Oxford movement. The preaching of a bloody sacrificial once-for-all atonement for sin served to identify evangelicals as anti-liberal and anti-ritualist.

P. T. Forsyth (1848–1921)

Alongside all of this, a voice was heard that had not sided with liberalism and yet was not fundamentalist either. Peter Taylor Forsyth was a Congregationalist from a remote corner of Scotland. Though not from a privileged background, his sermons, lectures, and prolific publications during the first two decades of the twentieth century went on to earn him a lasting place in theological reflection, which has continued to the present day.[3] In fact, so great was his oratory ability and his literary flourish (he reportedly labored over every sentence he wrote) that some of the sharpest criticisms were directed against his rhetorical skills. Sometimes the fine words would obscure rather than enhance his meaning, one critic describing his writing as leaving the reader "dazed by a series of electric flashes which did not succeed in dispelling the obscurity that gathered around the subject."[4]

Having studied under Albrecht Ritschl in Germany, he had fully imbibed German liberalism but held this in tension with a professedly evangelical faith. However, following a bout of severe ill-health beginning around 1893, his theology became much more focused on the terrible importance of the cross.[5] By 1899, in an address in Boston, his new agenda was clear: "The Cross is the final seat of authority, not only for the Church, but for all human society."[6] In an address at the Congregational Union of

---

3. Highlights include: Trevor Hart (ed), *Justice the True and Only Mercy: Essays on the Life and Theology of Peter Taylor Forsyth* (1995), Leslie McCurdy, *Attributes and Atonement: The Holy Love of God in the Theology of P. T. Forsyth* (1999), and Jason Goroncy, *Hallowed Be Thy Name: The Sanctification of All in the Soteriology of P. T. Forsyth* (2013).

4. Higgsinson, "The Theology of P. T. Forsyth and its Significance for us Today," 75, citing A. S. Peake in the *Holborn Review*.

5. The turning point was marked by a sermon at the Congregational Union in Leicester in 1896 called "Holy Father." Andrews, Jessie Forsyth, "Memoir," in Forsyth, *The Work of Christ* (1965 ed.), 18.

6. Andrews, "Memoir," in Forsyth, *The Work of Christ*, 21.

1905, which was described by one eye witness as the "greatest public utterance to which he had ever listened,"[7] Forsyth spoke these words:

> The old orthodoxies can never again be what they were; but one thing in them draws me and sustains me amidst much that is hopelessly out of date. And it is this, that they had a true eye for what really mattered in Christianity; and especially that they did grapple with the final facts of human nature, the abysses of moral experience, the wickedness of the human heart, and its darling self-will. They closed with ultimates. They did not heal lightly the wound of the people. . . . It is the grace of Israel we need; for the grace of Greece fails heart, and flesh and moral will. It is subjective sand when we want objective rock. It does not enable us to keep our feet. We need a hand to lift us by the hair, if need be, and hurt us much in the doing of it, if only it sets us on the Rock of Ages.[8]

In an address that would be published in 1908 as *Positive Preaching and the Modern Mind,* Forsyth was explicit about the change that had taken place in him: "I was turned from a Christian to a believer, from a lover of love to an object of grace. And so, whereas I first thought that what the Churches needed was enlightened instruction and liberal theology, I came to be sure that what they needed was evangelization."[9] Forsyth had become a "prophet of the cross."[10]

The delicate balance between the progressive and the conservative that was in evidence in his speaking, was of a piece with his most characteristic phrase: holy love. In everything he wrote, he made continual reference to this phrase and variations on it in order to preserve the fundamental insight, recovered by liberalism, that God loves the world but also the terrible fact of God's holiness. This holiness was what made grace costly when holy love was most perfectly manifested in Christ crucified. He was not pitting the one attribute against the other and setting them bargaining for human salvation, as Scott-Lidgett had complained.[11] He was urging that God's love is only ever a holy love and that his holiness is only ever a loving holiness. Supremely it is Christ that helps us to grasp this: "If we cannot hold both sides in paradox we are not fit for the kingdom of heaven . . . but we can

7. Whale, "Foreword," in Forsyth, *The Work of Christ*, 8.

8. Ibid., 9.

9. Fosyth, *Positive Preaching and the Modern Mind*, 281–82.

10. Higginson, "The Theology of P. T. Forsyth and Its Significance for us Today," 68.

11. So Higginson: "Divine love did not mollify divine holiness." Higginson, "The Theology of P. T. Forsyth," 69.

grasp them by a faith of their reconcilement in a person with whom we have to do."[12] And how does this work? "[I]t was the Christ of the two natures cohering in one person that gave value to the cross."[13] And so, the cross is "the offering to God in man of a holiness possible only to God. He dies once for all, the just for the unjust, that He might bring us to His finality of God."[14] And this human and divine union on the cross must become the focus of faith "if life is to be unified out of its present distraction, if religion is to have a vital core, and cease to be a frame of pious moods and morals."[15] Salvation is to "enter Christ"[16] and thence, not to join some loose affiliation of like-minded people (the concept of church that was prevalent in Protestant Christianity in his day[17]), but to "enter the Church which is in Christ."[18]

Did he teach a penal doctrine? The answer would seem to be yes: "Christ bore God's penalty on sin. That penalty was not lifted even when the Son of God passed through it."[19] This is because, in Forsyth's theology, "where there is holiness there must be judgment."[20] This bearing of judgment, however, is integrated with a wider, more incarnational concept of Christ's obedience: "The atoning thing being the holy obedience to the Holy."[21] Forsyth's high regard for the Christ of Chalcedon was fully brought out in his most highly regarded work, *The Person and Place of Jesus Christ*.[22] Yet in none of his writings does the incarnation obliterate the atonement: "The incarnation has no religious value but as the background of the atonement."[23] Like Campbell, he is also insistent that, "The sacrifice is the result of God's grace and not its cause. It is given *by* God before it is given to Him."[24]

---

12. Forsyth, *This Life and the Next*, 27–28.

13. Forsyth, *The Cruciality of the Cross*, 43.

14. Ibid., 44.

15. Ibid., 43.

16. Forsyth, *The Church and the Sacraments*, 40.

17. Higginson, "The Theology of P. T. Forsyth and Its Significance for us Today," 68.

18. Forsyth, *The Church and the Sacraments*, 40.

19. Forsyth, *The Work of Christ*, 222.

20. Higginson, "The Theoloy of P. T. Forsyth," 69.

21. Forsyth, *The Work of Christ*, 222.

22. Forsyth, *The Person and Place of Jesus Christ*.

23. Forsyth, *Positive Preaching and the Modern Mind*, 182.

24. Forsyth, *The Cruciality of the Cross*, 52.

So in Forsyth, as in Campbell, some traditional lines are traced, yet these are placed within an exalted theology of incarnation that lifts the atonement of Christ from the narrow concerns of what God's justice supposedly cannot do. And not only is a more unified picture of the person and work of Christ given, but also a more unified picture of the Godhead as an undivided and overflowing fountain of holy love.

The Cross and Pentecostalism

The early twentieth century witnessed the mushrooming worldwide of a new form of Christianity that emphasized supernatural phenomena such as speaking in tongues and healing. The term "Pentecostal" eventually stuck, though plenty of late-nineteenth-century holiness groups had freely used this term for themselves. With the controversy that surrounded the Pentecostals, the term was soon dropped by such holiness organizations as the Pentecostal League of Prayer.

What is remarkable for such an influential movement as Pentecostalism is how little is original to it. Even its concept of a baptism in the Holy Spirit had already enjoyed a long prehistory within the holiness movement. And another Pentecostal concept with a long nineteenth-century prehistory was the doctrine that physical healing was available by faith on the basis of the atonement, in exactly the same way, and to the same degree, as the forgiveness of sins. The only logical reason to fail to be healed in response to prayer ministry, therefore, was a defective faith either in the minister or in the recipient of the ministry, since Christ's atoning work cannot be deficient.[25]

The first major work to appear that promoted this view had been that of A. J. Gordon, *The Ministry of Healing*, first published in 1882,[26] the title of which coined the now commonly used phrase, "ministry of healing."[27] The ideas behind this book, however, are traceable to the teachings of holiness preachers William Boardman and Carrie Judd Montgomery, which

---

25. Interestingly, according to research carried out among British Pentecostal ministers in 1999, while 86 percent of those surveyed agreed with the statement, "Physical healing is provided by Christ's atonement," 60 percent disagreed (some strongly) with the statement, "Divine healing will always occur if a person's faith is great enough." Kay, "Approaches to Healing in British Pentecostalism," 120–21.

26. Available in *Healing: The Three Great Healing Classics*.

27. Wilkinson, "Physical Healing and the Atonement," 151, n. 4.

first emerged around the year 1880.[28] It does not seem possible to trace healing in the atonement back any further than 1880. Although the origin of the Faith Cure movement (of which Boardman, Montgomery, and Gordon were a part) is traceable to Charles Cullis, whose ministry began in 1865, it is clear that, as late as 1879, Cullis was making no attempt "to provide a theological basis for his practice of healing."[29] The doctrine emerges gradually through various books and publications before reaching its fully developed form in A. J. Gordon. It seems likely that the original spark was provided by William Boardman noticing the way Psalm 103:3 juxtaposes physical healing with forgiveness.[30]

One of the aims of the early writers, all of whom were engaged in mass evangelism in America, was to elevate the status of healing ministry by placing it at the center of Christian theology, namely, in the cross.[31] Offering not only the opportunity to be born again but also to be physically healed was already drawing large crowds, but to link the offer of healing with the center-piece of the Christian faith was, in an age of virulent cessationism, to give healing ministries badly needed credibility.

Here is A. J. Gordon:

> He who entered into mysterious sympathy with our pain—which is the fruit of sin—also put Himself underneath our pain, which is the penalty of sin. In other words the passage [Isa. 53:4–5] seems

28. Petts, "Healing and the Atonement," 12–13. See also Dayton, *Theological Roots of Pentecostalism*, 115–41. Synan traces the origins to an undated book by Otto Stockmayer, *Sickness and the Gospel* (1878), though he agrees that A. J. Gordon was the one who "elevated divine healing to the level of the atonement." Synan, "A Healer in the House?" 191. Besides those of Petts, Dayton, Wilkinson, and Synan, other academically credible treatments of the subject of healing in the atonement (some in favor of it and some not) include: McCrossan, *Bodily Healing and the Atonement* (1930); Unger, "Divine Healing," (1971), Hubbard, *Isaiah 53: Is There Healing in the Atonement?* (1972); Moo, "Divine Healing in the Health and Wealth Gospel" (1988); Bokovay, "The Relationship of Physical Healing to the Atonement" (1991); Niehaus, "Old Testament Foundations"; Mayhue, "For What did Christ Atone in Isa 53:4–5?" (1995); Seet, "The Doctrine of Healing in the Atonement" (1996); Reichenbach, "By His Stripes We Are Healed" (1998); Menzies, "Healing in the Atonement." Interest in the subject now appears to be waning.

29. Wilkinson, "Physical Healing and the Atonement," 151, referring to Cullis' booklet of 1879 entitled, *Faith Cures, or Answers to Prayer in the Healing of the Sick*.

30. Petts, "Healing and the Atonement," 12, citing Mary M. Boardman, *Life and Labors of the Rev. W. E. Boardman*, 232.

31. Synan, "A Healer in the House?" 192.

to teach that Christ endured vicariously our diseases, as well as our iniquities.[32]

And A. B. Simpson:

> Therefore as he hath borne our sins, Jesus Christ has also borne away, and carried off our sicknesses; yea, and even our pains, so that abiding in Him, we may be fully delivered from both sicknesses and pain. Thus by His stripes we are healed. Blessed and glorious Burden-Bearer.[33]

Here is Pentecostal Carrie Judd Montgomery:

> If we trust fully to His finished work, sickness shall not be able to hold us captive, for Christ "himself took our infirmities, and bare our sicknesses."[34]

Anticipating Derek Prince's "wonderful exchange" teaching, F. F. Bosworth asserts:

> Sin and sickness have passed from me to Calvary—salvation and health have passed from Calvary to me.[35]

The main biblical source for the doctrine is Isaiah 53:4–5 and the New Testament citations of it in Matthew 8:17 and 1 Peter 2:24. If translated literally, Isaiah 53:4 would indeed yield phrases such as "our sicknesses" and "our pains" to describe what the servant bore. For Bosworth, the meaning is clear: "This prophecy, therefore, gives the same substitutionary and expiatory character to Christ's connection with sickness that is everywhere given to His assumption of our sins."[36] However, Isaiah seems to use the

32. Gordon, *The Ministry of Healing*, 16–17.

33. Simpson, *The Gospel of Healing*, 17.

34. Judd Montgomery, *The Prayer of Faith*, 58.

35. Bosworth, *Christ the Healer*, 26.

36. Ibid., 27. He marshals an impressive array of other lines of reasoning also, none of which clinch the argument alone but together present a formidable defence: "In Numbers 16:46–50 . . . Aaron, as priest, in his mediatorial office, stood for the people . . . and made an atonement for the removal of the plague. . . . Again, in Numbers 21:9, we read of the Israelites all healed by looking at the brazen serpent which was lifted up as a type of the Atonement. . . . Again, in Job 33:24, 25, we read: 'I have found a ransom . . . his flesh shall be fresher than a child's; he shall return to the days of his youth.' Here, we see Job's flesh was healed through an atonement. Why not ours?" Ibid., 20. He concludes: "Since the types of the Old Testament taught healing, it is certainly unwarranted and illogical to place the Antitype on lower ground." Ibid., 24. He goes on: "If Christ redeemed us from

word "sickness" (*ḥalah*) either as a poetic metaphor for the consequences of Israel's sin (Isa 17:11; 33:24) or as a reference to non-physical weakness and grief (Isa 14:10; 53:3; 53:10; 57:10).[37] Where Isaiah does use the word to refer to physical sickness it is in the case of Hezekiah's illness (Isa 38:1, 9; 39:1). Elsewhere in the Old Testament, instances where this word unambiguously refers to physical sickness are mostly in the historical books (e.g., 1 Sam 30:13; 1 Kgs 14:1; 2 Kgs 13:14; 20:1). The Prophets by contrast tend to use this words for physical sickness metaphorically (Jer 10:19; 12:13; 30:12; Ezek 34:4, 21; Hos 7:5; Amos 6:6; Mic 6:13; Nah 3:19). Mayhue concludes: "The obvious focus of Isaiah 53 is on sin, not on its immediate effects upon the body."[38]

And so some insist that the healing included in the atonement is purely "spiritual,"[39] or only for the future.[40] Nevertheless, some have been willing to include the thought of the servant vicariously bearing the consequences of sin, including, in some sense, sickness,[41] though this sickness element is generally left somewhat unresolved.[42] In a holistic culture there has been some giving of ground to the thought that Isaiah 53, if interpreted as referring to the work of Christ at all, must have some bearing on our physical wholeness: "The linkage between sin, sickness and death forms a background motif for Isaiah in the Servant song of chaps. 52–53. For

the curse of the law, and sickness is included in the curse, surely He redeemed us from sickness." Ibid., 31, "Man's future destiny being both spiritual and bodily, his redemption *must* be spiritual and bodily." Ibid., 32. In reply to the fact that Matt 8:17 refers, not to the atonement, but to the healing ministry of Jesus: "Christ was 'the Lamb of God slain from the foundation of the world.' He not only healed disease before Calvary, but he also forgave sins, and yet both of these mercies were bestowed on the ground of the Atonement yet future." Ibid., 28. (Incidentally, this is an argument also advanced by Carson, *Showing the Spirit*, 156–57.)

37. So Mayhue, "For What Did Christ Atone in Isa 53:4–5?" 121–41.

38. Ibid., 127.

39. Unger, "Divine Healing," 243. Though Unger was not a cessationist and did affirm physical healing, he insisted that such healings are, "direct and sovereign acts of God's gracious power released in view of Christ's redemptive work on Calvary but independent of it." Ibid., 243, 244.

40. Packer, "Poor Health May be the Best Remedy," 15.

41. Westermann makes a clear distinction between the sin and the punishment, or resultant suffering, of sin, both of which, he says, were borne by the servant. Westermann, *Isaiah 40–66*, 263.

42. Thompson concedes that "healing and health" are the result of the servant's sufferings, but does not seem to make any clear decision as to whether this is physical or spiritual; literal or metaphorical. Thompson, *Isaiah 40–66*, 103–4.

him there is no difficulty in moving between the two in prophetic poetic parallelism."[43] Indeed "atonement as healing" is a theory of the atonement in itself that is just beginning to be articulated in print.[44]

Theologically however, to relate present physical healing directly to the atonement is difficult to sustain, especially within the penal substitutionary framework within which it is normally cast. It is not necessary for substitution to take place in order for God's healing to flow in the same way that it is necessary, in the logic of penal substitution, for substitution to take place in order for there to be forgiveness. Jesus cannot have been punished for our sicknesses in the same way that he might be conceived to have been punished for our sins. It is a category mistake.[45] And so we are pushed back to a much less direct way of inferring physical healing from the atonement: "All that man lost in the fall was due to sin. All that he ever regains is through the atonement for that sin."[46]

David Petts postulates that a possible way of sustaining healing in the atonement is to adopt a different paradigm of atonement, one with which there are not such obvious logical and theological clashes as there are with penal substitution. Specifically he points to *Christus Victor:* "It is possible that a way forward for the doctrine may be found in terms of Christ having conquered the powers of darkness (and with them their authority to inflict sickness),"[47] but he does not develop this point. John Wimber never emphasized healing in the atonement as the theology behind his ministry, preferring the "already-but-not-yet" kingdom theology of George Eldon

43. Reichenbach, "By His Stripes We Are Healed," 553.

44. Ibid., 557–60, especially: "The Servant as healer takes the sickness/sin upon himself, thereby effecting a cure. Until he disposes of it the sickness/sin is on him, its virulence leading to his death. Atonement, in its deepest rhythms, necessitates the self-sacrifice of the healer to address the human predicament understood in terms of sickness and death." See also Brown, "The Atonement: Healing in Postmodern Society," 34–43, Flood, "Substitutionary Atonement and the Church Fathers," 142–59; Flood, *Healing the Gospel.*

45. So, Seet, "The Doctrine of Healing in the Atonement," 97; Wilkinson, "Physical Healing and the Atonement," 162; Stott, *The Cross of Christ,* 245. Against this, Baldwin uses Luke 5:17–26 (the healing of the paralytic) to prove that "Jesus sees the forgiveness of our sins and the healing of our bodies on the same level." Baldwin, *Healing and Wholeness,* 126–27. Bosworth states, "The salvation of any part of man without sacrifice is unknown in scripture." Bosworth, *Christ the Healer,* 18.

46. Cornish Jones, "Is Healing in the Atonement?" 646. So Moo, "Divine Healing in the Health and Wealth Gospel," 204; Bokovay, "The Relationship of Physical Healing to the Atonement," 35; Carson, *Showing the Spirit,* 175–76.

47. Petts, "Healing and the Atonement," *EPTA Bulletin,* 34.

Ladd. When he does touch upon the atonement in relation to healing he seems to deploy an atonement theology resembling recapitulation:

> Everything the devil introduced to men and women was undone by Jesus at the cross, which of course includes sickness. Jesus, the new Adam, came to restore us, to reproduce his new nature in us—which touches every part of our beings.[48]

He then goes on to integrate atonement with his kingdom theology:

> Because our sins are forgiven at the cross and our future bodily resurrections are assured through Christ's resurrection, the Holy Spirit can and does break into this age with signs and assurances of the fullness of the kingdom of God yet to come.[49]

However, besides the theological problems with healing in the atonement as classically expressed, there are obvious ethical and pastoral difficulties also. The first difficulty is with the nature of sickness. To tie healing so closely to sin implies a relationship between the two that Jesus himself never explicitly identified.[50] The second main pastoral difficulty is that if healing is given on the same basis as forgiveness, then everyone ought to be able to come to the cross and walk away physically healed.[51] The New Testament nowhere promises this.

It is perhaps the resurrection that could be invoked in the context of healing praxis, rather than the cross, as this is the New Testament standard of power (see Eph 1:20–22). It was the resurrection of Christ that ushered in the age that will eventually give way to the demise of disease and death altogether. Until then, as Wimber was so keen to point out, believers may taste the powers of the age to come as the resurrection of Christ is looked to as the ultimate demonstration of those powers. Believers can take comfort in the resurrection as the greatest of all miracles in the same way that Old Testament saints took comfort in the exodus as what was for them

---

48. Wimber and Springer, *Power Healing*, 165.

49. Ibid., 167.

50. In John 9:1–3 (the healing of the man born blind) Jesus is given the opportunity to make this link, a link that had been traditional in Judaism for centuries, yet refuses to do so.

51. Wilkinson is especially uncomfortable with this. Wilkinson, *Physical Healing*, 162–67.

the ultimate demonstration of God's saving power (e.g., Pss 66:1–7; 77; 136:10–15).[52]

David Petts completed his research into the subject drawing the conclusion that "healings occur as a work of the Spirit who is given to Christians as an *arrabōn* of their future inheritance."[53] The Holy Spirit is, in that case, the first installment of the future, the present in-breaking of it. In a similar vein, John Stott has offered 2 Corinthians 4:10–11, which speaks of the "life of Jesus" being manifested in the bodies of believers, as an alternative to healing in the atonement.[54] To this may be added Romans 8:11, which is susceptible of similar interpretation.[55]

Before we leave this interesting and controversial subject, it is worth our while to take a brief look at one particular exponent, and that is the renowned charismatic teacher Derek Prince (1915–2003). Part of his *Keys to Successful Living* series included such teachings as "The Exchange at the Cross,"[56] recorded in 1989, and "The Cross in My Life,"[57] recorded at Kensington Temple in 1992. Such talks then appeared as a small book in 1995, *The Divine Exchange,* and were finally collated into a larger work entitled *Atonement* in 2000. Throughout these, the same essential set of teachings is repeated. It is summed up in the form of "nine exchanges":

1. Jesus was punished that we might be forgiven.
2. Jesus was wounded that we might be healed.
3. Jesus was made sin with our sinfulness that we might be made righteous with His righteousness.
4. Jesus died our death that we might share His life.
5. Jesus was made a curse that we might receive the blessing.
6. Jesus endured our poverty that we might share His abundance.
7. Jesus bore our shame that we might share His glory.
8. Jesus endured our rejection that we might enjoy His acceptance.
9. Our old man died in Jesus that the new man might live in us.[58]

---

52. See McConville, "Exodus."
53. Petts, "Healing and the Atonement," iii.
54. Stott, *The Cross of Christ*, 245–46.
55. So, Tee, "The Doctrine of Divine Healing," 199.
56. Prince, "Redemption: Plan and Fulfilment. The Exchange at the Cross."
57. Prince, "Kensington Temple Sep 1992. The Cross in My Life."
58. Prince, *Atonement*, 37.

All of this teaching had its root in an encounter with two Christians in the back of a car during World War II in Suez. They offered prayer for his physical healing from a chronic skin condition. One of them spoke in tongues and delivered an interpretation that Prince describes as being in exquisite "Elizabethan English": "Consider the work of Calvary: a perfect work, perfect in every respect, perfect in every aspect."[59] Without having received healing at that point, these words soon led to a discovery:

> The essence of my discovery was this: On the cross a divinely ordained exchange was enacted in which all the evil due to our sinfulness came on Jesus, that in return all the good due to His spotless righteousness might be made available to us.[60]

He thus broadens his concept of the cross by amplifying the substitutionary element. He also reduces the penal element to only one aspect of a many-sided holistic exchange. He further takes the result of the atonement out of the eschatological sphere that it has tended to occupy in popular perception: there is no hint of the cross being a "ticket to heaven." He transfers the *telos* of the atonement well and truly into the existential sphere: the whole package is about a here-and-now quality of life that draws resources from a single source: "By this one sacrifice He made provision for all the needs of the whole human race in every area of our lives, for time and for eternity."[61]

When he does come onto physical healing as provided for in the atonement, he takes a familiar assured line: "It is finished! As far as God is concerned, healing has already been obtained. We are healed,"[62] and he is certain that, "If you do not believe that God has provided healing in the first place . . . you are not likely to appropriate it."[63] However, because his doctrine of healing in the atonement has been made to fit within a broader metanarrative of exchange, its logic is undergirded and its fault lines become less visible.

This way of resituating a controversial interpretation of the cross within an enlarged and less contestable theological construct is a strategy we have already seen in Forsyth and will see again in those that follow. In

59. Ibid., 24–25.
60. Ibid., 8.
61. Ibid., 45.
62. Ibid., 49.
63. Ibid., 45.

this way, the problematic elements are not removed; they simply become smaller. Prince locates healing as only one of nine great benefits afforded by the exchange at the cross, all of which operate in the same way and in response to faith.

Emil Brunner (1889–1966)

Based in Zurich, where he served as Professor of Systematic and Practical Theology (1924–53), Brunner was a highly significant figure in twentieth-century theology, largely because his works made it into English translation much more swiftly than other Neo-orthodox theologians, though today he has largely vanished from the radar in theological discourse.[64] Like McLeod Campbell, Brunner was a man with pastoral commitments and a passion for preaching.[65] And like Campbell, Brunner takes a thoroughly incarnational approach: "The centre and the foundation of the whole Christian faith is 'Christology,' that is, faith in Jesus Christ, the Mediator."[66] His Christology, however, is more dynamic than that of Chalcedon. He understands God's love to involve a movement towards humankind: "He is the Word God has to speak to us. Essentially, Jesus Christ is not a doctrine . . . but an act of God."[67] Christ is the supreme self-movement of God: "The God of the Christian faith, the Three in One, the Living God, is in Himself motion, because in His very nature He is Love."[68] As with Campbell, "The presupposition of this movement is the gulf between God and man."[69]

He comes out against Greek conceptions of God: "Here alone, therefore, do we perceive the complete contrast between this living personal God of Love and the unmoved rigid Being of the God of the philosopher,

---

64. So McKim, "Brunner the Ecumenist: Emil Brunner as a *Vox Media* of Protestant Theology," 91. Until now, the most recent book-length treatment of Brunner dated back to 1976: Humphrey, *Emil Brunner*. This has now thankfully been superseded by McGrath, *Emil Brunner*.

65. Nelson, "Emil Brunner," in Marty and Peerman, eds., *A Handbook of Christian Theologians*, 412–13. Also, Nelson, "Emil Brunner: Teacher Unsurpassed."

66. Brunner, *The Mediator*, 232. "Christ as Revealer crosses the epistemological divide between infinite God and finite man." Muller, "Christ-the Revelation or the Revealer?" 314.

67. Brunner, *The Mediator*, 232.

68. Ibid., 285.

69. Ibid., 291.

the mystic, and the moralist."[70] Nevertheless he is not averse to penal theories, and also comments agreeably on Anselm's famous dictum about the seriousness of sin ("you have not yet considered what a heavy weight sin is"): "We can see whether guilt is regarded seriously or lightly by the kind of energy or 'work' which is considered necessary in order to remove the separating obstacle from the path."[71] So, he returns to Anselm's[72] original burden of why such a sacrifice was necessary, and infers from the cost of it the seriousness of the plight from which it saves us.

By far the most significant thing about Brunner, however, is his contextualization of an otherwise highly conservative view of the atonement within the broader concerns of the incarnation of Christ. He unites the person of Christ with the work of Christ.

John Stott (1921–2011)

John Stott's contribution to atonement theology has been described as a "sophisticated and passionate" defense.[73] In Stott's own estimation,[74] one of the most important aspects of his landmark book *The Cross of Christ* is the attention it pays, not only to atonement theory, but to all aspects of the cross, especially the effect of the cross on personal discipleship. Especially memorable is his account of the Moravians, the "Easter People," who placed so much emphasis on the death and resurrection of Christ that they possessed very great reserves of personal assurance, even in the face of death.[75] It is easy to see that more of his "heart and mind" went into writing *The Cross of Christ* than any other of his books.[76] He wrote his book at a time

---

70. Ibid., 298.

71. Ibid., 451.

72. Brunner's Christology has been described as a "modified Anselmianism." Wolf, "Outline of Brunner's Theology," 133.

73. Wood, "Penal Substitution in the Construction of British Evangelical Identity," 120.

74. Interview with Art Lindsay, dated Summer 2001: http://www.cslewisinstitute. org/webfm_send/527 [accessed 3 Sep 2013]. "This is not a book on the atonement only, but on the cross." Stott, *Cross of Christ*, 11.

75. Stott, *Cross of Christ*, 293–94.

76. Interview with Art Lindsay.

when there was almost nothing else in print on the subject,[77] a situation that was soon to change beyond recognition.

Stott's main contribution to atonement theory has been his ability to situate classic penal substitutionary theory, not within Hodge's concept of inflexible divine justice and law, but within a much bigger, better concept: the need for God to "satisfy" himself.[78] The chapter in which he puts forward this satisfying of all divine attributes at the cross is called, significantly, "The Self-Substitution of God."[79] This signals, as with Derek Prince, an expanded logical underpinning of penal substitution that helps us to locate the atoning event within a bigger picture of the self-movement of God towards humanity (Brunner). The gospel, according to Stott, is indeed "full-orbed."[80] In Stott's presentation, the cross is an act of God in which any thought of the Father punishing the Son is overshadowed, though it is not at all eliminated. Like Anselm, Stott asserts that God "must be completely and invariably himself in the fullness of his moral being."[81] He "never contradicts himself."[82]

This absolute internal consistency within and among the divine perfections results in a cross when, in the language of Forsyth, "the holy love of God"[83] collides with "the unholy lovelessness of man."[84] God must substitute himself for man in order to assume the consequences for man of this unholy lovelessness. The person of the God-Man is therefore central: "At the root of every caricature of the cross there lies a distorted Christology."[85] And, "in giving his Son he was giving himself."[86]

In logic hard to resist, Stott points out: "For the essence of sin is man substituting himself for God, while the essence of salvation is God substituting himself for man."[87] And returning to the divine satisfying of himself: "How then could God express simultaneously his holiness in judgment and

---

77. Stott, *Cross of Christ*, 11.

78. Ibid., 133.

79. Ibid., 133–63.

80. Hood, "The Cross in the New Testament," 284.

81. Stott, *Cross of Christ*, 133.

82. Ibid.

83. Ibid.

84. Ibid.

85. Ibid., 160.

86. Ibid., 159.

87. Ibid., 160.

his love in pardon? Only by providing a divine substitute for the sinner, so that the substitute would receive the judgment and the sinner the pardon."[88] This last statement is perhaps a disappointing reversion to familiar explanations of penal substitution, and this so soon after introducing what promised to be a fresh, christological and theological vision of atonement. Leaving the Forsythian language of holy love, he seems to instinctively return to the old binary bargaining between two opposing attributes: "Divine love triumphed over divine wrath by divine self-sacrifice."[89]

Nevertheless, it is without doubt the case that Stott's book ensured that when penal substitution came under such bitter attack, as it did in less than twenty years after its publication, many who went on to defend the doctrine did so fore-armed by Stott. Stott was referenced again and again as the debate raged on. Defenses were so robust that as recently as 2009, Hood could remark that "the critics have failed to sustain the case against penal substitution,"[90] an assertion that, though arguably true earlier on, was already becoming out of date by the time of the publication of Hood's article.

I will now briefly introduce three areas of debate relevant to the subject of this chapter, before moving on to consider the subjective theories of atonement.

Recent Debates 1: Propitiation or Expiation?

The antiquated word "propitiaton," now hardly used in conversational English, refers to the soothing of anger, the act of pacifying someone, usually a deity, who has been offended. In Greek this is the *hilaskomai* word group. This, in turn, is derived from *hilarotēs,* "cheerful, hilarious" (cf. 2 Cor 9:7). In non-biblical Greek, *hilaskomai* normally referred to the act of appeasing a god by the offering of a sacrifice or other gift. Great fear would fill the minds of the Greeks and Romans that perhaps, out of all the many gods they worshipped, one had been left out, hence the altar in Athens entitled, "To the Unknown God" (Acts 17:23). The gods were seen as bad tempered and indifferent to human suffering. There was a need for continuous appeasement in order to avoid some calamity or misfortune. When gods were successfully propitiated they were understood to have undergone a change in attitude from displeasure to cheerfulness.

88. Ibid., 134.

89. Ibid., 159.

90. Hood, "The Cross in the New Testament," 284.

In connection with the atonement, the *hilaskomai* word group occurs only four times in the New Testament, yet this should not be understood as necessarily diminishing the significance of these occurrences. The most significant passage is Romans 3:25: Here the form is *hilasterion,* which can be translated as "place of" or "means of" propitiation. In the Septuagint, the very same word is translated "mercy seat," hence "place of propitiation." The other places are 1 John 2:2, 4:10, and Hebrews 9:5.

In 1935, C. H. Dodd wrote a book called *The Bible and the Greeks.* Having surveyed the way the *hilaskomai* word group is used in the Septuagint, he came to this conclusion:

> Hellenistic Judaism, as represented by the Septuagint, does not regard the cultus as a means of pacifying the displeasure of the Deity, but as a means of delivering man from sin, and it looks in the last resort to God himself to perform that deliverance thus evolving a meaning of ἱλασκεσθάι [*hilaskesthai*] strange to non-biblical Greek.[91]

In the light of this, Dodd argued for a revision of our understanding of this word in the New Testament. Regarding Romans 3:25, he says, "the meaning conveyed is that of expiation, not that of propitiation. Most translators and commentators are wrong."[92] Propitiation inescapably implies God's wrath, whereas expiation need not. Expiation is a subjective cleansing from the pollution of sin. The resulting adjustments to the Revised Version and New English Version of the Bible were part of a more general movement within theology away from crude ideas of God's wrath.

By the 1960s, the debate on this matter was still hot, Australian scholar Leon Morris having become a determined opponent of Dodd. Morris examined the evidence Dodd was relying on, and concluded, "as far as I know there are only two passages in the whole range of Greek literature that are suggested as possible exceptions [to the translation as 'propitiation' rather than 'expiation'] and neither of these is convincing."[93] Morris was insistent that the meaning of *hilaskomai* is the turning away of God's anger.[94] Morris was as keen as anyone to insist that the New Testament writers were not likening God's wrath to the capricious deities of paganism who must be bribed with gifts and sacrifices, but he was adamant that it is not to the

---

91. Dodd, *The Bible and the Greeks,* 93.

92. Ibid., 94.

93. Morris, *The Atonement,* 153.

94. See his thorough analysis: Morris, *The Apostolic Preaching of the Cross,* 144–47.

word *hilaskomai* that we should go if we want to argue that point.[95] He was equally concerned, however, that what Dodd appeared to be advocating was not merely the elimination of a misunderstood wrath from our theological vocabulary but the elimination of the idea of God's wrath altogether, despite over 580 references to it in the Old Testament alone.[96]

In the light of later work by Gunton[97] and McIntyre,[98] which drew our attention to the centrality of metaphor to the New Testament presentations of the death of Christ, including the metaphor of sacrifice, to argue over a single Greek word in this way now appears to be something of a storm in a teacup. The crucial thing is not the role of *hilaskomai* in the New Testament, but the role of the whole metaphor of sacrifice of which the word *hilaskomai* is but one part. And Morris was right to point out that the presence or otherwise of wrath in God's dealings with man cannot be settled by this Greek word, especially on the basis of the slender evidence for an alternative rendering that Dodd presented.

A similar and not unrelated debate arose over the meaning of the word "Blood" in Scripture, which began with the Bishop of Durham B. F. Westcott at the end of the nineteenth century. In his commentary on the letters of John of 1883[99] he claimed, on the basis of Leviticus 17, as well as parts of the Gospel of John, that the shed blood referred to in 1 John 1:7 signified life released rather than life taken: "The Blood always includes the thought of life preserved and active beyond death."[100] On the basis of John 6:56, "Participation in Christ's blood is participation in his life," yet, "it is only through death—His violent Death—that His Blood can be made available for men."[101] On this logic, the sacrificial metaphor cannot carry any atoning significance. The sacrifices were not substitutionary. They were not sacrifices for sin as such. Therefore, the death of Jesus, likewise, was to inaugurate a blood covenant in the sense of blood brothers intermingling their blood.[102] It was not a means of atoning for sin or propitiating God's wrath.

95. Ibid., 147–48.

96. Ibid., 148–49.

97. Gunton, *The Actuality of Atonement.*

98. McIntyre, *The Shape of Soteriology.*

99. Westcott, *The Epistles of John.*

100. Ibid., 36.

101. Ibid.

102. Seemingly quite independently of Westcott, and deriving its inspiration more from native American spirituality, this view of the blood covenant has enjoyed a

C. H. Dodd and B. F. Westcott were both eventually replied to in 1943 in a booklet by Alan Stibbs: *The Meaning of the Word "Blood" in Scripture.*[103] Morris also covers both sides of the argument in some detail in his *Apostolic Preaching.*[104] Perhaps the most profound statement that Stibbs makes in his short study is the following. He concludes that the significance of the biblical use of the term "blood" is that it is "a sign of life either given or taken in death. Such giving or taking of life is in this world the extreme, both of gift or price and of crime or penalty. Man knows no greater."[105]

Recent Debates 2: The New Perspective on Paul

In 1977, American scholar E. P. Sanders wrote a book called *Paul and Palestinian Judaism*. Its effect was not unlike that of the 95 *Theses* or of Karl Barth's *Exposition of the Book of Romans*. It inaugurated a Copernican Revolution. It was never again going to be possible to view Paul in quite the same way. His scholarship—especially the exhaustive use of Jewish sources—is intimidating. He dazzles the beginning reader, although, over time, plenty of scholars have found fault with his scholarship. Though many have disagreed with him, he is still casting an extremely long shadow over biblical scholarship.

Sanders' main point is this: in contrast to traditional views of the Pharisaism of Paul's day, Paul was not as antagonistic towards the law—especially if by this we understand simply the Torah—as might be supposed. The reason for this is that in Jewish understanding, membership of the covenant was on the basis of God's electing grace. The law therefore was never about getting into the covenant but about staying in. Hence, "Their [the rabbis'] legalism falls within a larger context of gracious election and assured salvation."[106] So, whatever Paul was battling in, say, Galatians (in

---

resurgence in recent decades, led mostly by Word of Faith advocate Kenneth Copeland, who is himself part native American. See his *Covenant of Blood*. The instigator of the idea seems to have been H. Clay Trumball and his book of 1885, which was reprinted in 1975: Trumbull, *The Blood Covenant*.

103. Stibbs, *The Meaning of the Word "Blood" in Scripture*, now republished as *His Blood Works: The Meaning of the Word "Blood" in Scripture*.

104. Morris *Apostolic Preaching*, 112–28. See also his earlier, "The Biblical Use of the Term 'Blood,'" 216–27.

105. Stibbs, *The Meaning of the Word "Blood,"* 33.

106. Sanders, *Paul and Palestinian Judaism*, 181. The whole section from 181–82 is a very useful summary of what much of the book is about.

different epistles it may well have been a slightly different enemy), it cannot have been a mainstream Jewish idea about salvation by works since, apparently, no such concept existed within the Palestinian Judaism of Paul's day. Instead, Sanders attempts to unify all forms of Palestinian Judaism under the one system of "covenantal nomism," which he explains thus:

> Covenantal nomism is the view that one's place in God's plan is established on the basis of the covenant and that the covenant requires as the proper response of man his obedience to its commandments, while providing means of atonement for transgression.[107]

This new perspective on Paul naturally has the effect of making the "Lutheran Paul" begin to crumble. We begin to see that the version of Paul that we understand to have been relentlessly on the war path against a religion of works might not be as true to his likeness as we had thought. Penal substitutionary theory begins to look precarious too since it rests so heavily upon this concept of keeping God's law, that is, the concept of trying to keep it in a carnal way in the hope of earning salvation, and then, in response to seeing its sanctions fulfilled in the death of Christ, making a new response based on faith alone.

However, Sanders has rightly been accused of smoothing over the variations within the Judaism of Paul's day.[108] More seriously, even on his own terms, and using the very sources he cites, frequent instances can be found of the picture of first-century Judaism that we are told is a Lutheran-influenced caricature. In other words, examples keep turning up of God's ledger tallying good works against evil works, and these not exactly in the most obscure places.[109] There is the further difficulty of Diaspora (that is, non-Palestinian) Judaism, which is immensely important to any understanding of Paul, yet not the focus of Sanders' study. In Diaspora Judaism, the sacrificial cultus (due to the obvious geographical distance from the Jerusalem temple) had to be replaced with something. Typically, the presentation of animals for atonement was replaced by such good works as

---

107. Sanders, *Paul and Palestinian Judaism*, 75.

108. Quarles, "The New Perspective and Means of Atonement in Jewish Literature of the Second Temple Period," 40.

109. E.g., *Jubilees* 5:13; 6:17; 16:29–30; 28:6; 30:19; 39:6; *Mishna, m. 'Abot* 3:16; 4:22; *b. Sanhedrin* 81a. Quarles, "The New Perspective and Means of Atonement," 41–42. See also, Westerholm, *Perspectives Old and New on Paul*, 343. Das, *Paul, the Law and the Covenant*, 32–36, Kim, *Paul and the New Perspective*, 146–52.

prayer, fasting, and almsgiving.[110] Giving to the poor was felt to have particular atoning power. And again, examples of this in the literature of the time are not tucked away somewhere difficult but are within the Apocrypha of many people's Bibles.[111]

However, to his credit, Sanders has not merely taken something away from our understanding of Paul. He has also added something of great value. He has drawn our attention to an emphasis in Paul that we couldn't see so clearly in the Lutheran Paul, although recent studies of Luther have found it there too. And that is the doctrine of participation in Christ:

> Paul has a more radical conception of sin than that it is transgression. Humans are not just sinners, they are enslaved by a power: Sin. Repentance and acquittal of individual transgressions do not fully meet the human problem. People are not just guilty, they are enslaved, and they need to escape. Paul thought that the power of Sin was so great that one must die to be free of it, and accordingly he reinterpreted Christ's death. People who become one person with Christ share his death and thus escape bondage, and they share his life being freed from the power of Sin. Herein lies Paul's distinctive contribution to thought about the death of Christ.[112]

In what follows, Sanders offers an insight that, if true, is quite momentous for atonement theology. It is the idea that the sacrificial and legal language that we tend to associate with Paul's explanations of the cross is not, as it were, his native language. Paul has merely borrowed these ideas from what was "received" by him from the tradition (1 Cor 15:3). In the single most sustained treatment of the death of Christ that we find in Paul, namely Romans 6:1–11, the language is unrecognizably different. And it is unmistakably the language of a participation in Christ, of a mystical union with his death: "although Paul knew and employed forensic or judicial ideas . . . the heart of his thought lies in another set of ideas: participation in Christ and a change of one's state from being under sin to living in the Spirit."[113]

N. T. Wright, at once a champion and a critic of Sanders, adds something more to what we are to see in Paul's concept of the atonement: "The

---

110. Quarles, "The New Perspective and Means of Atonement," 43.

111. Tobit 4:9–11; 12:8–10; Ben Sirach (Ecclesiasticus) 3:3, 30; 20:28; 35:1–15; 45:23.

112. Sanders, *Paul: A Very Short Introduction*, 93. So Ziesler, "Paul's major contribution to the theology of the cross and resurrection is that believers participate in them." Ziesler, *Pauline Christianity*, 91.

113. Sanders, *Paul: A Brief Insight*, 130.

crucifixion of the Messiah is, we might say the *quintessence* of the curse of exile, and its climactic act."[114]

In Wright, Jesus is a corporate figure who does something for the nation of Israel. Yet Wright points out that Christ's bearing of Israel's exile, his bearing of their curse was, in effect, the bearing away of the exile of all humankind, not just Israel. By way of context, we perhaps need to remind ourselves of the perplexity that post-exilic Jews felt having endured the judgment of God on their unfaithfulness to God and having been allowed to return to their land only to find themselves still under the yoke of oppressive foreign powers. They must have wondered what had really changed. There was a sense in which they had never truly returned from exile and awaited a Messiah to make this happen for them.

Both Sanders and Wright help to minimize the idea of an impersonal transaction and amplify the ideas of personal and corporate union with a representative Christ whose death and resurrection we in some way participate in. The work of these biblical scholars thus confirms many of the insights that systematic theologians have been offering.

Recent Debates 3: The Lost Message

Some evangelicals today (like the liberal theologians of the nineteenth century) are rejecting penal substitution altogether as being too barbaric and susceptible of crude interpretations. Others are happy to include it, but only as one theory among other, equally valid, theories. Still others, while accepting that the cross is like a many-faceted diamond that can indeed be viewed from many different angles, would, nonetheless, give penal substitution a privileged place as the theory that makes sense of, and unites together, all the others. However, there is in evidence a very strong contingent within evangelicalism that still wishes to defend the third option: penal substitution is not only one option among many but is an organizing principle that explains all other theories and therefore must occupy a central and normative place. It has quasi-creedal status.

A debate in the UK in the mid-2000s is of particular interest in this regard. The controversy is traceable to a single comment made by Steve Chalke and Alan Mann on page 182 of their book *The Lost Message of Jesus*, where it is implied that common presentations of the cross are tantamount

---

114. Wright, *The Climax of the Covenant*, 191. See also a helpful summary of Wright's thought in Kruse, *Paul, the Law and Justification*, 49–50.

to "cosmic child abuse," a criticism that, in response to widespread reactions, Chalke soon made explicit.[115] The furor resulting from his book brought a rash of publications.[116] Somewhat prophetically, an illuminating article by Paul Wells was published on the very eve of the debate that neatly summarized the objections that were already being raised. These five points were already easy to observe in the wake of the 1995 Atonement Symposium at St. John's College[117] and its reply at the Annual School of Theology at Oak Hill College in 2000.[118] Wells listed them as follows. Penal substitution is:

1. Ontological and objective, not demonstrative or subjective (liberalism);

2. Unethical, as sin and guilt are personal and non-transferable (Socinianism);

3. Untrinitarian, or implies tri-theistic divisions in God;

4. Self-contradictory, since God the Father cannot act for and against Christ at one and the same time;

5. Finally, a wrong interpretation of biblical data. Sacrifice does not imply penal substitution. Various images are merged in a totalizing way and the legal model is given a non-biblical pre-eminence.[119]

As the *Lost Message* debate progressed these five points were reiterated with the possible exception of point 4. Point 5 received considerable attention from all sides, while, instead of point 4, a new objection was made, especially by Chalke himself, which was the issue of cultural dissonance. The

115. Chalke, "Cross Purposes," 4–5.

116. Sach and Ovey, "Have We Lost the Message of Jesus?" (June 2004); James, "Cross Purposes?" (September 2004); Chalke, "Cross Purposes" (September 2004); Haslam, "The Lost Cross of Jesus" (November 2004); Allen, "Crossfire" (March 2005); Peck, "Why Did Jesus Die?" (September 2005); Pugh, "'The Lost Message of Jesus' What Is All the Fuss About?" (October 2005); James, "Atonement and Unity" (March-April 2006); Williams, "Penal Substitution: A Response to Recent Criticisms" (2007); Jeffrey et al., *Pierced for Our Transgressions* (2007); Holmes, *The Wondrous Cross* (2007); Tidball et al., eds., *The Atonement Debate*. Most recently a Durham PhD has appeared that also addresses the subject: Wood, "Penal Substitution in the Construction of British Evangelical Identity" (2011). An exhaustive literature review that covers the wider debate within English-speaking evangelicalism as whole over a similar period is provided by Hood, "The Cross in the New Testament."

117. Published as Goldingay, ed., *Atonement Today*.

118. Published as Peterson, ed., *Where Wrath and Mercy Meet*.

119. Wells, "A Free Lunch at the End of the Universe?"

very phrase "cosmic child abuse" had its source, not in feminist theology, but in a conversation Chalke had had in a London pub with a Welshman who derisively described the message he had been exposed to in the Welsh Valleys as precisely that.[120] This dissonance with the cultural categories now at home in British social life was such that the very idea of the Father punishing his innocent Son on the cross had now become unacceptable to most people. This issue refused to go away and has not gone away since. In fact, the new cultural perspective has so changed that increasing numbers now wonder whether advocates of penal substitution are, at least unwittingly, endorsing or valorizing the abuse of women and children.

By the Autumn of 2004, less than a year after its publication, *The Lost Message* had generated so much controversy that the Evangelical Alliance knew they had to act fast.[121] They were receiving a tidal wave of complaints.[122] As a result, on 7 October 2004, a debate was hosted at Westminster's Emmanuel Chapel in London. "About a hundred and fifty people" was the figure the Evangelical Alliance had in mind. To their amazement, some 700 people signed up for it, necessitating a change of venue, which was promptly filled to capacity. The atmosphere was calm and considered,

---

120. Wood, "Penal Substitution in the Construction of British Evangelical Identity," 128–29. Wood interviews Chalke about this and records Chalke's answer in n. 124. With regards to cultural change, Wood's interview with Derek Tidball is also highly illuminating. Tidball speaking: "Postwar Britain is very structured and institutional. It is rule-bound and there are authority figures that you don't question. So the whole concept of law and guilt and punishment and grace was, until the sort of mid-60s onwards, considered to be the fabric of society. . . . So the sense of the Cross as God's law which we have broken, which we deserve therefore to be punished for; ah, but somebody else is going to take our punishment and therefore we, though guilty, can be pardoned and justified, fits perfectly with this wider social climate. But then in the '60s you get this tremendous moral and social transformation going on. . . . You go to the period where all that is called into question, where authorities begin to be, not only questioned, but lampooned . . . where law, which had been enshrined, begins to be changed and you think it's not so fixed. Where in the '60s under Roy Jenkins as Home Secretary, you begin to abolish capital punishment and hanging and those things, the sense of punishment begins to go. So actually the world does become very different and still talking about the Cross in those terms seems to relate to a past decade at least, if not a past generation.'" Wood, "Penal Substitution in the Construction of British Evangelical Identity," 108–9.

121. It had already been banned from sale at that year's Keswick Convention. Wood, "Penal Substitution in the Construction of British Evangelical Identity," 131.

122. There were frequent calls for him to resign from the EA, though Chalke maintains that he never was a member in the first place. His organization had corporate membership but he had no personal subscription. Wood, "Penal Substitution in the Construction of British Evangelical Identity," 130, and n. 128.

even though feelings were clearly running high. A three day conference was planned to follow this. Accordingly, "Why Did Christ Die?" a gathering of theological heavy-weights, ministers, and students, including Steve Chalke and Alan Mann, was convened at the London School of Theology from 6–8 July 2007. The attendance figures alone proved that Lost-Message-Fever had still not died down. There were 200 delegates (including myself), the most the college could possibly house and feed. Many could not be accommodated or were asked to buy their own food in town (thankfully, not me).

Those who were against this way of looking at the cross objected that the theory leads to a neglect of the life of Jesus, a neglect of other ways of looking at the cross, and a neglect of how a Christian is supposed to live his life once he's saved. These all fall within Wells' point 1 and point 5: the objections that the model is too objective and that it is not biblically balanced. More seriously, as alluded to earlier, the anti-penal substitution camp accused those who hold this view of unwittingly endorsing abuse. Further, they said, this doctrine places a division in the Trinity. The Father turns against his innocent Son. The Son, in turn, tries to wrest forgiveness for the human race from a begrudging Father who coldly requires all his laws to be fulfilled before he can give it. These are point 3: the un-Trinitarian objection, and the new point: the cultural dissonance objection.

Howard Marshall offered the strongest defense.[123] He walked the delegates through the biblical support for the idea that God is a God of justice and wrath who actively visits his judgment upon sinful humanity. Marshall was clear that this was not to say that God required the death of his Son before he could forgive. Rather, the very act of giving his Son was an act of love on the part of a God who was under no obligation to save us, yet had to uphold his justice, or else cease to be just at all. He was equally keen to point out that "God was in Christ reconciling the world to himself"(2 Cor 5:19). The Father and the Son were united in the work of the cross, both equally willing. The Father, far from victimizing his Son, was well pleased with him precisely because he was willing to go to the cross, otherwise he would have left him in the tomb. Though this does not answer all the classic objections, Marshall was able to swing the vote. Even Alan Mann himself publicly stated on the third day of the conference that he was not against

---

123. It is available at http://evangelicalarminians.org/i-howard-marshall-the-theology-of-the-atonement/ [accessed 3 Sept 2013] and is entitled "The Theology of Atonement." See also Marshall's *Aspects of the Atonement*.

penal substitution and that he regretted much of what he had implied in his co-authoring of the book.

To finish, and without, for now, attempting any final judgment on the matters that have been raised, here are some very fine extracts from some spokesmen for the theory, two of whom we have heard from already:

> [O]ur most merciful Father, seeing us to be oppressed and over-whelmed with the curse of the law . . . sent His only Son into the world and laid upon Him all the sins of everyone, telling Him to be Peter the denier, to be Paul the persecutor and blasphemer and op-pressor, to be David the adulterer, to be the sinner who ate the fruit in Paradise, the thief who hung on the cross—in short, to be the person who has committed the sins of everyone. The law comes along and says, "I find Him a sinner . . . let Him die on the cross.[124]

> Our Lord came forth as true man and took the person and name of Adam in order to take Adam's place in obeying the Father, to present our flesh as the price of satisfaction to God's righteous judgment, and, in the same flesh, to pay the penalty that we had deserved.[125]

> Jesus Christ our Lord, moved by a love that was determined to do everything necessary to save us, endured and exhausted the destructive divine judgment for which we were otherwise inescap-ably destined, and so won for us for us forgiveness, adoption and glory. To affirm penal substitution is to say that believers are in debt to Christ specifically for this, and that this is the mainspring of all their joy, peace and praise both now and for eternity.[126]

Here is someone, equally eloquent, who is vehemently against it:

> The theological consequence of such a view is to throw the unity of Father and Son in character, will and action into jeopardy, the pastoral consequence is to attack our confidence in the Father's own love for us at its heart. The result can be that we are left with a cringing guilt-ridden religion which has to hide behind the love of Jesus in order to be saved from the only just contained wrath of an angry God.[127]

124. Luther, *Galatians,* (1998), 153.

125. Calvin, *Institutes* 2.12.3.

126. Packer, *Celebrating the Saving Work of God,* 105, originally published as, "What Did the Cross Achieve?" 25.

127. Smail, *Forgotten Father,* 129.

Summary and Evaluation

By way of evaluation, it does appear that atonement theory took a slightly wrong turn when the satisfaction model became the penal substitution model. The satisfaction model itself is, of course, not free of difficulty, but it maintains a balancing christological nexus. It shares with the New Testament itself a fascination with the God-Man. It takes its bearings from the fact of Jesus Christ. Penal substitution, losing this coordinating meeting point between the self-movement of God into humanity and the priestly representation of man into the presence of God, splits into two. Sometimes, penal substitution is about God—not really about anything else in fact. In the hands of the Princeton divines, as well as some of the Calvinism that Campbell was contending with, the unalterable demands of divine law become a most diverting way of insisting ever more stridently upon the logical inviolability of the doctrine. And in the thought of such theorists, the trajectory of the act of atonement is ever increasingly a direction of movement from the Father to the Son (the Father punishing him), rather than from the Son to the Father (the Son satisfying him)—also problematic, but less so. There is a fixation with what God cannot do and a blindness to how distasteful—even terrifying—the resulting picture of God actually is.

This form of penal substitution is all about the Father; it is the patrocentric doctrine of Princeton. The earlier Reformation version of the theory (and the two seem to be quite distinct) is salvation-centric, it is focused on dealing with the mistaken notion that people can save themselves. It is a justification-eye-view of the atonement, but it is still not centered on Christ. It is centered on letting people know how powerless they are and how real their peril is and how faith in the cross is the only answer, an answer that must admit of no rivals. Penal substitution thus keeps veering off towards one of its two magnetic poles: the vindication of God's justice at one end, or the justification of the sinner at the other end. It never finally alights to admire that man on that cross: the Redeemer himself.

For this reason, I commend all those that have sought to restore the Chalcedonian Christ as the center and meaning of atonement. Specifically, I refer to Campbell and the sufficiency of the God-Man, to Forsyth and the holy love of God in Christ, and to Brunner and the Christ whose work is coterminous with his person and his person with his work. Into this cluster we can also gather some others: Irenaeus and Anselm. Penal substitution itself would appear to be at least in need of modifying in the direction of one of these authors, some of whom continued to affirm penal substitution. Even Chalke's derisive "penal substitution-lite" will not do, as he rightly says. Even John Stott's masterfully nuanced portrayal of the doctrine may perhaps only amount to a polished but still rather ugly doctrine.

One way in which we have been testing the theories is to place them in a contemporary context to see whether they hold anything timeless enough to give them a voice in a new situation. My explorations have been brief, suggestive forays. But supposing we take this further and, with Derek Prince, insist that the cross is the great place in history for the meeting of a whole range of human needs. This too might be a good way of judging the merits of a theory. We could ask: what does this do for people?

If Christ himself is the "way through the maze," as I seem to be suggesting, then it is not so much the case that "the cross is all our theology" (Luther) but that "*the Christ* of the cross is all our theology." Already, we have noted how Ireneaus' recapitulation theory in conjunction with *theosis* meets the needs of the disconnected. People are at such a distance from God that many do not even believe that he is there. Step on to the bridge between humans and God, and God becomes a present God because he is in Christ reconciling the world to himself. Anselm's theory, with its overabundant supererogatory outcome, is good news for the those who feel perpetually deficient, that they are never enough. Satisfaction itself means "a doing enough." To them we can offer the news that Christ has done enough. He has measured up, gone the distance, bridged the gap. For those who feel the crushing weight of guilt and crave the assurance that God has forgiven them, Campbell comes and proclaims a Christ who has come from God to bridge the gulf and offer to God the life we couldn't offer, the "sorry" we didn't give, the repentance we couldn't muster. We take him as our forgiving grace and the power to reach God. For those who have found a sentimental subjective spirituality inadequate, Forsyth offers a holy love embodied in a divine human carrying the weight of human evil to God on the cross.

Someone once said, "the history of thought is the laboratory of the thinker." If this is so then it seems we are already in the very finest laboratory of all. What is already clear at this stage is that atonement theology is by far the richest seam in the history of theological and religious ideas. We find that we have struck gold. We find that, at the cross, we have gained a perspective that allows us to see into and speak into a panoramic range of human need and experience. When Scott reached the South Pole, there was nothing there—except a rather discouraging Norwegian flag. But when we reach the heart of God, as Horace Bushnell said, we discover a cross.[128] But also, when we reach the cross, as Moltmann will tell us, we discover the heart of God.

128. "[T]here is a cross in God before the wood is seen upon Calvary." Bushnell, *The Vicarious Sacrifice*, 53.

PART THREE

Subjective Theories

THE SUBJECTIVE VIEWS OF THE atonement comprise all those ways of see-ing the cross that emphasize its affect upon us. The moral influence of the cross, sometimes understood as being augmented by the work of the Spirit, is the heart of this view. On this view, the cross is orientated towards hu-mankind. Unlike the *Christus Victor* views, which focus on Christ as King, and the objective views that focus on Christ's priestly office, the subjective views correspond to Christ's prophetic office. The cross speaks, revealing God to us, and this revelation alone is understood to save us and change us without the need for any kind of objective transaction taking place on our behalf. Where this is understood pneumatologically, the focus of this view is the Holy Spirit acting upon humans to bring home to them the message of the cross. Its focus is not the evil powers, as in the *Christus Victor* ap-proaches, or on the Father as in the dominant objective approaches, but on the human condition.

7

The Cross as Transformative Revelation

HERE WE CONSIDER THE ORIGIN and development of the moral influence theory and other approaches that are either directly indebted to it or that similarly see the work of Christ as speaking to human subjectivity. In these theories, it is this address to the human soul, and the human response, that is understood to be the main thing the cross achieves, and, in many cases, the sum and total of it.

The Early Emergence of the Subjective Angle

It is generally accepted that no one consciously attempted to set down a doctrine of the atonement in the first centuries of Christianity,[1] such a task being largely left to Anselm. McIntyre has suggested that the sacramentalism of the patristic period made speculation unnecessary. The cross was regularly applied to the faithful in an entirely straightforward way: eating and drinking. There was little to provoke speculation or argument.[2] Unlike the christological debates, there was a general absence of heterodox views

---

1. E.g., McIntyre, *The Shape of Soteriology*, 24–25. The standard histories agree, e.g., Grensted, *A Short History of the Doctrine of the Atonement*, 11; McDonald, *The Atonement of the Death of Christ*, 115; MacIntosh, *Historic Theories of Atonement*, 80, 83.

2. McIntyre, *The Shape of Soteriology*, 8–12.

that might have demanded a clear definition.[3] This point can't be pressed too far, however, since when atonement theory did begin to be clarified, with Anselm, there was still nothing remotely like the kind of controversy that had surrounded Christology during the patristic period.

The very earliest patristic writings, especially those of the Apostolic Fathers, lean towards a moralistic interpretation of the cross.[4] McDonald elaborates a highly plausible reason for this exemplarist feel to the very earliest post-apostolic descriptions of the cross. The answers lie, for McDonald, in the fact that this was the persecuted church. On the one hand, part of the reason for the persecution were the moral accusations that Christians faced from pagans, who widely misunderstood their practices and famously judged them guilty of incest (due to their emphasis on "brotherly love"), cannibalism (due to their consumption of the "body and blood" of Jesus), and atheism (due to their refusal to worship the recognized deities). It was therefore necessary for them to live to the most impeccable of moral standards so as not to add to these accusations. Secondly, and perhaps more significantly, many Christians were being called upon to be faithful to the point of death, and what better example to look to in order to strengthen their resolve as they faced the lions of the arena than the crucified Christ himself?[5]

There is, however, evidence of penal substitution in these writings for those who are looking for it,[6] though some have clearly had to look very hard indeed to find this.[7] A key issue is whether a genuinely penal theory is

3. Ibid., 15–21.

4. Here again, the standard histories are in agreement, even those not authored by Abelardians, e.g., McDonald, *The Atonement of the Death of Christ*, 11–12, 115–18.

5. McDonald, *The Atonement of the Death of Christ*, 116.

6. Most notably in the recent literature the point-proving exercise of Jeffery et al., *Pierced for Our Transgressions*, 161–204. See also Derek Flood's devastating critique of their work: Flood, "Substitutionary Atonement and the Church Fathers," passim. See also Garry Williams' rebuttal of Flood: Williams, "Penal Substututionary Atonement in the Church Fathers," 195–216, and Flood's rejoinder to Williams' rebuttal: Flood, "The Abolishment of Retribution in the Church Fathers," on his blog: *The Rebel God*: http://therebelgod.com/FathersAbolishRetribution.pdf [accessed 13/09/2013]. There has also been a very favorable response to Jeffrey et al.: Vlach, "Penal Substitution in Church History," 199–214. Also worth considering are Peter Ensor's four articles that attempt a similar undertaking to that of Jeffery et al., but with more detail and a much higher standard of scholarship: "Justin Martyr and Penal Substitutionary Atonement," "Clement of Alexandria and Penal Substitutionary Atonement," "Penal Substitutionary Atonement in the Later Ante-Nicene Period," and "Tertullian and Penal Substitutionary Atonement."

7. Ensor, "Clement of Alexandria and Penal Substitutionary Atonement," 19–35.

detectable or whether what we are really looking at is various early forms of substitutionary atonement, without the penal element.[8] The penal element specifically involves the Father punishing the Son on the cross, which is very difficult to find in these early writings.

Likewise, there has been at least one recent attempt to prove at length that "moral transformation" was "the original Christian paradigm of salvation."[9] This work consists of a totally one-sided presentation of biblical and historical data followed by conclusions based on that data using phrases like: "From the above passages, we see that the New Testament authors believed that . . ."[10] The authors go one step beyond the obvious moral and devotional tendencies of post-apostolic reflections on the death of Christ to claim that this in fact had been the New Testament paradigm all along.

Some typical examples of references to the atonement in the five Apostolic Fathers and others of a similar period will suffice. The five truly Apostolic Fathers: that is, those thought to have derived their authority directly from one of the apostles, are: Clement of Rome, Ignatius of Antioch, Polycarp of Smyrna, the anonymous author of the *Didache*, and the Shepherd of Hermas.

Here is Clement of Rome in what is the very earliest Christian document to be written after the writing of the last of the documents that would later constitute the New Testament canon: Clement's letter to Corinth dated around AD 96: "Let us fix our gaze on the Blood of Christ, and let us know that it is precious to his Father, because it was poured out for our salvation, and brought the grace of repentance to all the world."[11] And here again: "In love did the Master receive us; for the sake of the love which he had towards us did Jesus Christ our Lord give his blood by the will of God for us, and his flesh for our flesh, and his soul for our souls."[12]

Meanwhile, Ignatius of Antioch (martyred between AD 98 and 117) gives us a taste of the thoroughly sacramental approach to the atonement

---

This is a very scholarly, and honest, piece of work on Clement, but which in the end detects penal substitution in but one passage in Clement: "For thee I contended with Death, and paid thy death, which thou owedst for thy former sins and thy unbelief towards God." Ensor, "Clement of Alexandria and Penal Substitutionary Atonement," 31, citing *Quis Dives Salvatur?* Section 23.

8. Flood, "Substitutionary Atonement and the Church Fathers," passim.

9. Wallace and Rusk, *Moral Transformation*.

10. Ibid., 187.

11. *1 Clement* 7:4. Kirsopp Lake's translation. So throughout.

12. *1 Clement* 49:6.

that permeated church life in the first two centuries of Christianity. Written en route to Rome to face execution by wild beasts in the arena, here is an extract from one of seven letters he wrote to churches on his journey there:

> Be careful therefore to use one Eucharist (for there is one flesh of our Lord Jesus Christ, and one cup for union with his blood, one altar, as there is one bishop with the presbytery and the deacons my fellow servants), in order that whatever you do you may do it according unto God.[13]

Probably dating from about a hundred years later than *1 Clement*, the anonymous *Epistle to Diognetus* is a piece of apologetic writing known for having a strangely Protestant or evangelical ring to it. It is the source of the famous "in the world but not of it." Equally well known is the following, in which the "sweet exchange" phrase is first coined. It is also the passage from the first two centuries of Christianity that could be the most readily cited as an instance of nascent penal theory:

> But when our iniquity was fulfilled and it had become fully manifest, that its reward of punishment and death waited for it, and the time came which God had appointed to manifest henceforth his kindliness and power (O the excellence of the kindness and the love of God!) he did not hate us nor reject us nor remember us for evil, but was long-suffering, endured us, himself in pity took our sin, himself gave his own Son as ransom for us, the Holy for the wicked, the innocent for the guilty, the just for the unjust, the incorruptible for the corruptible, the immortal for the mortal. For what else could cover our sins but his righteousness? In whom was it possible for us, in our wickedness and impiety, to be made just, except in the Son of God alone? O the sweet exchange, O the inscrutable creation, O the unexpected benefits, that the wickedness of many should be concealed in the one righteous, and the righteousness of the one should make righteous many wicked![14]

The Nicene Creed, as the so called "Apostles' Creed" had also done, simply insisted on the facts, that Christ was "crucified under Pontius Pilate. He suffered and was buried, and the third day he rose again." The piecemeal emergence of ransom to Satan and recapitulation theories began with Irenaeus' *Against Heresies*, in the late second century. Yet, even after a thousand years there was still fluidity enough to allow the speculations of

13. *Ignatius to the Philadelphians* IV.
14. *Epistle to Diognetus*, 9:2–5.

Anselm and Abelard. It is a fluidity that still exists today and is responsible for the sheer richness of atonement theology. To Abelard we now turn.

Peter Abelard (1079–1142) and the Love of God

A contemporary and opponent of Anselm, Abelard's writings were driven by two concerns. The first was his interest in romantic love. Love letters to his beloved Heloise (pronounced like "Eloise" of the 1968 pop song), with whom he had a hapless and rather tragic love affair (which, even more tragically, resulted in self-castration) have been preserved to the present day.[15] In fact, it is probably quite accurate to say that, "Abelard found God through his own human life story."[16] The second concern of his was with ethics. His most famous works were on this subject.[17] When he came to the atonement, the two concerns flowed together: the cross changes our ethical behavior because there, in the crucified Christ, we come to understand something of God's love for us. This love motivates us to change the way we live. This, rather than some barbaric sacrifice for the sins of others, is how we are saved from our sins:

> Indeed, how cruel and wicked it seems that anyone should de-
> mand the blood of an innocent person as the price for anything, or
> that it should in any way please him that an innocent man should
> be slain—still less that God should consider the death of his Son so
> agreeable that by it he should be reconciled to the whole world?[18]

Abelard has a fairly unsubtle way of translating a number of key Pauline terms into concepts that all basically equate to *caritas:* "love," for instance: "faith in Jesus Christ, meaning the love which comes from faith in our salvation through Christ."[19] Even Paul's "righteousness of God" means, "love,"[20] according to Abelard.

15. Radice, trans., *The Letters of Abelard and Heloise.*

16. Murray, *Abelard and St. Bernard*, 13.

17. In particular, his *Ethica* of c. 1138: Luscombe, ed., *Peter Abelard's Ethics*, but his *Commentary on Romans* also falls within his works on ethics: King, "Abelard's Intentionalist Ethics." The other two philosophical subjects that Abelard addressed in his works were logic and physics: King, "The Metaphysics of Peter Abelard," 65.

18. Abelard, *Commentary on Romans*, Book II: Rom. 3:19–26, Section II, in Fairweather, ed., *A Scholastic Miscellany*, 283. His commentary dates to around 1134.

19. *On Romans* IV: Rom. 3:27, 285.

20. "[A] righteousness of God—something which God approves and by which we are

Like Anselm, his Christology is vitally Chalcedonian. The fully human/fully divine orthodoxy of Chalcedon is not merely assumed but plays an essential part in his theology, as in the following extract where also a strong attachment to the mystical union with Christ is clear:

> By the faith which we hold concerning Christ, love is increased in us, by virtue of the conviction that God in Christ has united our human nature to himself and, by suffering in that same nature, has demonstrated to us that perfection of love of which he himself says, "Greater love than this no man hath," etc. So we, through his grace, are joined to him as closely as to our neighbor by an indissoluble bond of perfection.[21]

The note of mystical participation in Christ, in particular, does much to balance the exemplarist overtones of Abelard's view of the atonement. In fact, it is clear that Abelard is no Pelagian[22] but takes sides with Paul in Romans on his insistence that grace cannot be obtained by the works of the law: "All such as fulfill the law merely according to the flesh and not according to the spirit will be accounted righteous in men's sight, perhaps . . . but not in God's."[23] He is clear that the Christian life is "not a matter of the display of outward works."[24]

Despite these strong features of Abelard's soteriology, Bernard of Clairvaux criticized Abelard for teaching that,

> Christ lived and died for no other purpose than that he might teach us how to live by his words and example, and point out, by his passion and death, to what limits our love should go. Thus he did not communicate righteousness, but only revealed to us what it is.[25]

---

justified in God's sight, namely love—has been manifested." *On Romans* I: Rom 3:21, 278.

21. *On Romans* I: Rom. 3:21, 278.

22. Weingart, *The Logic of Divine Love*, 125.

23. *On Romans* I: Rom. 3:19, 277.

24. *On Romans* I: Rom. 3:21, 278. This chimes exactly with his more extended treatment of what constitutes moral worth in his *Ethica*. There he argues that a deed in and of itself, has no moral value apart from the intentions of the one doing the deed: *Ethica* 28. See also King, "Abelard's Intentionalist Ethics," 218–22.

25. *Contra quaedam Capitula errorum Abaelardi* VII, 17.

This has been a criticism that has echoed down the ages.[26] Yet, despite these, McGrath[27] follows Taylor[28] in insisting that Abelard did not teach an exemplarist doctrine of the atonement. By this he means that nowhere does Abelard insist that being aroused to follow Christ's example of love is the thing that saves us: "Abelard is an exemplarist if, and only if, it can be shown that he understands Christ to be our example, *through whose imitation we are redeemed.*"[29] McGrath thinks that Abelard is referring to the urge to follow Christ *after* having been saved. However, if we take into account the general tenor of Abelard's thought, incorporating, for instance his *Ethica,* which came a few years after *Romans,* it becomes more difficult to disentangle Abelard's soteriology from the exemplarist framework that he is so frequently associated with. In *Ethica* he makes explicit some of the things that had been only implicit in *Romans.* He makes clear that his concept of sin is "contempt of God." This contempt of God is dealt with only by the repentant sigh: "In this sigh we are instantly reconciled to God and we gain pardon for the preceding sin."[30] The repentant sigh is, by definition, a renunciation of prior contempt for God and a "turning to God in love."[31] This ability to turn to God in love, however, is itself a gift of God's love.[32] But the point is that the answering love that we already see superimposed onto all of Paul's soteriological terms in *Romans* comes prior to reconciliation with God and, though a gift, is a precondition of it. Further, this love that is aroused in response to the crucified Christ is the thing that "delivers us from the bondage of sin."[33] If this is not an exemplarist theory of the atonement then it is certainly very close to one, and Hastings Rashdall was probably not as far off-beam as McGrath implies.[34] We also have Abelard's

---

26. Abelard's supporters also have tended to limit his theory to precisely the exemplarist idea that Bernard has set up as his object of derision: Franks, *A History of the Work of Christ* I, 146; Rashdall, *The Idea of Atonement* 26; Weingart, "The Atonement in the Writings of Peter Abailard," 408. One paper argues that both Bernard and Abelard held "propitiatory and exemplary elements" in tension, the two figures being much closer to one another in belief than is commonly supposed: Beeke, "'Cur Deus Homo?' A Closer Look at the Atonement Theories of Peter Abelard and Bernard of Clairvaux," 44.

27. McGrath, "The Moral Theory of the Atonement," 206–9.

28. Taylor, "Was Abelard an Exemplarist?" 207–13.

29. McGrath, "The Moral Theory of the Atonement," 209, italics original.

30. Abelard, *Ethica* 19, 88–89.

31. McMahon's summary: McMahon, "Penance and Peter Abelard's Move Within," 4.

32. Abelard, *Ethica* 20, 91.

33. *On Romans* I: Rom. 3:27, 284.

34. McGrath, "The Moral Theory of the Atonement," 205–6, commenting on

famous and very strident repudiation of substitutionary atonement to reckon with, cited at the start of this chapter, as well as Abelard's principle that a model of the atonement must be "neither unintelligible, arbitrary, illogical nor immoral."[35] It seems clear that Anselm's satisfaction theory presented Abelard with a moral problem that is resolved in his exemplarist theory.

A third medieval writer, besides Anselm and Abelard, is also of some significance. In fact, he is a giant of theology, dwarfing both Anselm and Abelard, both in intellectual influence and in physical size: a belly-shaped semi-circle cut out of his desk accommodated his ample reserves of visceral fat. His name is Thomas Aquinas. Like Augustine, despite his vast influence on theology generally, he is not the originator of an atonement theory, so he has received but little coverage in this book. Aquinas is significant, however, in that he synthesized Anselm and Abelard. In a process that has been likened to evolution,[36] Anselm adapted the patristic approaches, Abelard adapted Anselm's approach, and Aquinas took elements from both.[37] I would prefer likening the process to Hegelian dialectics: thesis, antithesis, synthesis, since Abelard was doing more than merely adapting Anselm: he was his antithesis.

And so we come back to the necessity of the cross. If it was only a demonstration of love, to what purpose this extravagance? Is it not in the nature of love to rescue from some tangible danger and provide for real needs, and, if necessary, to pay the ultimate price in doing so? Did this "demonstration" really achieve that? James Denney provides the illustration that if I were sitting on Brighton Pier relaxing on a deck chair and, from nowhere, a stranger runs past me and flings himself into the water and drowns, and if I was then informed that the stranger had done this because he loved me, I would not be benefited in any way. In fact, I would think he was a lunatic.[38] If, on the other hand, I was in the water being

---

Rashdall, *The Idea of Atonement*, 358–64.

35. See Quinn, "Abelard on Atonement," 281–300.

36. Siekawitch, "The Evolution of the Doctrine of the Atonement in the Medieval Church," 3–30.

37. Walters, "The Atonement in Medieval Theology," 249. For the best in scholarship on Aquinas and the atonement see works by Stump: "Atonement according to Aquinas," in Morris, ed., *Philosophy and the Christian Faith*, 61–91, and "Atonement according to Aquinas," in Rea, ed., *Oxford Readings in Philosophical Theology, Vol. 1*, 267–93.

38. Mackintosh speaks in similar terms giving the illustration of two friends beside a raging torrent: "It is difficult to imagine anything so stagey, indeed so insane, as a friend saying to his fellow, 'I love you deeply! I must give you proof of it! And therefore for your

swept out to sea and in imminent danger of drowning and the stranger dived in to save me at the cost of his own life, then I would understand, yes this is love indeed.

Faustus Socinus (1539–1604), Hugo Grotius (1583–1645), and the Governmental Theory

Dutch jurist Hugo Grotius, student of the great Jacobus Arminus (1560–1609), set out to defend orthodoxy against the Unitarian pioneer Faustus Socinus. This Socinus had recently penned *De Jesu Christo Servatore* (*On Jesus Christ the Savior*),[39] a work so powerful that its effect upon the Calvinists of his day has been described as "mesmeric."[40] Someone of equal brilliance was needed who could offer a defense, and that person was Hugo Grotius. In the end, both theologians started to sound not unlike one another.[41]

Socinus, a Catholic, was a moral influence theorist who was especially rigorous in his critique of penal substitution, leaving none of its possible weaknesses unaddressed. His main purpose was to undermine the concept of justice upon which both Anselm's satisfaction theory and its Protestant modifications hung so tenaciously: "If we could but get rid of this justice, even if we had no other proof, that fiction of Christ's satisfaction would be thoroughly exposed, and would vanish."[42]

This fiction appears to have consisted in the thought that, if sin is punished then it is not forgiven. Likewise, if it is forgiven, then there is no need for punishment. The idea, therefore, of Christ needing to vicariously

---

sake I will risk everything by leaping into this dangerous torrent.'" Mackintosh, *Historic Theories of the Atonement*, 19–20.

39. Published in 1594. See Gomes' "'De Jesu Christo Servatore': Faustus Socinus on the Satisfaction of Christ," 209–31.

40. Packer, "What Did the Cross Achieve?" 2, also in *Celebrating the Saving Work of God*, 86.

41. Mackintosh reckoned that Grotius' departure from orthodoxy was completely unintentional: "He says something quite different from what he believes he is saying." Mackintosh, *Historic Theories of the Atonement*, 171, cf. 181, 183. However, there is evidence from other works of Grotius that he deliberately borrowed extensively from Socinus' thought: Henk, ed., *Hugo Grotius, Theologian*, 46–48, 68. Indeed, Socinus' followers considered Grotius to be one of their own number: Bloemendal, "Huogo Grotius (1583–1645)," 345. See also the more recent study: Heering, *Hugo Grotius as Apologist for the Christian Religion*.

42. Socinus, *De Jesu Christo Servatore*, III, i.

bear punishment, or even (as in Anselm) to vicariously avert punishment by paying God an equivalent, becomes redundant.[43] Christ is thus, "an example of man's best rather than the bearer of man's worst."[44]

He also asserted "that compassion which stands opposed to justice is the appropriate characteristic of God."[45] Ultimately, however, it is neither God's justice, nor his mercy that dictates the method by which God saves people, for Socinus, but only his will. Hence, the specific insight that Socinus appears to have given Grotius is the insight that, in Grotius' words, God's law "is not something inward in God, or in the Divine will and nature, but only the effect of his will."[46] From this, Grotius develops the principle, "All positive laws are relaxable."[47] So it is that, in his reply to Socinus of 1617, Grotius presents for the first time a theory of the atonement hailed by Franks as "one of the most important in the whole history of our doctrine,"[48] the Governmental or Rectoral theory.

> The end of the matter which is being discussed, as to the intention of God and of Christ, is twofold: the display of the Divine justice; and, so far as we are concerned, the remission of sins, that is, our release from punishment. For if you take the exaction of penalty impersonally, its end is the display of the Divine justice; but if personally, that is, why Christ is punished, its end is that we may gain release from punishment.[49]

The vestiges of a penal view are clearly present,[50] though, for the most part, Grotius seems to merely use the same language yet mean something else by it. In his phrase, "the display of the Divine justice," we find the key to his thought. It is the "deterrent purpose"[51] that the cross has that is central to the theory. The cross is a demonstration of the seriousness of the law.

It is in Grotius that we find one of the underlying reasons for the reactionary inflexible approach that would later be in evidence in Charles

43. Aptly summarized by McDonald, *The Atonement of the Death of Christ*, 197.

44. Ibid., 197.

45. Socinus, *Paelectiones Theologicae*, xvi; *Bibliotheca Fratrum Polonorum* I, 566.

46. Grotius, *Defensio Fidei Catholicae de Satisfactione Christi*, 3.

47. Ibid., 3.

48. Franks, *A History of the Work of Christ* II, 48.

49. Grotius, *Defensio Fidei Catholicae de Satisfactione Christi*, 1.

50. McDonald describes his theory as "a sacrifice of satisfaction to the necessities of a relaxed law." McDonald, *The Atonement of the Death of Christ*, 205.

51. Grensted, *A Short History of the Doctrine of the Atonement*, 294.

Hodge. Grotius removed the discussion of the atonement from the role of God the Father as Judge, and instead, focused on his role as Governor or Ruler. In this capacity, God is free to relax or even to abrogate entirely any laws he chooses. A judge upholds the law; a ruler makes the laws. So what we saw in Hodge, writing some two hundred years later, by which time Grotian theory had acquired some popularity in New England, is an attempt to return the discussion of the atonement to God's role as Judge. To do this, it was necessary for Hodge to emphasize the immutability of the divine attribute of justice, and therefore the unalterable nature of the laws that flow from it. It is not surprising then that what results, from the pen of Hodge, is a new and extreme form of penal theory.

For Grotius, God as Governor is not bound to uphold the law but does so only to meet "the ends of His own good government."[52] In that case, the punishment of crimes is not a matter of the abstract fulfillment of justice but is a lot more to do with deterring others:

> There is therefore no wrong in this, that God, who has supreme power as to all things not unjust in themselves, and who is liable to no law, willed to use the torments and death of Christ for the setting up of a weighty example against the immense faults of us all.[53]

It is not for nothing that this theory has been dubbed "penal example" or "penal non-substitution."[54]

Since Grotius' day, the governmental theory of the atonement has been held by as significant a figure as Charles Finney,[55] and was reinvented with a much higher dosage of "substitution" language by Methodist John Miley,[56] a contemporary of Finney's, and supported by other Wesleyans of that time, such as Nathanael Taylor[57] (as well as more recent Wesleyans[58]). It soon became associated with the nineteenth-century Calvinist New England

---

52. Ibid., 293.

53. Grotius, *Defensio Fidei Catholicae de Satisfactione Christi*, 4.

54. Crisp, "Penal Non-Substitution."

55. See his *Lectures on Systematic Theology*, 2nd ed., 264–81, and his *Lectures on Moral Government*.

56. Miley, *Atonement in Christ*, chapter 8. Also his *Systematic Theology*, Vol. 2, Part 5.

57. *Lectures on the Moral Government of God* (1859)

58. Grider, *A Wesleyan-Holiness Theology*, chapter 12; also his article, "The Governmental Theory," in which he claims: "The governmental theory can incorporate into itself everything that Scripture teaches about the atonement."

theology.[59] Today, interest in the theory has gone into decline. Recent studies of Grotius theology tend to be more interested in his apologetics.

However, in many ways, this theory arrives at a place every bit as distasteful as the worst forms of penal substitutionary theory. In fact, the picture painted of God the Father is, by implication, even worse than what would later show in Hodge's penal substitution. Here, the Father puts his Son through unimaginable torture, not for some inescapably just necessity, but merely so that he can say to humanity: "Now, let that be a lesson to you." In dealing with one problem: the idea that God is bound by his laws, Grotius creates another: a picture of the Father as Governor that is every bit as austere as the picture of him as Judge that the theory tries to replace. On the positive side, Grotius has released atonement theory from our various insistences about what God must or must not do. He has highlighted that any notion of the atonement that turns upon the payment of exact mercantile equivalents belittles God and obscures the generosity of his self-movement towards us in Christ.

Albrecht Ritschl (1822–89) and Liberal Protestantism

Moving now to the *Aufklärung*, or the German Enlightenment, we find the moral influence theories of the atonement taking on a new lease of life, beginning with the works of Gothelf Steinbart in 1778.[60] A fairly typical example of Steinbart, which set the tone for much that followed, is this: "No one who has clear ideas of an absolutely perfect righteousness can be persuaded that the father of the world will ever inflict upon anyone penal evils, except such as are necessary for his reformation."[61]

There was a growing insistence that the power of the atonement cannot possibly lie anywhere but in the effect that it produces within the interior life of a person to reform them. Specifically, this effect was thought to entail deliverance from a misunderstanding about the nature and attitude of God towards us.[62]

With the full flowering of the liberal tradition in the century that followed, the figure of Albrecht Ritschl looms large. Franks described him as

59. Summarized in a long "Introductory Essay," by Park, *The Atonement*, vii–lxxx.

60. McGrath, "The Moral Theory of the Atonement," 210.

61. Steinbart, *System de reinen Philosophie oder Glücklichkeitslehre des Christenthums*, 162. Translation by McGrath, "The Moral Theory of the Atonement," 211.

62. McGrath, "The Moral Theory of the Atonement," 211.

"the most important German theologian since Schleiermacher."[63] Ritschl's most important work in relation to the atonement was his *The Christian Doctrine of Justification and Reconciliation*, which was the third in a trilogy of works on the same theme[64] in which he applies a new method to historic Christian doctrines, inspired mostly by Kant, but also by some aspects of Schleiermacher's work. It is summed up in his dictum: "the immediate object of theological knowledge is the faith of the community."[65] In other words, religious knowledge can only be verified (or falsified) by its usefulness or otherwise to the community of the faithful. This signaled a radically empirical approach to Christian doctrine that excluded metaphysical speculation, scholastic reasoning, and mysticism, in favor of the religious and ethical experience of the believing community. That being the case, all notions of a satisfaction for sin or of any kind of transaction taking place outside of human experience was excluded from his doctrine of the atonement.

Ritschl's doctrine of sin and judgment showed all the cautions that we now associate with the liberal Protestantism of which he was a leading architect:

> The authority of Holy Scripture gives us no right to relate the wrath of God to sinners as such, for *ex hypothesi* we conceive sinners to be known and chosen by God, as partakers in His kingdom, and objects of His redemption from sin. . . . God loves even sinners in view of their ideal destiny, to realize which He chooses them.[66]

For Ritschl, the punishment for sin was its guilt, and its guilt—that is, a regretful sense of not attaining to fellowship with God—was its punishment. That being the case, Christ, who lived in perpetual God-consciousness and perfect harmony of will with the Father, cannot have endured punishment for sin. The possibility of a transfer of guilty status from humans to Christ is excluded: "For Christ had no sense of guilt in His sufferings, consequently He cannot have regarded them as punishment, nor even as punishment accepted in the place of the guilty."[67] To the contrary, "these

---

63. Franks, *A History of the Work of Christ* II, 329.

64. The other two are: Ritschl, *A Critical History of the Doctrine of Justification and Reconciliation* (1872) and the as-yet-untranslated work of biblical theology: *Die christliche Lehre von der Rechtfertigung under Versöhnung: Zweiter Band* (1874).

65. Ritschl, *Justification and Reconciliation*, 209.

66. Ibid., 320.

67. Ibid., 479.

sufferings, which, by His enduring of them to the death, He made morally His own, are manifestations of His loyalty to His vocation."[68] Because guilt is such a subjective experience, all that is needed for full reconciliation with God is the removal of the "mistrust"[69] of God that this subjective guiltiness produces in us. Once this is done, ethical goodness can begin to flow again, which is realized in the context of the community gathered around Christ, which he defines as the kingdom of God.

Grensted's sympathy for this type of theory is undisguised, and he sums it up well:

> Thus the death of Christ is regarded as having exactly the same purpose as His life. It was one great manifestation of perfect holiness, perfect obedience, perfect fellowship with God. And by this manifestation sin was condemned. It could not stand the presence of the light.[70]

Yet his perception of the greatest flaw in the moral theories is equally clear, and is worth reproducing here:

> [W]e are left with a great difficulty, the difficulty that must always face all purely ethical theories of the Atonement—How is man enabled to receive this manifestation of Divine fellowship? The Example is there indeed, but how shall eyes blinded with sin perceive it, how shall those who are chained by sin—and the metaphor is no mere metaphor—rise up and follow? That Liberal Protestantism of to-day which takes its inspiration from Ritschl has yet to give us an answer.[71]

In fact, Grensted did not seem fully aware that one of his own contemporaries had already supplied an answer to this, for Robert Campbell Moberly had already begun to look at the place of the Spirit within the moral theory in his work of 1901, *Atonement and Personality*,[72] a work that Grensted clearly appreciated. Before we come to Moberly, there is one last heading under which to explore the cross as transformative revelation: Neo-orthodoxy.

68. Ibid., 448.

69. Ibid., 85.

70. Grensted, *A Short History of the Doctrine of the Atonement*, 336.

71. Ibid., 337.

72. Moberly, *Atonement and Personality*, 1901. Grensted critiques Moberly's work, but does not do justice to his pneumatology: Grensted, *A Short History of the Doctrine of the Atonement*, 364–72.

The Cross and Neo-Orthodoxy: The Suffering God Revealed

As with most other topics of Trinitarian thought in twentieth-century theology, Karl Barth was responsible for kicking off discussion about the role of the obedient suffering of the Son on the cross in the Spirit as a revelation of the Trinity. It goes like this: man is the prodigal who has gone off into a far country in disobedience to the Father. In order to save man, the Father sends the Son into the far country. The eternally begotten Son, thus becomes the suffering, obedient human Son, identifying himself with lost humanity, bearing the consequences of its disobedience: "in becoming a human obedient son Jesus identifies himself with the human sons of God (notably Israel), who are disobedient and thus under judgment."[73] This causes suffering in the Son, as he bears the Godforsakenness of prodigal man. It also involves extreme suffering on the part of the Father as he loses his Son:

> It is not at all the case that God has no part in the suffering of Jesus Christ[;] . . . it is God the Father who suffers in the offering and sending of his Son, in his abasement. The suffering is not his own, but the alien suffering of the creature, of man, which he takes to himself. But he does suffer it in the humiliation of his Son with a depth with which it never was or will be suffered by any man— apart from the One who is his Son. This fatherly fellow-suffering of God is the mystery, the basis, of the humiliation of his Son; the truth of that which takes place historically in his crucifixion.[74]

All of this reveals a close relationship between the Father and the Son within the being of God, and the way the Father and the Son act in the world. The cross is the high point of the Son's obedience to the Father, revealing most clearly his sonship to the Father.

Barth is criticized by Paul Fiddes for not going far enough. Barth tries to preserve the impassibility of God (the idea that God cannot suffer), saying that the suffering is not his own, as well as claiming that God suffers and dies on the cross. How can God be passible and impassible? Barth's solution is that God is passible in the world, that is, in the economic Trinity, but impassible in himself, the immanent Trinity. There is thus, according to Fiddes' critique, "an untouched hinterland in the immanent being of

73. Barth, *Church Dogmatics* IV/1, 171.

74. Barth, *CD* IV/2, 357.

God"[75] He goes on, "Such a driving of a wedge between God in his essence and his works does not match Barth's own insight that God corresponds to himself."[76] There is, however, strength in Barth's argument, echoing Luther, that the glory of God is revealed in its opposite—the cross. The very forsakenness reveals the otherwise perfect unity of Father and Son.

The resurrection is the confirmation of the Son's deity. In the cross the Son is active, in the resurrection the Father is the principle actor while the Son is mostly passive. In our experience of the revealing of the Christ-event, it is the Spirit who is active. For Barth, therefore, reconciliation is certainly a Trinitarian accomplishment, but is the cross itself a fully Trinitarian event? For it to be so, we would need to be able to confirm that the Spirit is revealed at the cross. All we have biblically is Hebrews 9:14: the Eternal Spirit empowers Christ on the cross to make his offering. For Barth, the Spirit is "their [the Father's and Son's] free but also necessary fellowship of love."[77]

Hans Urs von Balthasar is among those who have drawn out the implications of Barth and sought to build something more with the raw materials he provided

> God causes God to go into abandonment by God, while accompanying him on the way with his Spirit. The Son can go into the estrangement from God of hell, because he understands his way as an expression of his love for the Father, and can give to his love the character of obedience, to such a degree that in it he experiences the complete godlessness of lost man.[78]

Balthasar incorporates the descent into hell described in the Apostles' Creed into his theology of the cross. The Son's descent into hell serves a similar function in his theology to the picture of the Son going onto the "far country" in Barth. Hell, for Balthasar, is the place of the self-damned:

> [O]n Holy Saturday there is the descent of the dead Jesus to hell, that is (put very simply) his solidarity in the period of nontime with those who have lost their way from God. Their choice—with which they have chosen to put their I in the place of God's selfless love—is definitive. Into this finality (of death) the dead Son descends, no longer acting in any way[,] . . . he is (out of an ultimate

75. Fiddes, *The Creative Suffering of God*, 121.

76. Ibid.

77. *CD* IV/1, 209.

78. Balthasar, "Trinity and Future," *Elucidations*, 51.

love however) dead together with them. And exactly in that way he disturbs the absolute loneliness striven for by the sinner: the sinner, who wants to be "damned" apart from God, finds God again in his loneliness.[79]

A further contribution to Barthian interpretation comes from Karl Rahner.[80] He sees the sending of the Spirit and the Son into the world as a single "concept."[81] As love, God is eternally moved towards self-communication. Revealing himself to the world by sending his Son would not be a complete act of communication unless the recipient was able to respond. The sending of the Spirit returns this communication. The Spirit causes the response of faith to rise from the addressees, the men and women that God has created to receive this communication.[82] The sending of the Son and the sending of the Spirit are, therefore, two sides of one work of redemption and not to be separated.

Another brilliant interpreter of Barth is Eberhard Jüngel. He, like Balthasar, develops Spirit-Son reciprocity specifically with reference to the cross.[83] For Jüngel, the cross is the defining moment of God's revelation in Christ, not simply the incarnation. Echoing Augustine, the Spirit is essential to Jüngel's theology as the bond of love uniting Father and Son during the crisis of the cross. For him, the statement "God is love" is about the Father's identification in the Spirit with the crucified Christ.[84] The Spirit, as the bond of that love, prevents there arising any fissure in the unity of Father and Son within the Trinity during that moment of agony.[85]

Jürgen Moltmann, famous for his book *The Crucified God* (1974), which mainly addressed the subject of theodicy,[86] further explored the possibilities of the cross as Trinitarian revelation:

---

79. Kehl and Löser, *The von Balthasar Reader*, 150–53.

80. Rahner, *The Trinity*.

81. Ibid., 85.

82. McFarland is very similar, using the analogy of speech. The Father speaks the Word, the Son is the Word and the Spirit is the "Amen" of response: McFarland, "Christ, Spirit and Atonement," 90.

83. See Jüngel, *God as the Mystery of the World*, 368–96.

84. Ibid., 326.

85. Ibid., 346.

86. The aspect of apologetics that addresses the "why suffering?" question. For Moltmann, the cross was a symbol of divine solidarity with a suffering world and was therefore the answer to "protest atheism."

The Son suffers in his love being forsaken by the Father as he dies. The Father suffers in his love the grief of the death of the Son. In that case, whatever proceeds from the event between the Father and the Son must be understood as the Spirit of the surrender of the Father and the Son, of the Spirit which creates love for forsaken man, as the Spirit which brings the dead alive.[87]

The event of the crucifixion reveals a God whose love has the power to absorb into itself all that is opposite to itself so as, ultimately, to take believers into the fellowship of the Trinitarian community:

For in the hidden mode of humiliation to the point of the cross, all being and all that annihilates has already been taken up in God and God begins to become "all in all." To recognise God in the cross of Christ, conversely means to recognise the cross, inextricable suffering, death and hopeless rejection in God.[88]

Christian faith is nourished on such a view of the cross:

In that case the doctrine of the Trinity is no longer an exorbitant and impractical speculation about God, but is nothing other than a shorter version of the passion narrative of Christ. . . . It protects faith from both monotheism and atheism because it keeps believers at the cross.[89]

In this incorporation of all things into God—known as panentheism—God takes part in the history of the world and changes with it. For Moltmann, the cross is not only a definition of the inner life of God but the inaugural moment of God's eschatological future. The very fact that God has opened himself up to the world in this way in order to redemptively draw the world into himself means that he has also become involved in its progress through history.[90] God has freely chosen to be so involved with the world he came to save as to be caught up in its very destiny. The world's becoming is therefore God's becoming. This, of course, serves Moltmann's liberationist agendas very well.[91] Concepts of immutability and impassibil-

87. Moltmann, *The Crucified God*, 245.

88. Ibid., 277.

89. Ibid., 246.

90. This theme emerges prominently in Moltmann, *The Trinity and the Kingdom of God*, esp. 94–96, also Moltmann, *The Church in the Power of the Spirit*, 53–56.

91. That Moltmann's eschatology is focused on this-worldly hopes of Utopia is seen as the main weakness of his theology by Williams, "The Problem with Moltmann," 158–59. Badcock sees Moltmann's eschatology as simply not biblical: Badcock, *Light of Truth and*

ity leave God too remote from human suffering for Moltmann, who was himself the victim of a wartime trauma.[92]

Moltmann, then, successfully presents a God that has connected with human pain in a decisive way at the cross. He is less persuasive in his efforts to portray the cross as a definitive revelation in history of God as Trinity.[93] In him, as in Barth and Balthasar, the cross seems more of a Binitarian event. Answers may well lie in the suggestions that the Spirit is the *vinculum* or bond of love between Father and Son, as Moltmann himself explains: "the common sacrifice of the Father and the Son comes about through the Holy Spirit, who joins and unites the Son in his forsakenness with the Father."[94] One author has further enlarged upon this idea, putting forward what he describes as a *pnumatologia crucis*.[95] In this model, drawing as the Neo-Orthodox all did from the Cry of Dereliction, the Spirit enters into the gulf that is characterized by the absence of God ("why have you forsaken me?") and replaces that absence with presence. The Spirit thus holds together the Trinity in a moment when a momentous and mysterious fissure seems to open up between Father and Son. In Jüngel the Spirit prevented the breach, here, the breach happens—which is what makes the cry of "why have you forsaken me" a very truthful one—but the Spirit dives into the gap.

It is interesting that the cross always brings us to these discussions of liminality: the Son bridging the gap between the divine the human; the Spirit bridging a gap between Father and Son; the Son making up to the full, and more, the gaping moral deficit of lost humanity. This is perhaps where rational explanation stops and theological aesthetics begin.

Fire of Love, 210. He also cites William Hill, who highlights the striking weakness that if God's very being is defined in terms of dying, suffering, and progressing with man, then what happens to his being once the *eschaton* has arrived? Badcock, *Light of Truth*, 210–11, citing Hill, *The Three-Personed God*, 175.

92. The story and that of his ensuing conversion is movingly told in Muller-Fahrenholz, *The Kingdom and the Power*, 15–25. Tomlin notes, interestingly, how theologies of the cross are a significantly postwar phenomenon. In the case of Germany and Japan, the cross has been essential as a tool to reflect on loss and suffering. On the part of the victors, the cross has served to correct heady optimism, Tomlin, *The Power of the Cross*, 3–4.

93. Jowers questions whether the cross is self-evidently Trinitarian in this sense: Jowers, "The Theology of the Cross as Theology of the Trinity," 263–264.

94. Moltmann, *The Trinity and the Kingdom of God*, 83. Cf. Moltmann, *The Church in the Power of the Spirit*, 126.

95. Dabney, "*Pneumatologia Crucis*," 524.

8

"The Spirit Comes from the Cross"

The Pneumatological Synthesis

The Cross and the Spirit: R. C. Moberly

OXFORD-BASED ANGLICAN THEOLOGIAN R. C. MOBERLY (1845–1903),[1] a contributor to the *Lux Mundi* publication, is a somewhat overlooked atonement theorist. His work is a sprawling magisterial tome that tries to keep together divergent polarities and, out of the tension involved in that, produces a striking new synthesis. At the time of his writing, there were only two main poles to the arguments surrounding atonement theory: the objective and the subjective: the penal versus the moral. Not until Aulén's work would a third alternative, the *Christus Victor* model, be presented. The profound influence of Aulén's threefold typology somewhat overshadowed Moberly's synthesis—and Aulén does not provide a synthesis in the way that Moberly does, but simply a third alternative.

---

1. Moberly, *Atonement and Personality*, 343–67. One of the main burdens of Moberly's work is, in the words of former Archbishop George Carey's review of his book, "an impassioned plea for a recovery of the work of the Spirit in the ministry of the Son on the cross." Carey, *The Gate of Glory*, 187. In Moberly's own words, "An exposition of atonement which leaves out Pentecost, leaves atonement unintelligible—in relation to us." *Atonement and Personality*, 151.

Moberly's book seems to achieve two things. First, it undermines the liberal protestant critique of objective views, especially of Anselm's satisfaction theory, but then it also strengthens the inadequacies of the subjective views. It mainly corrects and strengthens subjective views, but also takes some of the heat off the objective views, by drawing attention to the essential element within them all: that of the representative solidarity of Christ with his people.

Moberly's defense of the objective views is achieved by way of an assertion that Moberly says is the central claim of the whole book. Put simply it is that no man is an island. Liberal Protestantism had been too strident in its claims that no man can represent or substitute for another. The liberals had been claiming this, not only on the basis of justice (criminals must bear their own penalties), but also on the basis of a scientific assumption, widely queried today,[2] that an individual is a closed system. Though he shares with the liberals an aversion to mysticism, he insists that some room at least should be allowed for unions between persons.

Just so, Christ as the God-Man, was able to unite the divine to the human in his own person and in his representative work. Moberly also keeps before him the liberal insistence upon an actual moral transformation in the individual as the primary purpose of the atonement. And, because unions between personalities can happen, this is achieved by the person of the Spirit dwelling with the person who responds to the cross and influencing him or her in the right direction. And it will be the right direction because that Spirit is at once one with the Godhead and united to the human person.

So, the possibility of solidarity is affirmed and, on that basis, the role of the Spirit in the human response to Calvary is given due place. The subjective views are at once corrected and reinforced, while objective views are not dismissed outright.[3]

Seemingly without any awareness of Moberly, a writer at the heart of the Charismatic Renewal in the UK in the 1960s and 70s went on to develop the pneumatology of atonement still further.

---

2. Some interesting work has been done neurologically in the area of "emotional intelligence." People's "limbic" systems are wired in such a way that they are an open loop. People need one another for emotional rescue—something that we see at its most basic in a mother's ability to soothe a crying baby. Basch and Fisher, "Affective Events-Emotions Matrix."

3. As we saw in an earlier chapter, Moberly was sympathetic towards John McLeod Campbell's vicarious repentance approach.

Pentecost Meets Easter: Thomas Smail (1928–2011)

It has been said that the place that the cross occupies in charismatic church life is "a kind of natural background music,"[4] though even this is perhaps a little too generous. It has often enough been observed that charismatic Christianity's emphasis on immediacy[5] leaves little place for a theology of the cross, or indeed any theology at all.[6] Many have identified the danger of a one-sided emphasis on the things of the Spirit. Smail himself warned that where such one-sidedness exists, "Christless mysticism" and "charismatic excess" were among the dangers to be faced.[7] Old Testament scholar, John Goldingay was sure that only as the charismatic emphasis on the experience of Pentecost is "systematically linked to the cross" can charismatic spirituality avoid being "a baptizing of the spirit of the age."[8] At its height, the charismatic movement became a site of moral panic.

Smail, though a leading light in the Renewal in the UK, was relentless in his criticism of the Charismatic Renewal as having failed to adequately integrate the message of the cross with the message of Pentecost.[9] Referring to the British school education system of the time, he derisively described Pentecostal and charismatic Christian initiation as taking place in two-stages: "O" Level, corresponding to an Easter faith, and "A" Level—a fully-fledged faith in Pentecost.[10]

Smail, and others who spoke at the 1995 St. John's College Symposium on the atonement, were vehemently against the idea of penal substitution.[11]

4. Runia, "The Preaching of the Cross Today," 53.

5. This word "immediacy" was the linchpin of Yves Congar's critique of the charismatic movement. Congar, *I Believe in the Holy Spirit* Vol. II, 165.

6. Smail bemoaned the fact that the Charismatic Renewal not only lacked a theology, but was not even looking for one. Smail, "The Cross and the Spirit," 49. Pawson ably highlighted the same weakness: Pawson, *The Fourth Wave*, 65–71.

7. Smail, *The Giving Gift*, 132.

8. Goldingay, "Charismatic Spirituality," 7.

9. This critique began, in book form, with his *Reflected Glory*. The book was written, says Smail, "in reaction to the tendency in Pentecostalist teaching to cut loose the work of the Spirit from the work of the Son." Smail, *Giving Gift*, 44.

10. Smail, "The Cross and the Spirit," 57. The pastoral problem created by there being, by implication, two classes of Christian was close to the heart of James Dunn's work, *Baptism in the Holy Spirit* (1970). By the time of his *Jesus and the Spirit* (1975), it was clear that he had begun to think along the lines of Spirit-Christology, much as Smail would go on to articulate in his *The Giving Gift* (1988).

11. Goldingay, *Atonement*, 3–127. Cf. *The Forgotten Father*, 129: Smail rejects the

Smail was not only a critic, however. Like Moberly, he added something overlooked yet profoundly significant. He was heavily indebted to Karl Barth and spent a year in Basel being taught by him. He was especially receptive to Barthian thought that had been modified through the filters of T. F. Torrance and Jürgen Moltmann. Though receiving an experience of the Spirit under charismatic leader Dennis Bennett, his Reformed theology compelled him to reject Bennett's two-stage framework by which to interpret charismatic experience.[12] This conviction that the saving cross and the empowering Spirit were not to be separated was confirmed by an experience he had not long after receiving what he described as his baptism in the Holy Spirit. It happened when Smail exercised the gift of tongues in public for the first time: "The interpretation was given by a young woman, and I have never forgotten what she said, 'The way to Pentecost is Calvary; the Spirit comes from the cross.'"[13]

All of his thinking from that time on appears to have been an exploration of this idea. In his writings, he works his way back from the cross into the Trinitarian life of God himself, and then back out to Calvary again. Much of this reflection took place during his time as Chairman of the Fountain Trust, editor of *Renewal* magazine and of the doomed *Theological Renewal*,[14] and as Vice-Principal of the Anglican St. John's College, Nottingham. The result of his thinking is a trilogy of books on each member of the Trinity written between 1975 and 1988: *Reflected Glory* (on the Son), *The Forgotten Father* (on the Father), and *The Giving Gift* (on the Spirit). In these works, his greatest concern is how best to integrate the work of the Spirit with the work of the Son. Having worked his way back from Calvary to the Trinity, he discovered the statement of Jesus concerning the ministry

---

view of the cross as a satisfaction for sin, saying that it leaves us with "a cringing guilt-ridden religion which has to hide behind the love of Jesus in order to be saved from the only-just-contained wrath of an angry God." The St. John's College Symposium was replied to five years later at the Oak Hill College annual School of Theology in a conference entitled "Proclaiming Christ Crucified Today," later published as Petersen, ed., *Where Wrath and Mercy Meet*.

12. Smail, "The Cross and the Spirit," 53.

13. Ibid., 55. A slight variant of the account is in *Reflected Glory*, 105: "the interpretation was given by a young woman, unknown to me before or since, who said, 'There is no way to Pentecost except by Calvary; the Spirit is given from the cross.'"

14. This ran from 1975 to 1980 and was scrapped through what Wright considers to be a very telling lack of interest in theology on the part of charismatics at that time: Wright, "The Charismatic Theology of Thomas Smail," 6. Also Stibbe, "The Theology of Renewal and the Renewal of Theology," 71.

of the Holy Spirit in John 16:14: "He will glorify me, for he will take of mine and declare it to you." As he admits in *The Giving Gift*,[15] Smail was initially so keen on this thought as a way of correcting faults that he perceived in Pentecostalism[16] that he emphasized it almost to the point of minimizing the full personhood of the Spirit in *Reflected Glory*. By the time he wrote *The Giving Gift*, his thinking has matured and is expressed thus:

> On the one hand, the Spirit depends upon the Son for the content that he conveys to us: without the Son the Spirit would have nothing to convey, because he brings no content of his own. On the other hand, without the Spirit, what the Son has would be shut up in himself.[17]

On that basis, the work of the Son is utterly definitive of the work of the Spirit. The Spirit's mission is to reveal the cross. And so, working back from the Trinity to the cross again, this idea is communicated in his writings in the form of various slogans:

> The Spirit reveals himself not as a new object of our knowledge, but as the one who makes it possible for us to know and receive Christ crucified. . . . The Holy Spirit is himself the living water that flows from the side of Christ. . . . The deed done on Calvary long ago has its contemporary effect in the present inrushing of Pentecostal power.[18]

On the basis of this arguing from the cross to the Trinity and back again, Smail produces his critique of Charismatic Renewal, which, if applied to some aspects of the present day charismatic scene, still sounds quite pertinent: "If in our thinking we loosen the connection between Christ and the Spirit, we are in danger of severing one of the nerve-centres of the New Testament gospel."[19] Elsewhere he explains:

> The more the renewal relates itself to the central things of the gospel, e.g., the person and work of Christ rather than just tongues

15. Smail, *Giving Gift*, 44.

16. Wright has a point, however, in querying whether or not this apparently Christless pneumatology in Pentecostalism that Smail has such a problem with might actually be a straw man: "very rarely, if at all, does he cite Pentecostal authors. . . . Instead there is an assumption concerning what Pentecostal theology might claim." Wright, "Thomas Smail," 10.

17. Smail, *Giving Gift*, 51.

18. Ibid., 63, 81, 134.

19. Ibid., 125.

or healing, the more its contribution becomes recognisable and receivable by the rest of the Church, and the more it is delivered from its own idiosyncrasies and eccentricities.[20]

In articulating these ideas of Spirit-Son mutuality and relating them to the atonement, Smail provides a theological framework by which a way back can be found to greater Christ-centeredness. He makes clear the reasons why the atonement of Christ ought to be emphasized by those who profess to be given to the Spirit. The reason is that the cross is on the mind of that very Holy Spirit that a Pentecostal or charismatic would claim to be filled with. Smail helps to define a true Pentecostal as someone who knows what the Spirit's greatest boast is, what his greatest concern is, what his mission in the church and in the world actually is: to glorify Christ and his work.

Summary and Evaluation

In sum, the subjective views of the atonement have in common a yearning for the tangible and the measurable. This is partly a reaction against the Anselmian turn towards a totally extrinsic, objective view of the cross, and partly a response to the empiricism of the Enlightenment. The subjective approaches seek to correct the objectivity by introducing an ethical or experiential imperative, or in other words, a right response to the cross.

In Abelard, the right response was elicited by the love revealed at the cross. With this Socinus and the German liberals agreed. When God's love is revealed in such a maximal way our mistrust of him is dealt with and an obedient response to Christ's example is secured. With Grotius, the important thing was the way God's justice is revealed. The cross serves as a sobering example of what sin really deserves, inspiring us all to see the full horror of our sin and duly repent. In the Neo-Orthodox we saw the very Godhead itself revealed. For them, the cross was an earthed, non-abstract demonstration of the Triune God. We can thus respond to the being of God in a way that guards us from the exorbitant metaphysics of the kind of Trinitarian theology that ignores the cross. Further, in Moltmann, it is the divine empathy and solidarity revealed at the cross that elicits the right response. Moltmann's God is far from impassible. At the cross he got so involved with humankind that the whole Godhead was opened up to humans and

20. Ibid., 18.

the destiny of God became bound up with the race. In the ruins of postwar Germany, to which Moltmann returned after his spell in a prisoner of war camp, any theology that did not begin with the Cry of Dereliction could not begin at all. For a suffering world, only the theology of the cross was a recognizable Christian theology. Protest atheism is the only response to be anticipated from a crossless Christianity. Finally, we saw the right response being brought forth, not merely by something divine being revealed, but by God's Spirit being imparted. Initiated by Moberly and further explored by Smail (and more than hinted at in the Neo-Orthodox), this is the one version of the subjective view that allows for something supernatural to happen, and indeed insists upon it. Since Moberly first wrote his work, the bloodiest century in history confirmed the shocking depravity of our race and rebuked the naïve optimism of German liberal theology. Unless the Spirit brings forth the right response to the cross, it very likely does not come forth at all, even though we might be ever so moved by it. The free flowing tears of thousands of cinema-goers during showings of Mel Gibson's *The Passion of the Christ* is probably a good case in point.

PART FOUR

A New Option?
Anthropological Theories

9

The Story of Nonviolent Atonement

THERE ARE TWO MAIN STRANDS to nonviolent atonement theory,[1] one older, the other more recent, and now, with the advent of Non Violent Atonement (NVA)[2] seminars and conferences that bring together both strands, there is a merging together of the two, exemplified by the collection of essays published in 2006 called *Stricken by God?*[3] We have already met the older strand when we looked at some of the re-appropriations of *Christus Victor.* Walter Wink takes his place alongside John Howard Yoder as possessing godfather status within that part of the movement.[4] It is a robust form of nonviolent atonement theory that stresses that Christ's death was not a non-

1. There is possibly a third, discernable in the work of Anthony Bartlett and his use of the moral influence theory and "abyssal compassion": Bartlett, *Cross Purposes.*

2. These began in January 2007 with a two day NVA Conference organized by Preaching Peace (http://www.preachingpeace.org)

3. Jersak and Hardin, eds., *Stricken by God?* Peters notes that in Girard's work there is already evidence of a coming together of the two perspectives, Girard himself making full use, however unconsciously, of the *Christus Victor* ideas about evil being tricked into overreaching itself. He cites Girard: "What violence does not and cannot comprehend is that, in getting rid of Jesus by the usual means, it falls into a trap that could only be laid by innocence." Peters, "Atonement and the Final Scapegoat," 178, citing Girard, *Things Hidden Since the Foundation of the World,* 209. Two other collections of essays in a similar vein to *Stricken by God* are Trelstad, ed., *Cross Examinations,* and Sanders, *Atonement and Violence.*

4. A much cited text of Wink's on violence is: "Facing the Myth of Redemptive Violence." Wink coined the now widely used phrase, "myth of redemptive violence." Yoder is best known for his *The Politics of Jesus.*

violent acceptance of evil perpetrated against him; it was no acquiescence to abuse, neither was it a pretext for other victims of abuse to not stand up for themselves.[5] It was, rather, a nonviolent resistance of evil—in the manner, say, of the nonviolent civil disobedience of Gandhi, Luther King, Tutu, and Mandela.[6] It amounts to a refusal to deal with evil in an evil way; a refusal to deal with violence in a violent way, but not a refusal to deal with it at all. God in Christ took positive action to conquer evil and carried out his plan in the best way possible: by absorbing the worst that humans could do, and inevitably did do, and then by rising again as the founder of a new way of being, all the time extending his reign by gentleness and persuasion, not by force or violence.

The second strand is inspired by the writings of French literary critic, Réné Girard (b. 1923). He began articulating his unique view of human social life as early as 1977, following his own return to the Christian faith sparked by his new insight into the Gospel passion narratives. Not until the translation into English in 1998 of his *I See Satan Fall Like Lightning*,[7] which is the clearest of his many statements of his theory, did his ideas enter wide circulation within English-speaking theology. To his theory we now turn.

---

5. Significant feminist literature critiquing the sanctioned violence of some atonement theories includes the following: Brock, *Journeys by Heart* (she coins the term "cosmic child abuse" on page 56), Brown and Parker, "For God So Loved the World?"; Crysdale, *Embracing Travail*; Brock and Parker, *Saving Paradise*. In this literature, the charge is repeatedly made that notions of penal substitution or of Anselmian satisfaction are complicit in the fostering of abuse by men of women and children and of further fostering the passive acceptance of abuse by victims. This is a plausible argument but, considering the very strident and repetitious nature of the claim it is surprising and frustrating how little concrete evidence is ever mustered to support this idea. It stands almost entirely on the strength of its emotive appeal. One feminist writer puts the case aptly: "For thousands of years before and after Christ suffered crucifixion, male homo sapiens has not needed the Jewish or Christian idea of sacrifice or suffering in order to keep women submissive." Trost, "On Suffering, Violence, and Power," 36.

6. Chenoweth and Stephan, *Why Civil Resistance Works*.

7. Girard, *I See Satan Fall Like Lightning*. See also his *Violence and the Sacred*, *The Scapegoat*, *Things Hidden Since the Foundation of the World*, and his contribution to Bukert et al., *Violent Origins*.

Girardian Theory

There are two main planks to Girard's theory. Firstly, humans have a tendency towards "mimetic" desire. Mimetic desire is desire that is brought about by "mimesis" or the imitation of other people. We desire something simply because others have made it look desirable. We mimic other people's desire. Satan then puts "stumbling blocks" in the way of our desire so that we cannot obtain it: "opposition exacerbates desire."[8] Mimetic rivalry ensues in which we see others as a threat, especially if they are competing for the same thing. As this process carries on and frustrations intensify, whole communities can become filled with violence. Girard speaks of "reciprocal escalation and one-upmanship."[9] "Internal violence," he says, is "the number one problem of every human community."[10] It is the war of all against all. Satan's next tactic is to be the answer to the cycle of violence, and here is the second plank. Satan presents to the community a marginal person who is slated as being the true cause of all the unrest. The whole community then turns on that person to destroy them. A temporary peace is achieved. This second component is called the "scapegoat mechanism."

Both of these factors, mimetic desire and the scapegoat mechanism, are then presented by Girard as the dominant factors involved in the genesis of civilizations. Girard speaks, for instance, of the "founding sacrifice," the initial scapegoated victim whose death at the hands of a mob brought about enough peace for a stable society to begin to take shape. This need for violence at the founding of civilizations is, according to Girard's research, axiomatic in all the great foundational myths of literature. Not only that but it stands to reason that, unless cycles of desire-fuelled violence are dissipated, there can only be a descent into self-destructive chaos and no ascent into civilization.

Because mimetic desire and scapegoating are foundational they are also definitive, and this is the most difficult thing about Girard's ideas to accept. At no point does Girard merely allow us to observe that rivalry and scapegoating are an all-too-familiar aspect of culture. This we could probably all agree is the case. In Western culture today scapegoating might not involve communal killings, but it is alive and well in the political realm, where senior figures are pressured into resigning in response

8. Girard, *I See Satan Fall*, 10.

9. Ibid., 9.

10. Ibid.

to media-generated controversy. They are our fiends, our public enemies. However, plenty of actual communal killings have occurred within this context also, the most obvious example being in the 1930s when prosperous Jews were scapegoated for Germany's economic depression, and the attempted genocide that soon followed. For Girard, these things are not only sad examples of a more general depravity but are definitive, without remainder, of the total human condition.

The work of Christ, then, is a kind of salvation, but not from sin as classically understood. It is salvation from violence. In fact, it is not even individuals, in the first instance, that need saving, but societies. Jesus is the one who fully absorbed all this community violence when he was scapegoated. Crucially, it is not God that does the scapegoating. He is on the side of the victims of scapegoating, not the one engineering the crucifixion of the Son of God: "There is nothing in the Gospels to suggest that God causes the mob to come together against Jesus. Violent contagion is enough."[11] This is what makes the Girardian approach fully and unashamedly anthropological. There is, strictly speaking, nothing theological about this approach at all.

Christ was then vindicated by his resurrection, thus fully exposing our scapegoating tendencies for what they really are: the victimization of the innocent. These violent tendencies depend for their very survival on not being exposed, they "cannot survive such a revelation."[12] We hide this jealous quality more ingeniously than any other human quality. And for as long as our hypocrisy goes undetected, Satan is able to perpetuate the violence.

According to this view, then, Jesus was not a sacrifice that saves us. To the contrary, he saved us from sacrificing. We are not in need of being saved *by* a sacrifice—humankind has been doing that from time immemorial through the scapegoat mechanism. Humankind needs to be saved *from* sacrifice.[13] It needs saving from the whole myth of redemptive violence, the very idea that the answer to bad violence is good violence, which we see never-endingly played out in global politics to this day.

Following in the footsteps of Girard and his scapegoat theory has been a plethora of studies that focus our attention on the trial and execution of Jesus, not as something that God did, but as something that humans did.[14]

11. Ibid., 21.

12. Ibid., 189.

13. See Heim, *Saved From Sacrifice*.

14. Peters, "Atonement and the Final Scapegoat," 151–81, Baillie, *Violence Unveiled*;

In the words of Raymund Schwager, "It is not God who must be appeased, but humans who must be delivered from their hatred."[15] Brad Jersak aptly cites Andre Harden:

> As I just look at what really happened in the physical realm on Good Friday, I don't see God's anger. If police were called to the scene, they would have found no "second shooter." . . . People killed him out of hate, spite and fear—plain and simple—really. Whatever theological theory we overlay, we must remember that the historical act was plain and simple and that humanity was responsible for it.[16]

God, however, was clearly not uninvolved, and Girardians seem to feel compelled to allow more of a place than Girard himself did, for a pre-ordained divine plan, some divine purpose that pre-empts the crucifixion, but articulated in a way that carefully side-steps attributing any violent intentions to God: "Jesus didn't volunteer to get into God's machine. God volunteered to get into ours."[17] Even the familiar New Testament language of Christ dying "for us" need not, for Girardians, be abandoned or altered to "by us," though a new twist must be added:

> Christ dies for us, to save us from what killed him. And what killed him was not God's justice but our redemptive violence. He stepped in between our violence and our victims, and has been a haunting presence there ever since.[18]

Similarly, we are accustomed, perhaps, to the language of "vindication" that surrounds the resurrection but would normally associate it with Christ's status as the divine Son of God. In Girardian theorists such as Heim, the concept is put to fresh use as the vindication of victims: "a resurrection that witnesses to the triumph over death is at the same time the

---

Volf, *Exclusion and Embrace*; Alison, *The Joy of Being Wrong*; Collins, "Girard and Atonement"; Heim, *Saved from Sacrifice*; Love, "Abyssal Compassion or Acquiescence to Violence?"; Love, *Love, Violence, and the Cross*; Nessen, "The Cross as Foundation for the Ministry of Reconciliation."

15. Schwager, *Must There be Scapegoats?* 209.

16. Andre Harden, *Agora Newsgroup* (Nov 2, 2006), cited in Jersak, "Nonviolent Identification and the Victory of Christ," in Jersak and Hardin, eds., *Stricken by God?* 28.

17. Heim, *Saved from Sacrifice*, xi.

18. Ibid., 306.

vindication of the victim. It is at once a promise about a life to come and a radical transformation in life here and now."[19]

There is no doubt that Girardian theory is completely fresh, totally fascinating, and extremely inviting. And Heim, for one, has presented Girard's ideas in an especially convincing way, relatively free of the angry polemics that can be seen in some of the *Stricken by God* essays. It is tempting to become a Girardian. Before that step is taken, however, it is worth pointing out the two preliminary steps that need to be taken. The first step will be hard for anyone of a theologically conservative bent since it requires a new hermeneutic. Girard's reading of Scripture requires that we see an emerging nonviolence in the Old Testament that comes to full flowering in the new. The genocides of the Old Testament, for instance, are understood as misguided human attempts to please God at a time when we all took him to be just another run-of-the-mill bloodthirsty deity. We should focus our attention instead on the more remarkable narratives where God seems to be saying, "No. You're wrong. I'm not like that." Examples range from God stopping Abraham from sacrificing Isaac, to Joseph's forgiving non-retaliation, to God's command that Gideon whittle down his army to 300 men, who go on to win the battle, not by fighting, but by smashing pitchers and blowing trumpets, while the enemy troops slaughter one another. And this selectivity does not necessarily follow some chronological or evolutionary pattern of progressive revelation. In the New Testament itself, we are asked to similarly forgive the misguided theology of the writer to the Hebrews, who mistakenly thought that Christ's death was a divinely instituted sacrifice for sin rather than a humanly perpetrated victimization. Girard-devotee Michael Hardin makes the interesting point that the Bible itself is self-critical and does not therefore intend itself to be used as an inflexible law of life. Claims of inerrancy can reinforce the use of Scripture as a pretext for some very undesirable things; "Jews and Christians don't need a perfect Bible; the perfect Bible will ultimately be distorted as a myth," by which he means a myth of redemptive violence.[20]

The second decision that a true Girardian must make, at least according to one of their number,[21] is that he or she must reject Platonism, or at

19. Heim, *Saved from Sacrifice*, 306.

20. Hardin, "Out of the Fog: New Horizons for Atonement Theory," in Jersak et al., *Stricken by God?* 60.

21. And he does seem to have identified accurately a tendency within Girard adherents: Hardin, "Out of the Fog: New Horizons for Atonement Theory," in Jersak et al, *Stricken by God?* 58–59.

least a certain take on Platonism. This entails the rejection of some ideas that are so deeply embedded within Western culture that we barely notice them. Plato's thought, as it has filtered down to us, has tended to result in a mindset that divides the world of what can be known into two realms: the ideal and the real, essences and particular instances, ideal forms and specific examples, theory and practice. Justice, for instance, is the ideal form, while law is the specific way in which the ideal of justice is imperfectly worked out in life. The result tends to be that the ideal always takes precedent over the particular. *It* is the thing that really matters. *It* is the thing we must attempt to grasp by our reasoning. We are to reach for it in a way that is analogous to the way Hollywood urges us to reach for our dreams of greatness, or we must yearn for it in the way plantation slaves sang spirituals about the hope of heaven across the Jordan of death. Western society has become programmed to distinguish sharply between the two worlds, and to consider the one more important than the other. When we watch films we accept terrible on-screen violence because it's "part of the plot," the plot is everything; the killing doesn't matter. In the Crusades knights in shining armor could kill for God and the hope of heaven. In ethics, we call these tendencies the end justifying the means. And this way of thinking, according to Girardians, has been so pervasive within atonement theology as to require comprehensive revision, revision that will come only as the whole way in which we think prioritizes the particular over the ideal, the concrete over the abstract.

A case in point has been the way atonement theory by its very nature is "theory." It abstracts from the horrific violence of the trials and crucifixion of Jesus a transcendent divine plan and purpose. In the end the transcendent divine purpose receives so much priority that we fail to connect it back again to the events themselves. The result is that we become blind to the obvious. It is obvious, for instance, to an outsider that penal substitution impugns God as sadistic and demanding, while an insider to the notion has got so caught up with the abstractions of exchange between debts and penalties and immutable divine justice that they cannot see how unattractive the thing is that they are so ardently defending. Girardian views refuse to let us move too quickly beyond the events surrounding the crucifixion itself. We are to gaze at those events until we all see ourselves reflected in the jeers of the mockers and the cries of "Crucify him!" from the mob. The particularity of the crucifixion takes priority over the abstractions of atonement theory. It is, in effect, the end of atonement theories, a declaration of their bankruptcy.

Summary and Evaluation

So it is, then, that our very last atonement theory is a negation of them all. We have probably all had times when we want to sweep everything off our desk: papers, books, computer—and start all over again with a completely clear desk. This quest for a clear desk is really part of a wider quest for the historical Jesus, and Girard seems just as guilty as the Jesus Seminar, for instance, of assuming that the Jesus of history is distinguishable from the Christ of faith. Gunton was wise when he counseled us that the atonement comes to us pre-interpreted. Even before it happens, Christ is predicting that he would be a "ransom for many" (Mark 10:45). So, even in the Gospels we cannot escape from an interpreted cross. We cannot finally tease out some core of truth that is truer or more reality-depicting than the metaphors of redemption, sacrifice, reconciliation, justification, or victory that the New Testament gives us. And it is upon these metaphors—constantly interpreted in new ways for new generations, that atonement theories largely rest. There is value in a quest for a New Testament theology of the atonement, which I hope to embark on myself very soon, but it is questionable whether Girard has finally seen past the metaphors to the reality behind them. After all, is that not itself a rather Platonic way of thinking?

Further, even on its own terms, Girardian theory is not completely satisfying. Almost all of the evidence that Girard gathers is from the world of ancient myths. His body of evidence is the literature. We are then asked to rely on his reading of these myths as cleverly concealing the innocence of the scapegoats portrayed in the stories. The authors portray the scapegoats as really guilty of something. Girard insists that this conceals the true barbarity of the acts portrayed. Somehow, in the retelling of these ancient myths, the truth was distorted. More importantly, no evidence is presented that might corroborate this reading of the literature: no archeological evidence, for instance, that might point to founding human sacrifices as a pattern in the formation of human societies.[22]

---

22. McClymond goes further still, claiming that this particular interpretation of human sacrifices superimposes ideas from Christianity itself: McClymond, *Beyond Sacred Violence.* See also Goode, "Beyond Sacred Violence," 476–86.

Regarding human nature, Girard might initially seem brutally honest about our hidden violent tendencies. The picture is very unflattering. It has been pointed out, however, that in the response that Girard anticipates, namely that we all become aware of our fault and turn from it, what we actually have here is a gospel for nice people.[23] Nice people might well look upon the crucifixion, recognize themselves in it, change their ways, and become champions for scapegoats in our world today.[24] But what about bad people? What about the kind of human nature described by Paul in Romans 7 that, when the tenth commandment shows the full extent of its sinfulness, reacts by becoming yet more sinful? We are left with the same deficiency as the moral influence theories, without the Moberly factor.[25]

There is much that is of value here, however. Perhaps the greatest favor that Girard has done for us is to open up our eyes to see the cross from a completely different angle, and having done so, we shall never be the same again. And this is what causes him to rank with the very most influential names mentioned in this book who also originated decisive new ways of seeing the cross. Heim expresses well just how stark this new perspective is:

> The gospels make it clear that it is Jesus' antagonists who view his death as a redemptive sacrifice, one life given for many. . . . Here is a caution for Christian theology. We must beware that in or reception and interpretation of the Gospel we do not end up entering the passion story on the side of Jesus' murderers.[26]

23. For Placher, Girard reduces the cross to "good news for basically good people." Placher, "Christ Takes Our Place," 6.

24. "He seems to assume that once we have understood the problem, it practically fixes itself." Ibid., 9.

25. Boersma goes as far as to say that to remove the penal element from justice, as nonviolent advocates seem to recommend, is to perpetuate cycles of violence, and is a violation of a victim's sense of justice. He asserts that penal substitution, properly nuanced, gives a solid hope of forgiveness and restoration to the perpetrators as well as the victims: Boersma, "Eschatological Justice and the Cross."

26. Heim, *Saved from Sacrifice*, 125–26.

10

The Way through the Maze

Some Initial Deductions

NOW THAT WE HAVE SURVEYED these Girardian approaches it does seem as though we have here a new kind of atonement theory—or perhaps more of an anti-theory—that has only just begun to emerge: an anthropological theory of the atonement.

Added to this is the fact that, with Moltmann's restatement of Luther's theology of the cross, we also perhaps have a small group of theories that are specifically theological, in the sense that they are really not about what Christ was achieving on the cross, but they are actually about God. This perhaps is a pole, a theological pole, with anthropological theories giving us the opposite pole. If so, these two poles allow us to update Aulén's threefold paradigm. What I propose is that, instead of three great big groupings that swallow up everything in a loosely chronological order, what we actually have are precisely two poles. On the extreme end is a pole under which we would place the truly theological theories. These use the cross to describe *God*. At the other end would be the anthropological theories. These use the cross to describe *human nature*. Right in the middle we would need to place those theories that are truly christological. They are neither about God nor man but about *the God-Man*. These are those theories that make a very clear attempt to place the work of Christ into the person of Christ and insist that the person of Christ is our only cipher for understanding the work of Christ as mediator. Here is a diagram that illustrates this as well as postulating where some of the theorists might fit.

Theological	Demonological	Christological	Soteriological	Ethical	Anthropological
Luther	Nyssa	Anselm	Luther	Abelard	Girard
Moltmann	Aulèn	McLeod Campbell	Calvin	Socinus	Heim
Hodge	J. Denny Weaver	P. T. Forsyth	Hodge	Grotius	
		Emil Brunner		Ritschl	
			Moberly	Moberly	

This is tentative, yet I hope it helps us to see that, while no theory of the atonement is without validity, it is probably the case that those that are the closest to the middle, and which therefore focus on the God-Man himself and what he, as a total life, achieves for us, have a potential advantage.

The work does not define the person—in that case we would have a Christ who came only to die; rather, his person defines his work. Whatever can be said about the Son of God, nothing more or less than that can be said of the death and resurrection of the Son of God. The person defines the work. One of N. T. Wright's more memorable quotes is the following: "The silhouette of the cross against a darkened sky is more, not less, evocative for our having studied the portrait of the man who hung there."[1] Pannenberg is similar: "Soteriology must follow from Christology, not vice versa."[2] The same would be true of any life. A novelist will go to some length to create and describe a character capable of and likely to perform the feats he or she will later become embroiled in as the plot unfolds.

This christological or incarnation-centered approach results in the least problematic outcomes. To let the Father define the work results in difficult moral problems that too easily impugn the Father's nature. To let our humanity define the work results in theories that are inadequate for explaining the extremity of the solution. To place the person of Christ himself at the center is to highlight the unbridgeable gulf between the divine

---

1. Wright, "The Reasons for Jesus' Crucifixion," in Jersak & Hardin, eds., *Stricken by God?* 149.

2. Pannenberg, *Jesus: God and Man*, 48.

and the human, whatever its causes. Into this breach comes the "Word," the "Son of God," the "Son of Man," the mediator between God and men.

Conclusion

A KEYBOARD PLAYER WHO IS suddenly given a grand piano might struggle at first to make full use of the entire range of notes that is now on offer. Similarly, many of us are accustomed to play only the familiar, if rather dreary, sonatas of our particular tradition. In some cases, we can only play endless renditions of *Chopsticks*. What I hope has become clear is that there is a wealth of melody, harmony, and rhythm accessible to us. There are some big fat Rachmaninovian chords to play. Some parts chime well with contemporary culture and deserve to be played more loudly than before, while other movements in the piece seem to need to be played more softly than we are used to. And it is here, in discerning where the emphasis ought to lie, that I have sought to find some answers and so show the way through the maze. If Christ himself is kept at the center then there is freedom to accommodate freely to the twists and turns of culture. Compared to other controlling options within atonement theory, his person is not easy to compromise, especially in the wake of all the recent work done on thoroughly contextualizing him within first-century Palestine so that we do not mistake him for a white Western theologian. And with the historical Jesus, the Christ of faith, firmly in place, our culture may yet be arrested by the claims a crucified and risen savior.

Jesus Christ himself, then, is the way through the maze, and it is only to the extent that we take our gaze off him and try to focus instead either on what we think the cross ought to be fixing, or on what we think it implies about God the Father, that we miss its central message. Calvary is full of mystery and contradiction, and our minds cannot fully cope with God on a cross, yet there is a central message, and it is the message that God has come near. And this divine embrace has become proximate not only to everyday human life but its extremes also. The cross and resurrection embrace the extremes of despair and joy, of pain and release. This embrace of extremes and of everything in between bridges the chasm, the liminal place, between humans and God. Forever into God has human being been taken up and forever into human being divine being has entered.

There is more than merely a bridge across which I may walk, impossibly great though that alone would be. There is a total penetration, a total mutuality, a total possibility of a total relationship. Creator and creature are reconciled, but more than reconciled. They can now be joined in a way that was never possible before. What I am saying describes both the incarnation and the cross, it is true, and this is just the way it should be, for the one movement of God towards lost humanity: Jesus Christ.

Bibliography

Abelard, Peter. *Commentary on Romans,* Book II: Rom 3:19–26, Section II. In *A Scholastic Miscellany: Anselm to Ockham,* translated by Gerald E. Moffatt and edited by Eugene Fairweather, 276–87. London: SCM, 1956.

Alexander, A. B. *The Shaping Forces of Religious Thought.* Glasgow: Maclehose, Jackson & Co., 1920.

Allen, David. "Crossfire," *Joy* 126, March 2005, 24–26.

Althaus, Paul. *The Theology of Martin Luther.* Translated by Robert C. Schultz. Philadelphia: Fortress, 1966.

Andrews, Jessie Forsyth. "Memoir." In *The Work of Christ,* by P. T. Forsyth, 11–29. London: Collins, 1965.

Anon. *Alcoholics Anonymous: The Story of How Many Thousands of Men and Women Have Recovered from Alcoholism.* 1939. Reprint. New York: AA World Services, 2001.

Anselm of Canterbury. *Basic Writings.* Translated by S. N. Deane. La Salle, IL: Open Court, 1962.

———. *A Meditation on Human Redemption.* In *Anselm of Canterbury,* Vol. 1, edited by Jasper Hopkins and Herbert Richardson, 276–87. London: SCM, 1974.

Armstrong, Brian G. *Calvinism and the Amyraut Heresy: Protestant Scholasticism and Humanism in Seventeenth-Century France.* Madison, WI: University of Wisconsin Press, 1969.

Arnold, Clinton E. *Powers of Darkness: Principalities and Powers in Paul's Letters.* Downer's Grove, IL: InterVarsity, 1992.

———. *3 Crucial Questions about Spiritual Warfare.* Grand Rapids: Baker, 1997.

Asiedu, F. B. A. "Anselm and the Unbelievers: Pagans, Jews and Christians in the *Cur Deus Homo.*" *Theological Studies* 62.3 (2001) 530–48.

Athanasius. *On the Incarnation of the Word.* In *Nicene and Post-Nicene Fathers,* Series II, Vol. 4. Edited by Philip Schaff. Online: http://www.ccel.org/ccel/schaff/npnf204.

Atkinson, William. *The Death of Jesus: A Pentecostal Investigation.* Leiden: Brill, 2009.

———. "The Nature of the Crucified Christ in Word-Faith Teaching." *Evangelical Review of Theology* 31.2 (2007) 169–84.

———. "A Theological Appraisal of the Doctrine that Jesus Died Spiritually, as Taught by Kenyon, Hagin and Copeland." PhD diss., Edinburgh University, 2007.

Aulén, Gustav. *Christus Victor: An Historical Study of the Three Main Types of the Idea of the Atonement.* Translated by A. G. Herbert. London: SPCK, 1931.

Badcock, G. D. *Light of Truth and Fire of Love: A Theology of the Holy Spirit.* Grand Rapids: Eerdmans, 1997.

Baillie, Gil. *Violence Unveiled.* New York: Crossroad, 1995.

Bainton, Roland. *Here I Stand.* New York: Mentor, 1950.

Baldwin, R. *Healing and Wholeness.* Milton Keynes: Word, 1988.

Bibliography

Balthasar, Hans Urs von. "Anselm." In *The Glory of the Lord: A Theological Aesthetics Vol. II: Studies in Theological Style: Clerical Styles.* Translated by Andrew Louth et al., 211–57. Edinburgh: T. & T. Clark, 1984.

———. *Elucidations.* London: SPCK, 1975.

Barnes, C. "Necessary, Fitting, or Possible: The Shape of Scholastic Christology." *Nova et Vetera* 10.3 (2012) 657–88.

Barth, K. *Church Dogmatics* Vol. VI/1. Translated and edited by G. W. Bromiley. Edinburgh: T. & T. Clark, 1936.

Bartlett, Anthony. *Cross Purposes: The Violent Grammar of Christian Atonement.* Harrisburg, PA: Trinity, 2001.

Basch John, and Cynthia Fisher. "Affective Events-Emotions Matrix: A Classification of Job-Related Events and Emotions Experienced in the Workplace." In *Emotions in the Workplace: Research, Theory and Practice,* edited by N. Ashkanasy et al., 36–48. Westport, CT: Quorum, 2000.

Basil of Caesarea. *On the Holy Spirit.* In *Nicene and Post-Fathers.* Series II, Vol. 8. Edited by Philip Schaff. Online: http://www.ccel.org/ccel/schaff/npnf208.

Baudrillard, Jean. *The Gulf War Did Not Take Place.* Translated by P. Patton. Sydney: Power, 1995.

———. *Simulations.* Translated by P. Foss et al. New York: Columbia University Press, 1983.

Beckwith, S. *Christ's Body: Identity, Culture, and Society in Late Medieval Writings.* London: Routledge, 1993.

Beeke, Jonathan. "'Cur Deus Homo?' A Closer Look at the Atonement Theories of Peter Abelard and Bernard of Clairvaux." *Puritan Reformed Journal* 1.2 (2009) 43–56.

Bell, M. Charles. "Calvin and the Extent of the Atonement." *Evangelical Quarterly* 55 (1983) 115–23.

———. "Was Calvin a Calvinist?" *Scottish Journal of Theology* 36 (1983) 535–40.

Bell, Daniel. "God Does Not Demand Blood: Beyond Redemptive Violence." In *God Does Not Entertain, Play "Matchmaker," Hurry, Demand Blood, Cure Every Illness,* edited by D. Brent Laytham, 39–61. Grand Rapids: Brazos, 2009.

Bell, Rob. *Love Wins.* London: Collins, 2011.

Bennett, Lance W. "Changing Citizenship in the 'Digital Age.'" *Civic Life Online: Learning How Digital Media Can Engage Youth* 1 (2008) 1–24.

Bernard of Clairvaux. *Contra Quaerdam Capitula Errorum Petri Abaelardi* VII, 17. In *Patrologia Latina Database* 182.21. Online: http://pld.chadwyck.com/.

Bewkes, Eugene. *Legacy of a Christian Mind: John McLeod Campbell.* Philadelphia: Judson, 1937.

Bielo, James. *Emerging Evangelicals.* New York: New York University Press, 2011.

Billings, J. Todd. *Calvin, Participation, and the Gift: The Activity of Believers in Union with Christ.* Oxford: Oxford University Press, 2007.

———. *Union with Christ: Reframing Theology and Ministry for the Church.* Grand Rapids: Baker, 2011.

Blacketer, Raymond A. "Definite Atonement in Historical Perspective." In *The Glory of the Atonement: Biblical, Historical & Practical Perspectives,* edited by Charles E. Hill and Frank A. James III, 304–23. Downers Grove, IL: InterVarsity, 2004.

Bloch, Marc, and F. L. Ganshof. *Feudal Society.* Translated by L. A. Manyon. London: Routledge & Kegan Paul, 1961.

Blocher, Henri. "Agnus Victor: The Atonement as Victory and Vicarious Punishment." In *What Does it Mean to be Saved? Broadening Evangelical Horizons*, edited by John Stackhouse, 67–91. Grand Rapids: Baker, 2002.

———. "The Atonement in John Calvin's Theology." In *The Glory of the Atonement*, edited by Charles Hill & Frank James III, 279–303. Downers Grove, IL: InterVarsity, 2004.

Bloemendal, Jan. "Huogo Grotius (1583–1645): Jurist, Philologist, and Theologian. A Christian Humanist, His Works, and His Correspondence." *Dutch Review of Church History* 82.2 (2002) 342–49.

Boardman, Mary M. *Life and Labors of the Rev. W. E. Boardman*. New York: Appleton, 1887.

Boersma, Hans, "Calvin and the Extent of the Atonement." *Evangelical Quarterly* 64 (1992) 333–55.

———. "Eschatological Justice and the Cross: Violence and Penal Substitution." *Theology Today* 60 (2003) 186–99.

———. "Irenaeus, Derrida and Hospitality: On the Eschatology of Overcoming Violence." *Modern Theology* 19.2 (2003) 163–80.

———. *Violence, Hospitality and the Cross: Reappropriating the Atonement Tradition*. Grand Rapids: Baker Academic, 2004.

Bokovay, Kelly W. "The Relationship of Physical Healing to the Atonement." *Didaskalia* 3.2 (1991) 26–35.

Bond, David. "Amyraldianism and Assurance." In *Christ for the World: Affirming Amyraldianism*, edited by Alan C. Clifford, 92–108. Norwich, UK: Charenton Reformed, 2007.

Bornkamm, Heinrich. *Luther's World of Thought*. Translated by Martin H. Bertram. Saint Louis, MI: Concordia, 1958.

Bosworth, F. F. *Christ the Healer*. Old Tappan, NJ: Revell, 1973.

Bowman, R. M. "'Ye Are Gods?' Orthodox and Heretical Views on the Deification of Man." *Christian Research Institute Journal* 1.0018 (1994). No pages. Online: http://www.iclnet.org/pub/resources/text/cri/cri-jrnl/web/crj0018a.html.

Boyd, Greg. "Christus Victor View." In *The Nature of the Atonement: Four Views*, edited by James Beilby and Paul R. Eddy, 23–49. Nottingham, UK: InterVarsity, 2006.

———. *God at War: The Bible and Spiritual Conflict*. Downer's Grove, IL: InterVarsity, 1997.

Bracken, Jerry. "Thomas Aquinas and Anselm's Satisfaction Theory." *Angelicum* 62 (1985) 501–30.

Brock, Rita Nakashima. "And a Little Child Will Lead Us: Christology and Child Abuse." In *Christianity, Patriarchy, and Abuse: A Feminist Critique*, edited by Joanne Carlson Brown and Carole R. Bohm, 42–61. New York: Pilgrim, 1989.

———. *Journeys by Heart: A Christology of Erotic Power*. New York: Crossroad, 1988.

Brock, Rita Nakashima, and Ann Parker. *Saving Paradise: How Christianity Traded Love of this World for Crucifixion and Empire*. Boston: Beacon, 2009.

Brown, Charles E. "The Atonement: Healing in Postmodern Society." *Interpretation* 53.1 (1999) 34–43.

Brown, Elizabeth. "The Tyranny of a Construct: Feudalism and Historians of Medieval Europe." *American Historical Review* 79 (1974) 1063–68.

Brown, Hunter. "Anselm's *Cur Deus Homo* Revisited." *Eglise et Théologie* 25 (1994) 189–204.

Bibliography

Brown, Joanne, and Rebecca Parker. "For God So Loved the World?" In *Christianity, Patriarchy, and Abuse*, edited by Joanne Brown and Carole Bohn, 1–30. Cleveland, OH: Pilgrim, 1993.

Browning, Robert. "Bishop Bougram's Apology." In *Browning: The Poetical Works 1833–64*, edited by Ian Jack, 650. Oxford: Oxford University Press, 1970.

Brunner, Emil. *The Mediator: A Study of the Central Doctrine of the Christian Faith.* Translated by Olive Wyon. London: Lutterworth, 1934.

Bukert, Walter et al. *Violent Origins: Ritual Killing and Cultural Foundations.* Redwood City, CA: Stanford University Press, 1987.

Buren, Paul van. *Christ in Our Place: The Substitutionary Character of Calvin's Doctrine of Reconciliation.* Grand Rapids: Eerdmans, 1957.

Burnhope, Stephen. "Beyond the Kaleidoscope: Towards a Synthesis of Views on the Atonement." *Evangelical Quarterly* 84.4 (2012) 363–64.

Bushnell, Horace. *The Vicarious Sacrifice.* London: Sampson Low, 1866.

Butler, Samuel. *The Way of All Flesh.* London: Penguin, 1966.

Byassee, Jason. "Abounding in Hope." *Theology Today* 66 (2010) 411–14.

Bynum, C. W. "The Blood of Christ in the Later Middle Ages." *Church History* 71.4 (2002) 685–714.

Calvin, John. *Commentary on Romans.* Calvin's New Testament Commentaries 8. Grand Rapids: Eerdmans, 1995.

———. *Institutes of the Christian Religion.* 2 Vols. Translated by Henry Beveridge. London: James Clarke, 1962.

Campbell, John McLeod. *The Nature of the Atonement.* London: Macmillan, 1865.

———. *Sermons and Lectures.* 2 vols. Greenock, UK: Lusk, 1832.

Campbell, Richard. "The Conceptual Roots of Anselm's Soteriology." In *Anselm: Aosta, Bec and Canterbury*, edited by D. Luscombe & Gillian R. Evans, 256–63. Sheffield, UK: Sheffield Academic, 1996.

Campbell, T. "The Doctrine of the Holy Spirit in the Theology of Athanasius." *Scottish Journal of Theology* 27 (1974) 408–40.

Camporesi, P. *Juice of Life: The Symbolic and Magic Significance of Blood.* Translated by R. Barr. New York: Continuum, 1995.

Carey, George, *The Gate of Glory.* London: Hodder & Stoughton, 1986.

Carlson Brown, Joanne, and Rebecca Parker. "For God So Loved the World?" In *Christianity, Patriarchy, and Abuse,* edited by Joanne Carlson Brown and Carole Bohn, 1–30. New York: Pilgrim, 1989.

Carr, Wesley, *Angels and Principalities.* Cambridge University Press, 1981.

Carson, D. A. *Becoming Conversant with the Emerging Church.* Grand Rapids: Zondervan, 2005.

———. *Showing the Spirit.* Grand Rapids: Baker, 1987.

Chalke, Steve. "Cross Purposes." *Christianity,* September 2004, 4–5.

Chalke, Steve, and Alan Mann. *The Lost Message of Jesus.* Grand Rapids: Zondervan, 2003.

Chenoweth, Erica, and Maria Stephan. *Why Civil Resistance Works: The Strategy of Nonviolent Conflict.* New York: Columbia University Press, 2011.

Clifford, Alan, C. *Amyraut Affirmed, or "Owenism a Caricature of Calvinism."* Norwich: Charenton Reformed, 2004.

Cohen, Nicholas. "Feudal Imagery or Christian Tradition? A Defense of the Rationale for Anselm's *Cur Deus Homo.*" *The Saint Anselm Journal* 2.1 (2004) 154–71.

Colin Kruse. *Paul, the Law and Justification.* Leicester, UK: Apollos, 1996.

Collins, Robin. "Girard and Atonement: An Incarnational Theory of Mimetic Participation." In *Violence Renounced*, edited by Willard Swartley, 132–56. Telford, PA: Pandora, 2000.

Collins-Mayo, Sylvia et al. *The Faith of Generation Y.* London: Church House, 2010.

Cone, James. *God of the Oppressed.* New York: Seabury, 1975.

Copeland, Kenneth. *Covenant of Blood.* Fort Worth, TX: Kenneth Copeland, 1987.

———. "The Gates of Hell Shall Not Prevail." *The Believer's Voice of Victory* 25.4, April 1997, 4–7.

———. *Jesus Died Spiritually.* Fort Worth, TX: Kenneth Copeland Ministries, nd.

———. *Jesus in Hell.* Fort Worth, TX: Kenneth Copeland Ministries, nd.

Cornish, Jones W. "Is Healing in the Atonement?" *Elim Evangel,* October 13, 1962, 646.

Cremer, Hermann. "Der germanische Satisfactionsbegriff in der Versöhnungslehre." *Theologische Studien und Kritiken* 66 (1893) 316–45.

———. "Die Wurzeln des Anselm'schen Satisfactionsbegriffes." *Theologische Studien und Kritiken* 53 (1880) 7–24.

Crisp, Oliver. "Penal Non-Substitution." *Journal of Theological Studies* 51.1 (2008) 140–68.

Cross, Richard. "Atonement without Satisfaction." *Religious Studies* 37 (2001) 397–416.

Crysdale, Cynthia. *Embracing Travail: Retrieving the Cross Today.* New York: Continum, 1999.

Culleton, Alfredo. "Punishment and Human Dignity in the *Cur Deus Homo* by Anselm of Canterbury (1033–1109)." In *Anselm of Canterbury (1033–1109): Philosophical Theology and Ethics,* edited by R. H. Pich, 143–51. Porto Alegre, Brazil: Fédération Internationale des Instituts d'Etudes Médiévales, 2011.

Cullman, Oscar. *Christ and Time.* Translated by F. V. Wilson. London: SCM, 1962.

Cunningham, William. *The Reformers and the Theology of the Reformation.* Carlisle, PA: Banner of Truth, 1967.

Dabney, D. L. "*Pneumatologia Crucis:* Reclaiming *Theologia Crucis* for a Theology of the Spirit Today." *Scottish Journal of Theology* 53.4 (2000) 511–24.

Dale, R. W. *The Atonement: The Congregational Union Lecture for 1875.* London: Congregational Union of England and Wales, 1897.

Das, Andrew. *Paul, the Law and the Covenant.* Peabody, MA: Hendrickson, 2001.

Dayton, Donald W. *Theological Roots of Pentecostalism.* Grand Rapids: Zondervan, 1987.

DeArteaga, William. *Quenching the Spirit: Examining Centuries of Opposition to the Moving of the Holy Spirit.* Altamonte Springs, FL: Creation House, 1992.

Deem, Michael. "A Christological Renaissance: The Chalcedonian Turn of St. Anselm of Canterbury." *The Saint Anselm Journal* 2 (2004) 42–51.

Delanty, G. *Modernity and Postmodernity.* London: Sage, 2000.

Dembele, Y. "Salvation as Victory: A Reconsideration of the Concept of Salvation in the Light of Jesus Christ's Life and Work Viewed as a Triumph over the Personal Powers of Evil." Phd diss., Trinity Evangelical Divinity School, 2001.

Denney, James. *The Atonement and the Modern Mind.* London: Hodder & Stoughton, 1903.

Dillistone, F. W. "A Biblical and Historical Appraisal of Theories of the Atonement." *Theology Today* 10 (1953) 185–95.

———. *Christianity and Symbolism.* London: SCM, 1955.

Dimock, N. *The Doctrine of the Death of Christ.* London: Stock, 1903.

Djaballah, Amar. "Calvin and the Calvinists: An Examination of Some Recent Views." *Reformation Canada* 5.1 (1982) 7–20.

Bibliography

Dodd, C. H. *The Bible and the Greeks*. London: Hodder & Stoughton, 1935.

Dunn, James D. G. *Baptism in the Holy Spirit*. London: SCM, 1970.

———. *Christology in the Making*. London: SCM, 1980.

———. *Jesus and the Spirit*. London: SCM, 1975.

Ebeling, Gerhard. *An Introduction to His Thought*. Translated by R. A. Wilson. Philadelphia: Fortress, 1970.

———. *Luther: Einführung in sein Denken*. Tübingen: Mohr, 1964.

Eckhart, Burnell. *Anselm and Luther on the Atonement: Was it "Necessary"?* San Francisco: Mellen Research University Press, 1992.

Edgar, Dickie. "Introduction." In *The Nature of the Atonement,* edited by John McLeod Campbell, xiii–xx. London: James Clarke, 1959.

Eisenbise, Kate. "Resurrection as Victory? The Eschatological Implications of J. Denny Weaver's 'Narrative Christus Victor' Model of the Atonement." *Brethren Life and Thought* 53.3 (2008) 9–22.

Ellis, Bill. *Raising the Devil: Satanism, New Religious Movements, and the Media*. Lexington, KY: University Press of Kentucky, 2000.

Elmore, Tim. *Generation iY: Our Last Chance to Save Their Future*. Atlanta: Poet Gardener, 2010.

Ensor, Peter. "Clement of Alexandria and Penal Substitutionary Atonement." *Evangelical Quarterly* 85.1 (2013) 19–35.

———. "Justin Martyr and Penal Substitutionary Atonement." *Evangelical Quarterly* 83.3 (2011) 217–32.

———. "Penal Substitutionary Atonement in the Later Ante-Nicene Period." *Evangelical Quarterly*. Forthcoming.

———. "Tertullian and Penal Substitutionary Atonement." *Evangelical Quarterly*. Forthcoming.

Espy, R. H. Edwin, ed. "In Celebration of Amsterdam 1939." Special edition of *Journal of Ecumenical Studies* 16 (1979).

Evans, Gillian. "*Cur Deus Homo*: The Nature of Anselm's Appeal to Reason." *Studia Theologica* 31.1 (1977) 33–50.

Evans, Gillian, R. "Anselm of Canterbury." In *The Medieval Theologians*, edited by Gillian R. Evans, 94–101. Oxford: Blackwell, 2001.

Evenson, George O. "A Critique of Aulen's *Christus Victor*." *Concordia Theological Monthly* 28.10 (1957) 738–49.

Fairweather, Eugene. "Incarnation and Atonement: An Anselmian Response to Auelen's *Christus Victor*." *Canadian Journal of Theology* 7.3 (1961) 167–75.

Ferri, M. et al. *Alcoholics Anonymous and Other 12-step Programmes for Alcohol Dependence*. The Cochrane Library, Issue 3. Oxford: Wiley, 2009.

Fiddes, Paul. *Past Event and Present Salvation: The Christian Idea of Atonement*. London: Darton, Longman, & Todd, 1989.

———. *The Creative Suffering of God*. Oxford: Clarendon, 1988.

Finger, Thomas. "Christus Victor and the Creeds: Some Historical Considerations." *The Mennonite Quarterly Review* 72 (1998) 31–51.

———. *A Contemporary Anabaptist Theology*. Downer's Grove, IL: InterVarsity, 2004.

———. "Pilgram Marpeck and the Christus Victor Motif." *Mennonite Quarterly Review* 78 (2004) 53–77.

Finlan, Stephen. *Problems with Atonement*. Collegeville, PA: Liturgical, 2005.

Finney, Charles. *Lectures on Systematic Theology.* 2nd ed. Edited by J. H. Fairchild. Whittier, CA: Colporter Kemp, 1946.

Flood, Derek. "The Abolishment of Retribution in the Church Fathers." Online: http://therebelgod.com/FathersAbolishRetribution.pdf.

——. *Healing the Gospel: A Radical Vision for Grace, Justice, and the Cross.* Eugene, OR: Cascade, 2012.

——. "Substitutionary Atonement and the Church Fathers: A Reply to the Authors of *Pierced for Our Transgressions.*" *Evangelical Quarterly* 82.2 (2010) 142–59.

Foley, George C. *Anselm's Theory of the Atonement.* London: Longmans, Green & Co., 1909.

Forde, G. O. *On Being a Theologian of the Cross: Reflections on Luther's Heidelberg Disputation of 1518.* Grand Rapids: Eerdmans, 1997.

Forsyth, P. T. *The Cruciality of the Cross.* Carlisle, UK: Paternoster, 1997.

——. *Positive Preaching and the Modern Mind.* London: Hodder & Stoughton, 1908.

——. *This Life and the Next: The Effect on This Life of Faith in Another.* London: Independent, 1946.

Fortin, John. "The Influence of Benedict's *Regula* on Anselm's Concept of Justice." *American Benedictine Review* 58.2 (2007) 154–71.

——. "*Satisfactio* in St Benedict's *Regula* and St Anselm's *Cur Deus* Homo." *Modern Schoolman* 79 (2002) 305–11.

France, Alan. *Understanding Youth in Late Modernity.* Maidenhead, UK: Open University Press, 2007.

Franks, R. S. *The Atonement.* Oxford: Oxford University Press, 1933.

——. *A History of the Work of Christ in its Ecclesiastical Development.* 2 vols. Nashville: Thomas Nelson, 1962.

Furlong, Andy, and Fred Cartmel. *Young People and Social Change: Individualization and Risk in Late Modernity.* Buckingham, UK: Open University Press, 1997.

Ganoczy, Alexandre. "Calvin's Life." In *The Cambridge Companion to John Calvin*, translated by D. Foxgrover and edited by Donald McKim, 3–24. Cambridge: Cambridge University Press, 2004.

Gansholf, F. L. *Feudalism.* (Original Belgian edition, 1944.) Translated by Philip Grierson. New York: Harper, 1961.

Gasper, Giles. "Anselm's *Cur Deus Homo* and Athanasius's *De Incarnatione Verbi*: Some Questions of Comparison." *Studia Anselmiana* 128 (1999) 147–64.

Gattrell, Victor, ed. *Crime and the Law: The Social History of Crime in Western Europe Since 1500.* London: Europa, 1979.

George, Sumner. "Why Anselm Still Matters." *Anglican Theological Review* 95.1 (2013) 25–36.

Gilbert, A. D. *Religion and Society in Industrial England: Church, Chapel and Social Change 1740–1914.* London: Longman, 1976.

Gilbert, Paul et al., eds. *Cur Deus Homo.* Rome: Pontificio Ateneo S. Anselmo, 1999.

Gillett, D. *Trust and Obey: Explorations in Evangelical Spirituality.* London: Darton, Longman & Todd, 1993.

Girard, Réné. *I See Satan Fall Like Lightning.* Maryknoll, NY: Orbis, 2001.

——. *The Scapegoat.* Baltimore, MD: Johns Hopkins University Press, 1986.

——. *Things Hidden Since the Foundation of the World.* Stanford, CA: Stanford University Press, 1987.

——. *Violence and the Sacred.* Baltimore: Johns Hopkins University Press, 1977.

Bibliography

Godfrey, W. Robert. "Reformed Thought on the Extent of the Atonement to 1618." *Westminster Theological Journal* 37 (1975) 133–71.

Goldingay, John, ed. *Atonement Today.* London: SPCK, 1995.

———. "Charismatic Spirituality: Some Theological Reflections." *Theology* 789 (1996) 178–87.

Gomes, Alan. "'De Jesu Christo Servatore': Faustus Socinus on the Satisfaction of Christ." *Westminster Theological Journal* 55.2 (1993) 209–31.

Gomocz, Wolfgang. "Anselm von Aosta als Schecken der 'europäischen' Anthropologie? Anmeldung der philosophischen Pficht, 'Cur Deus Homo' zu durchkreuzen." In *Entwicklungslinien mittlalterlicher Philisophie. Vorträge des V. Kongresses der österreichen Gesellschaft für Philosophie,* edited by G. leibold and W. Löffler, 73–86. Vienna: Hölder-Plichler-Tempsky, 1999.

Goode, Leslie. "Beyond Sacred Violence: The Challenge of Karthryn McClymond for Christian Apologetics." *Theology Today* 66 (2010) 476–86.

Gordon, A. J. *The Ministry of Healing.* In *Healing: The Three Great Healing Classics.* Edited by Jonathan F. Graf. Camp Hill, PA: Christian, 1992.

Gore, Charles, ed. *Lux Mundi: A Series of Studies in the Religion of the Incarnation.* 13th ed. London: Murray, 1892.

Goroncy, Jason. *Hallowed Be Thy Name: The Sanctification of All in the Soteriology of P. T. Forsyth.* London: T. & T. Clark, 2013.

Gorringe, Timothy. *God's Just Vengeance.* Cambridge: Cambridge University Press, 1996.

Greathouse, M. "Sanctification and the Christus Victor Motif in Wesleyan Theology." *Wesleyan Theological Journal* 38.2 (2003) 217–29.

Greef, W. de. *The Writings of John Calvin.* Translated by L. D. Bierma. Grand Rapids: Baker, 1993.

Green, Joel, and Mark Baker. *Recovering the Scandal of the Cross.* Downer's Grove, IL: InterVarsity, 2000.

Gregory of Nazianzus. *Theological Orations.* Edited by Philip Schaff. *Nicene and Post-Nicene Fathers,* Series II, Vol. 7. Online: http://www.ccel.org/ccel/schaff/npnf207.

Gregory of Nyssa, *Great Catechism.* Edited by Philip Schaff. *Nicene and Post-Nicene Fathers* Series II, Vol. 1. Online: http://www.ccel.org/ccel/schaff/npnf205.

Grensted, L. W. *A Short History of the Doctrine of the Atonement.* Manchester: University of Manchester Press, 1920.

Grider, J. Kenneth. "The Governmental Theory: An Expansion." Online http://www.libraryoftheology.com/writings/atonement/Governmental_Theory_Explained-KenGrider.pdf.

———. *A Wesleyan-Holiness Theology.* Kansas City, KS: Beacon Hill, 1994.

Gritsch, Eric. *Martin Luther's Anti-Semitism: Against His Better Judgment.* Grand Rapids: Eerdmans, 2012.

Grotius, Hugo. *Defensio Fidei Catholicae de Satisfactione Christi.* Translated by Holtze Mulder. Edited by Edwin Rabbie. Assen: Van Gorcum, 1990.

Grudem, Wayne. "He Did Not Descend into Hell: A Plea for Following Scripture Instead of the Apostle's Creed." *Journal of the Evangelical Society* 34.1 (1991) 103–13.

Guelich, Robert. "Spiritual Warfare: Jesus, Paul and Peretti." *Pneuma* 13.1 (1991) 33–64.

Gunton, Colin. *The Actuality of Atonement: A Study of Metaphor, Rationality and the Christian Tradition.* Edinburgh: T. & T. Clark, 1988.

———. "*Christus Victor* Revisited: A Study in Metaphor and the Transformation of Meaning." *Journal of Theological Studies* 36.1 (1985) 129–45.

Hagin, Kenneth. *Redemption*. Tulsa, OK: Faith Library, 1981.

Hall, Basil. "Calvin against the Calvinists." In *John Calvin*, edited by G. E. Duffield, 1–37. Appleford, UK: Sutton Courtenay, 1966.

Hannegraaff, Hans. *Christianity in Crisis*. Eugene, OR: Harvest House, 1993.

Harnack, A. von. *History of Dogma* Vol. II. Translated by N. Buchanan. Boston: Little Brown, 1901.

Harog, Paul. *A Word for the World: Calvin on the Extent of the Atonement*. Schaunberg, Austria: Regular Baptist, 2009.

Harper, Brad. "Christus Victor, Postmodernism and the Shaping of Atonement Theology." *Cultural Encounters* 2.1 (2005) 37–51.

Hart, David Bentley. "A Gift Exceeding Every Debt: An Eastern Orthodox Appreciation of Anselm's *Cur Deus Homo*." *Pro Ecclesia* 7 (1998) 333–49.

Hart, Trevor. "Anselm of Canterbury and John McLeod Campbell: Where Opposites Meet?" *Evangelical Quarterly* 62 (1990) 311–33.

———, ed. *Justice the True and Only Mercy: Essays on the Life and Theology of Peter Taylor Forsyth*. Edinburgh: T. & T. Clark, 1995.

Haslam, Greg. "The Lost Cross of Jesus," *Christianity*, November 2004, 18–23.

Hastings Rashdall. *The Idea of Atonement in Christian Theology*. London: MacMillan, 1919.

Heath, Mark. "Salvation: A Roman Catholic Perspective." *Review & Expositor* 79.2 (1982) 275–78.

Heering, J. P. *Hugo Grotius as Apologist for the Christian Religion: A Study of his Work:* De Veritate Religionis Christianae. Leiden: Brill, 2004.

Hefling, Charles. "A Perhaps Permanently Valid Achievement: Lonergan on Christ's Satisfaction." *Method: Journal of Lonergan Studies* 10 (1992) 51–76.

Heim, Mark. *Saved from Sacrifice*. Grand Rapids: Eerdmans, 2006.

Heller, Agnes. *Can Modernity Survive?* Berkeley: University of California Press, 1990.

Helm, Paul. "Calvin and the Covenant: Unity and Continuity." *Evangelical Quarterly* 55 (1983) 65–81.

———. *Calvin and the Calvinists*. Edinburgh: Banner of Truth. 1982.

———. "The Logic of Limited Atonement." *Scottish Bulletin of Evangelical Theology* 3 (1985) 47–54.

Henk, J. M. Nellen, ed. *Hugo Grotius, Theologian: Essays in Honour of G. H. M. Posthumus Meyjes*. Leiden: Brill, 1994.

Hiebert, Paul. *Anthropological Reflections on Missiological Issues*. Grand Rapids: Baker, 1994.

Higginson, Richard. "The Theology of P. T. Forsyth and Its Significance for Us Today." *The Churchman* 71.1 (1957) 66–75.

Hilborn, David, and Matt Bird, eds. *God and the Generations*. Carlisle, UK: Paternoster, 2002.

Hill, Bradley, N. "The Church and Gen Y: Missing the Signs." *Christian Century*, April 5, 2011, 28–33.

Hill, Charles, and Frank James III, eds. *The Glory of the Atonement*. Downers Grove, IL: InterVarsity, 2004.

Hill, William. *The Three-Personed God: The Trinity as a Mystery of Salvation*. Washington, DC: Catholic University of America Press, 1982.

Hobart Freeman. *Did Jesus Die Spiritually? Exposing the JDS Heresy*. Warsaw: Faith Ministries, nd.

Hodge, A. A. *Outlines of Theology.* London: Hodder & Stoughton, 1879.

Hodge, Charles. *Systematic Theology,* Vol. 2. London: James Clark, 1960.

Hogg, David. *Anselm of Canterbury: The Beauty of Theology.* Aldershot, UK: Ashgate: 2004.

Holder, R. Ward. "Calvin as Commentator on the Pauline Epistles." In *Calvin and the Bible,* edited by Donald McKim, 224–56. Cambridge: Cambridge University Press, 2006.

Holl, Karl, *Gesammelte Aufsätze zur Kirchengeschichte,* Vol. 3. Tübingen: Mohr Siebeck, 1948.

Holmes, Stephen. "Cur Deus Pomo? What Anselm can Teach us about Preaching the Atonement Today." *Epworth Review* 36.1 (2009) 6–17.

———. *The Wondrous Cross: Atonement and Penal Substitution in Bible and History.* Milton Keynes, UK: Paternoster, 2007.

———. "The Upholding of Beauty: A Reading of Anselm's *Cur Deus Homo.*" *Scottish Journal of Theology* 54 (2001) 189–203.

Hood, Jason. "The Cross in the New Testament: Two Theses in Conversation with Recent Literature (2000–2007)." *Westminster Theological Journal* 71 (2009) 281–95.

Hooker, Morna. *Not Ashamed of the Gospel: New Testament Interpretations of the Death of Christ.* Carlisle, UK: Paternoster, 1994.

Hopkins, Jasper. "God's Sacrifice of Himself as a Man: Anselm of Canterbury's *Cur Deus Homo.*" In *Human Sacrifice in Jewish and Christian Tradition,* edited by K. Finsterbusch et al., 237–57. Leiden: Brill, 2007.

Houston, Joseph. "Was the Anselm of *Cur Deus Homo* a Retributivist?" In *Cur Deus Homo,* edited by Paul Gilbert et al., 621–39. Rome: Pontificio Ateneo S. Anselmo, 1999.

Houts, Margo G. "Classical Atonement Imagery: Feminist and Evangelical Challenges." *Catalyst* 19.3 (1993) 1–6.

Hubbard, R. *Isaiah 53: Is There Healing in the Atonement?* Bromley, UK: New Life, 1972.

Hughes, T. H. *The Atonement.* London: Allen & Unwin, 1949.

Humphrey, J. Edward. *Emil Brunner.* Waco, TX: Word, 1976.

Ignatius. *Letter to the Philadelphians.* Translated by Kirsopp Lake. Loeb Classical Library 24: Apostolic Fathers I. Cambridge: Harvard University Press, 1912.

———. *Against Heresies.* In *Ante-Nicene Fathers,* Vol. 1, edited by Philip Schaff. Online: http://www.ccel.org/ccel/schaff/anfo1.

Iwand, Hans Joachim. *Nachgelassene Werke* II. Munich: Kaiser, 1966.

James, R. "Atonement and Unity." *Idea,* March/April 2006, 26–27.

———. "Cross Purposes?" *Christian Herald,* Week 36, September 4, 2004, 1.

Jay, E. *Faith and Doubt in Victorian Britain.* Basingstoke, UK: MacMillan, 1986.

Jeffery, Steve et al. *Pierced for Our Transgressions: Rediscovering the Glory of Penal Substitution.* Wheaton, IL: Crossway, 2007.

Jersak, Brad, and Michael Hardin, eds. *Stricken by God? Nonviolent Identification and the Victory of Christ.* Grand Rapids: Eerdmans, 2007.

Jones, Paul. "Barth and Anselm: God, Christ and the Atonement." *International Journal of Systematic Theology* 12 (2010) 257–82.

Jowers, D. W. "The Theology of the Cross as Theology of the Trinity: A Critique of Jürgen Moltmann's Staurocentric Trinitarianism." *Tyndale Bulletin* 52.2 (2000) 263–64.

Jüngel, Eberhard. *God as the Mystery of the World.* Edinburgh: T. & T. Clark, 1983.

Kay, William K. "Approaches to Healing in British Pentecostalism." *Journal of Pentecostal Theology* 14 (1999) 113–25.

Kehl, M., and W. Löser. *The von Balthasar Reader*. Edinburgh: T. & T. Clark, 1982.

Kempis, Thomas. *The Imitation of Christ*. London: Penguin, 1987.

Kendall, R. T. *Calvin and English Calvinism to 1649*. Oxford: Oxford University Press, 1979.

Kent, J. *Holding the Fort: Studies in Victorian Revivalism*. London: Epworth, 1978.

Kenyon, E. W. *The Bible in the Light of Our Redemption*. Lynnwood, WA: Kenyon Gospel Publishing Society, 1969.

———. *Identification: A Romance in Redemption*. Lynnwood, WA: Kenyon's Gospel Publishing Society, 1986.

———. *The Two Kinds of Life*. Washington: Kenyon's Gospel Publishing House, 2002.

———. *What Happened from the Cross to the Throne*. Lynnwood, WA: Kenyon's Gospel Publishing Society, 1989.

———. *The Wonderful Name of Jesus*. 1927. Reprint. Lynnwood, WA: Kenyon's Gospel Publishing Society, 1964.

Kiisel, Ty. "Gimme, Gimme, Gimme: Millennials in the Workplace." *Forbes*, June 16, 2012, Online: http://www.forbes.com/sites/tykiisel/2012/05/16/gimme-gimme-gimme-millennials-in-the-workplace/

Kim, Seyoon. *Paul and the New Perspective: Second Thoughts on the Origin of Paul's Thought*. Grand Rapids: Eerdmans, 2002.

King, Peter. "Abelard's Intentionalist Ethics." *The Modern Schoolman* 72 (1995) 213–31.

———. "The Metaphysics of Peter Abelard." In *The Cambridge Companion to Peter Abelard*, edited by Jeffery E. Brower and Kevin Guilfoy, 65–125. Cambridge: Cambridge University Press, 2004.

LaChance, Paul. "Understanding Christ's Satisfaction Today." *The Saint Anselm Journal* 2.1 (2004) 60–66.

Lane, A. N. S. "The Quest for the Historical Calvin." *Evangelical Quarterly* 55 (1983) 95–113.

Lane, Richard. *Jean Baudrillard*. London: Routledge, 2000.

Langston, Douglas. "Scotus' Departure from Anselm's Theory of the Atonement." *Recherches de Théologie ancienne et medievale* 50 (1983) 227–41.

Lawrence, James. *Engaging Gen Y: Leading Well across the Generations*. Cambridge: Grove, 2012.

Leahy, Frederick, S. "Calvin and the Extent of the Atonement." *Reformed Theological Journal* 8 (1992) 54–64.

Leftow, Brian. "Anselm on the Beauty of the Incarnation." *The Modern Schoolman* 72 (1995) 109–24.

———. "Anselm on the Cost of Salvation." *Medieval Philosophy and Theology* 6 (1997) 73–92.

———. "Anselm on the Necessity of the Incarnation." *Religious Studies* 31 (1995) 167–85.

Lenman, Bruce, and Geoffrey Parker. "The State, the Community and the Criminal Law in Early Modern Europe." In *Crime and the Law: The Social History of Crime in Western Europe Since 1500*, edited by Victor Gattrell, 11–48. London: Europa, 1979.

Letham, Robert. *The Work of Christ*. Leicester, UK: InterVarsity, 1993.

Lewis, C. S. *Mere Christianity*. London: Fount, 1977.

———. *Surprised by Joy*. London: HarperCollins, 2012.

Loewe, William, P. "'Irenaeus' Soteriology: *Christus Victor* Revisited." *Anglican Theological Review* 67.1 (1985) 1–15.

Loewenich, Walther von. *Luther's Theology of the Cross*. Translated by Herbert J. A. Bouman. Minneapolis, MN: Augsburg, 1976.

Lohse, Bernhard. *Martin Luther's Theology: Its Historical and Systematic Development*. Translated by Roy A. Harrisville. Edinburgh: T. & T. Clark, 1999.

Loofs, F. *Leitfaden zum Studien der Dogmengeschichte*. Halle: Niemayer, 1906.

Lortz, J. *Die Reformation in Deutschand*. Vol. 1. Freiburg: Herder, 1947.

Louth, Andrew. "Holiness and the Vision of God in the Eastern Fathers." In *Holiness Past and Present*, edited by Stephen Barton, 217–38. London: T. & T. Clark, 2003.

Love, Gregory Anderson. "Abyssal Compassion or Acquiescence to Violence? Reconfiguring Abelard for a Non-Violent Theory of Atonement." Paper presented at the American Academy of Religion: Joint Session of the Wesleyan Studies Group and the Open and Relational Theologies Consultation, November 3, 2008. Online: http://www.ctr4process.org/affiliations/ort/2008/LoveG-Abyssal%20Compassion%20or%20Acquiescence%20to%20Violence.pdf.

———. *Love, Violence, and the Cross*. Eugene, OR: Cascade, 2010.

Luscombe, D. E., ed. *Peter Abelard's Ethics: An Edition with Introduction: English Translation and Notes*. Oxford: Clarendon, 1971.

Luther, Martin. *D. Martin Luthers Werke: kritische Gesammtausgabe*. 120 vols. Weimar: Böhlau, 1883–1929.

———. *Galatians*. Edited by Alister McGrath and J. I. Packer. Wheaton, IL: Crossway, 1998.

Mackintosh, Robert. *Historic Theories of the Atonement*. London: Hodder & Stoughton, 1920.

Macquarrie, John. "Demonology and the Classic Idea of the Atonement." *Expository Times* 68 (1956) 5–6, 60–63.

———. "John McLeod Campbell 1800–72." *Expository Times* 83 (1972) 263–68.

Maimela, Simon. "The Atonement in the Context of Liberation Theology." *Journal of Theology for Southern Africa* 39 (1982) 45–54.

Mansini, Guy. "St. Anselm, 'satisfactio,' and the 'Rule' of St Benedict." *Revue Benedctine* 97 (1987) 101–21.

Mannermaa, Tuomo. "Theosis as a Subject of Finnish Luther Research." *Pro Ecclesia* IV.1 (1995) 37–48.

Marshall, I. Howard. *Aspects of the Atonement: Cross and Resurrection in the Reconciling of God and Humanity*. Milton Keynes, UK: Paternoster, 2008.

———. "The Theology of Atonement." Online http://evangelicalarminians.org/i-howard-marshall-the-theology-of-the-atonement/.

Martens, Peter. "The Quest for an Anabaptist Atonement: Violence and Nonviolence in J. Denny Weaver's *The Nonviolent Atonement*." *Mennonite Quarterly Review* 82 (2008) 281–311.

Martin, Grant. *Regaining Control: When Good Things Become Addictions*. Washington, DC: Victor, 1990.

Mayhue, Richard. "For What Did Christ Atone in Isa 53:4–5?" *The Masters Seminary Journal* 6.2 (1995) 121–41.

McAllister, Dawson. *Saving the Millennial Generation*. Nashville: Thomas Nelson, 1999.

McBrien, R., ed. *The Harper Collins Encyclopedia of Catholicism*. New York: Harper Collins, 1995.

McClymond, Kathryn. *Beyond Sacred Violence: A Contemporary Study of Violence*. Baltimore: John Hopkins University Press, 2008.

McConnell, Dan. *A Different Gospel*. London: Hodder & Stoughton, 1988.

———. *The Promise of Health and Wealth*. London: Hodder & Stoughton, 1990.

McConville, J. G. "Exodus." In *New International Dictionary of Old Testament Theology and Exegesis*, edited by W. Van Gemeren, 4:603–4. Grand Rapids: Zondervan, 1997.

McCrossan, T. J. *Bodily Healing and the Atonement*. Edited by R. Hicks and K. E. Hagin. Tulsa, OK: Kenneth Hagin Ministries, 1982.

McCurdy, Leslie. *Attributes and Atonement: The Holy Love of God in the Theology of P. T. Forsyth*. Carlisle, UK: Paternoster, 1999.

McDonald, H. D. *The Atonement of the Death of Christ*. Grand Rapids, 1985.

———. *Ideas of Revelation: An Historical Study AD 1700 to AD 1860*. London: Macmillan, 1959.

McDonough, Thomas. *The Law and the Gospel in Luther: A Study of Martin Luther's Confessional Writings*. Oxford: Oxford University Press, 1963.

McFarland, Ian A. "Christ, Spirit and Atonement." *International Journal of Systematic Theology* 3.1 (2001) 83–93.

McGrath, Alister. *Emil Brunner: A Reappraisal*. Oxford: Wiley Blackwell, 2013.

———. *Luther's Theology of the Cross*. Oxford: Blackwell, 1985.

———. "The Moral Theory of the Atonement: An Historical and Theological Critique." *Scottish Journal of Theology* 38.2 (1985) 206–9.

———. "Rectitude: The Moral Foundation of Anselm of Canterbury's Soteriology." *Downside Review* 99.2 (1990) 4–13.

McIntyre, Joe. *E. W. Kenyon and His Message of Faith: The True Story*. Lake Mary, FL: Creation House, 1997.

McIntyre, John. *St. Anselm and His Critics: A Re-interpretation of the* Cue Deus Homo. Edinburgh: Oliver & Boyd, 1954.

———. *The Shape of Soteriology: Studies in the Doctrine of the Death of Christ*. Edinburgh: T. & T. Clark, 1992.

McKnight, Scot. *A Community Called Atonement*. Nashville: Abingdon, 2007.

McLaren, Brian. *A New Kind of Christian*. San Francisco: Jossey-Bass, 2001.

McMahon, Kevin. "The Cross and the Pearl: Anselm's Patristic Doctrine of Atonement." In *Saint Anselm: His Origins and Influence*, edited by John Fortin, 57–69. Lewiston, NY: Mellen, 2001.

———. "Penance and Peter Abelard's Move Within." *The Saint Anselm Journal* 6.2 (2009) 1–7.

Megill-Cobbler, T. "A Feminist Rethinking of Punishment Imagery in Atonement." *Dialog* 35.1 (1996) 14–20.

Menzies, Robert. "Healing in the Atonement." In *Spirit and Power: Foundations of Pentecostal Experience*, edited by Robert and William Menzies, 160–68. Grand Rapids: Zondervan, 2000.

Mesch, Gustavo S., and Ilah Talmud. *Wired Youth: The Social World of Adolescence in the Information Age*. London: Routledge, 2010.

Milavec, Aaron. "Is God Arbitrary and Sadistic? Anselm's Atonement Theory Reconsidered." *Schola* 4 (1981) 45–94.

———. *Salvation Is of the Jews: Saving Grace in Judaism and Messianic Hope in Christianity*. Collegeville, MN: Liturgical, 2007.

Miley, John. *Atonement in Christ*. New York: Phillips & Hunt, 1881.

———. *Systematic Theology*, Vol. 2. New York: Eaton & Mains, 1894.

Moberly, R. C. *Atonement and Personality*. London: John Murray, 1924.

Möltmann, Jürgen. *The Church in the Power of the Spirit: A Contribution to Messianic Ecclesiology*. London: SCM, 1975.

———. *The Crucified God*. London: SCM, 1974.

———.*The Trinity and the Kingdom: The Doctrine of God*. New York: Harper and Row, 1981.

Montgomery, Carrie Judd. *The Prayer of Faith*. London: Victory, 1930.

Moo, Douglas. "Divine Healing in the Health and Wealth Gospel." *Trinity Journal* 9 (1988) 191–209.

Morris, Leon. *The Apostolic Preaching of the Cross*. Exeter, UK: Paternoster, 1965.

———. *The Atonement: Its Meaning and Significance*. Leicester, UK: InterVarsity, 1983.

———. "The Biblical Use of the Term 'Blood.'" *Journal of Theological Studies* 3 (1952) 216–27.

Muller, Richard. "Calvin and the 'Calvinists': Assessing Continuities and Discontinuities between the Reformation and Orthodoxy." *Calvin Theological Journal* 30 (1995) 345–75.

———. "Christ-the Revelation or the Revealer? Brunner and Reformed Orthodoxy on the Doctrine of the Word of God." *Journal of the Evangelical Theological Society* 26.3 (1983) 307–19.

Muller-Fahrenholz, G. *The Kingdom and the Power: The Theology of Jürgen Moltmann*. Edinburgh: T. & T. Clark, 2000.

Murray, A. V. *Abelard and St. Bernard: A Study in Twelfth-Century "Modernism."* Manchester: Manchester University Press, 1967.

Naylor, Charles B. "Bach's Interpretation of the Cross." *Theology* 78.662 (1975) 397–404.

Neelands, David. "Crime, Guilt, and the Punishment of Christ: Travelling Another Way with Anselm of Canterbury and Richard Hooker." *Anglican Theological Review* 88 (2006) 197–213.

———. "Substitution and the Biblical Background to *Cur Deus Homo*." *The Saint Anselm Journal* 2.2 (2005) 80–87.

Neil Howe, and Bill Strauss. *Millennials Rising: The Next Generation*. New York: Vintage, 2000.

Nellas, Panayiotis. "Redemption or Deification? Nicholas Kavasilas and Anselm's Question: 'Why did God become Man?'" *Sourozh* 66 (1996) 10–30.

Nelson, Robert. "Emil Brunner." In *A Handbook of Christian Theologians*, edited by Martin Marty and Dean Peerman, 412–13. Nashville: Abingdon, 1965.

———. "Emil Brunner: Teacher Unsurpassed." *Theology Today* 19.4 (1963) 532–35.

Nessen, Graig. "The Cross as Foundation for the Ministry of Reconciliation: Ending Violence in our Endangered Globe." *Currents in Theology and Mission* 40.2 (2013) 95–105.

Neuman, H. T. "Cultic Origins of the Word-Faith Theology within the Charismatic Movement." *Pneuma* 12.1 (1990) 32–55.

Ngien, Dennis. *Luther as a Spiritual Adviser*. Milton Keynes, UK: Paternoster, 2007.

———. *The Suffering of God according to Martin Luther's "Theologia Crucis."* New York: Lang, 1995.

———. "Ultimate Reality and Meaning in Luther's Theology of the Cross: No Other God, But the Incarnate Human God." *Andrews University Seminary Studies* 42.2 (2004) 383–405.

Nicole, Roger. "Covenant, Universal Call and Definite Atonement." *Journal of the Evangelical Theological Society* 43 (1995) 403–11.

———. "John Calvin's View of the Extent of the Atonement." *Westminster Theological Journal* 47 (1985) 197–225.

Niehaus, J. "Old Testament Foundations: Signs and Wonders in Prophetic Ministry and the Substitutionary Atonement of Is. 53." In *The Kingdom and the Power*, edited by G. S. Greig and K. Springer, 48–50. Ventura, CA: Regal, 1995.

Nieuwenhove, Rik van. "St. Anselm and St. Thomas on 'Satisfaction': or How Catholic and Protestant Understandings of the Cross Differ." *Angelicum* 80 (2003) 159–76.

Nimmo, Paul. "A Necessary Suffering? John McLeod Campbell and the Passion of Christ." *Theology in Scotland* XII.2 (2005) 57–70.

Noll, Mark. "Charles Hodge." In *Evangelical Dictionary of Theology*, edited by W. Elwell, 561. Grand Rapids: Baker, 2001.

Norris, F. W. "Deification: Consensual and Cogent." *Scottish Journal of Theology* 49.4 (1996) 411–28.

Origen. *On Matthew.* In *Ante-Nicene Christian Library: Additional Volume IX.* Edited by Allan Menzies. Edinburgh: T. & T. Clark, 1897.

Ovey, Michael. "Appropriating Aulén? Employing Christus Victor Models of the Atonement." *Churchman* 124.4 (2010) 297–330.

Packer, James I. *Celebrating the Saving Work of God: Collected Shorter Writings of J. I. Packer.* Carlisle, UK: Paternoster, 1998.

———. "Poor Health May Be the Best Remedy." *Christianity Today* 26.10, May 21, 1982, 15.

———. "What Did the Cross Achieve? The Logic of Penal Substitution." *Tyndale Bulletin* 25 (1974) 3–45.

Pannenberg, Wolfhart. *Jesus: God and Man.* Philadelphia, PA: Westminster, 1977.

———. *Systematic Theology,* Vol. 2. Translated by G. W. Bromily. Grand Rapids: Eerdmans, 1994.

Park, Edwards, A. *The Atonement.* Boston: Congregational Board of Publication, 1859.

Paul, R. S. *The Atonement and the Sacraments.* London: Hodder & Stoughton, 1961.

Pawson, David. *The Fourth Wave: Charismatics and Evangelicals: Are we Ready to Come Together?* London: Hodder & Stoughton, 1993.

Payne, Seth R. "Alma and Anselm: Satisfaction Theory in the *Book of Mormon*." Online: http://www.mormonstudies.net/html/payne/alma.html#_ftn8.

Peck, Andy. "Why Did Jesus Die?" *Christianity,* September 5, 2005, 12–15.

Perriman, Andrew. *Faith, Health and Prosperity.* Carlisle, UK: Paternoster, 2003.

Peters, Ted. "Atonement and the Final Scapegoat." *Perspectives in Religious Studies* 19 (1992) 151–81.

———. "The Atonement in Anselm and Luther, Second Thoughts about Aulen's *Christus Victor*." *Lutheran Quarterly* 24.3 (1972) 301–14.

Petersen, David, ed. *Where Wrath and Mercy Meet: Proclaiming the Atonement Today.* Carlisle, UK: Paternoster, 2001.

Petersen, Robert. *Calvin and the Atonement.* Fearn, UK: Christian Focus, 1999.

———. *Calvin's Doctrine of the Atonement.* Phillipsburg, NJ: Presbyterian and Reformed, 1983.

Peterson, David, ed. *Where Wrath and Mercy Meet: Proclaiming the Atonement Today.* Carlisle, UK: Paternoster, 2001.

Petts, David. "Healing & the Atonement." PhD diss., University of Nottingham, 1993.

———. "Healing and the Atonement." *EPTA Bulletin* XII (1993) 23-37.

Piggin, Stuart. *Firestorm of the Lord.* Carlisle, UK: Paternoster, 2000.

Pirie, M., and R. M. Worcester. *The Millennial Generation.* London: Adam Smith Institute, 1998.

Placher, William. "Christ Takes Our Place: Rethinking Atonement." *Interpretation* 53.1 (1999) 5–20.

Prensky, Marc. "Digital Natives, Digital Immigrants." *On the Horizon* 9.5 (2001) 1–6.

Prenter, Regin. *Luther's Theology of the Cross.* Philadelphia: Fortress, 1966.

Prince, Derek. *Atonement: Your Appointment with God.* Baldock, UK: Derek Prince Ministries UK, 2000.

———. *The Divine Exchange: The Sacrificial Death of Jesus Christ on the Cross.* Harpenden, UK: Derek Prince Ministries UK, 1995.

———. "Kensington Temple Sep 1992. The Cross in My Life." *Keys to Successful Living.* Audiotape. Enfield, UK: Derek Prince Ministries UK, 1992.

———. "Redemption: Plan and Fulfilment: The Exchange at the Cross." *Keys to Successful Living.* Audiotape. Fort Lauderdale: Derek Prince Ministries International, 1989.

Pugh, Ben. "A Brief History of the Blood: the Story of the Blood of Christ in Transatlantic Evangelical Devotion." *Evangelical Review of Theology* 31.3 (2007) 239–55.

———. "'Kicking the Daylights out of the Devil': The Re-appropriation of the Victory Motif in Some Recent Atonement Theology." *European Journal of Theology* 23.1 (2014) 32–42.

———. "'The Lost Message of Jesus': What is all the Fuss About?" *Direction,* October 2005, 16–18.

———. "The Mind of the Spirit: Explorations in the Reciprocal Relationship between the Work of the Spirit and the Work of the Son." *Journal of the European Pentecostal Theological Association* 32.1 (2012) 41–60.

———. "The Spirit and the Cross: Insights from Barth and Moltmann into the Holy Spirit's Relationship to the Cross of Christ." *Evangelical Review of Theology* 36.4 (2012) 292–301.

———. "What the Faith Teachers Mean by 'Faith'—An Evaluation of the Faith Teachers' Concept of Faith in the Light of Hebrews 11:1 and Mark 11:22–24." MA diss., University of Manchester, 2004.

Quarles, Charles. "The New Perspective and Means of Atonement in Jewish Literature of the Second Temple Period." *Criswell Theological Review* 2.2 (2005) 39–56.

Quinn, Philip. "Abelard on Atonement: 'Nothing Unintelligible, Arbitrary, Illogical, or Immoral about It.'" In *Reasoned Faith,* edited by Eleonore Stump, 281–300. Ithaca, NY: Cornell University Press, 1983.

Radice, Betty, trans. *The Letters of Abelard and Heloise.* London: Penguin, 1974.

Rahner, Karl. *The Trinity.* Tunbridge Wells, UK: Burns & Oates, 1970.

Rainbow, Jonathan H. *The Will of God and the Cross: An Historical and Theological Study of John Calvin's Doctrine of Limited Redemption.* San Jose, CA: Pickwick, 1990.

Rainer, Thom, and Jess Rainer. *The Millennials.* Nashville: B. & H., 2010.

Ray, Darby Kathleen. *Deceiving the Devil: Atonement, abuse and ransom.* Cleveland, OH: Pilgrim, 1998.

Reichenbach, Bruce. "By His Stripes We Are Healed." *Journal of the Evangelical Theological Society* 41.4 (1998) 551–60.

Rennie, I. S. "Fundamentalism and the Varieties of North Atlantic Evangelicalism." In *Evangelicalism: Comparative Studies of Popular Protestantism in North America, The British Isles, and Beyond 1700–1990,* edited by Mark Noll et al., 333–64. Oxford: Oxford University Press, 1994.

Reynolds, Susan. *Fiefs and Vassals: The Medieval Evidence Reinterpreted.* Oxford: Oxford University Press, 1994.

Richardson, H. G., and G. O. Sayles. *The Governance of Medieval England from the Conquest to Magna Carta.* Edinburgh: Edinburgh University Press, 1963.

Ritschl, Albrecht. *The Christian Doctrine of Justification and Reconciliation.* Edited by H. R. Mackintosh and A. B. Macaulay. Edinburgh: T. & T. Clark, 1900.

———. *A Critical History of the Doctrine of Justification and Reconciliation.* Translated by John S. Black. Edinburgh: Edmondson & Douglas, 1872.

———. *Die christliche Lehre von der Rechtfertigung under Versöhnung: Zweiter Band: Der biblische Stoff der Lehre.* Bonn: Marcus, 1874.

Riviere, Jean. *Le dogme de la Redemption.* Paris: Librairie Victor LeCoffre, 1914.

———. "Sur la Satisfaction du Christ." *Bulletin de Literature Ecclésiastique* 35 (1934) 174–87.

Robbins, Anna. "Atonement in Contemporary Culture: Christ, Symbolic Exchange and Death." In *The Atonement Debate: Papers from the London Symposium on the Atonement,* edited by Derek Tidball et al., 329–44. Grand Rapids: Zondervan, 2007.

Robson, Michael. "The Impact of *Cur Deus Homo* on the Early Franciscan School." In *Anselm: Aosta, Bec and Canterbury,* edited by David Luscome and Gillian Evans, 334–47. Sheffield, UK: Sheffield Academic, 1996.

Rodger, Symeon. "The Soteriology of Anselm of Canterbury: An Orthodox Perspective." *The Greek Orthodox Theological Review* 34 (1989) 19–43.

Rogers, Katherine. "Christ our Brother: Family Unity in Anselm's Theory of the Atonement." *American Catholic Philosophical Quarterly* 86 (2012) 223–36.

———. "A Defense of Anselm's *Cur Deus Homo* Argument." *Proceedings of the American Catholic Philosophical Association* 74 (2000) 187–200.

Ronald Nydam. "The Relational Theology of Generation Y." *Calvin Theological Journal* 41 (2006) 324, 328–29.

Root, Michael. "Necessity and Unfittingness in Anselm's *Cur Deus Homo.*" *Scottish Journal of Theology* 40 (1987) 211–30.

Rouwendal, P. L. "Calvin's Forgotten Classical Position on the Extent of the Atonement: About Sufficiency, Efficiency, and Anachronism." *Westminster Theological Journal* 70 (2008) 317–35.

Royce, James. "Alcohol and Other Drugs in Spiritual Formation." *Studies in Formative Spirituality* 8.2 (1987) 211–12.

Runia, Klaus. "The Preaching of the Cross Today." *European Review of Theology* 25.1 (2001) 53–64.

Rupp, Gordon. *The Righteousness of God: A Reconsideration of the Character and Work of Martin Luther.* London: Hodder & Stoughton, 1953.

Sach, A., and M. Ovey. "Have We Lost the Message of Jesus?" *Evangelicals Now!* June 2004, 27.

Salai, Sean. "Anselm, Girard, and Sacramental Theology." *Contagion: Journal of Violence, Mimesis, and Culture* 18 (2011) 953–1109.

Sanders, E. P. *Paul: A Brief Insight.* New York: Oxford University Press, 1991.

———. *Paul: A Very Short Introduction.* Oxford: Oxford University Press, 1991.

———. *Paul and Palestinian Judaism: A Comparison of Patterns of Religion.* London: SCM, 1977.

Sanders, John. *Atonement and Violence: A Theological Conversation.* Nashville: Abingdon, 2006.

Schaef, Anne. *Escape from Intimacy: Untangling the "Love" Addictions: Sex, Romance, Relationships*. New York: Harper Collins, 1992.

———. *When Society Becomes an Addict*. San Francisco: Harper Collins, 1988.

Schwager, Raymund. *Must There be Scapegoats?* San Francisco: Harper & Row,1987.

Scott-Lidgett, J. *The Spiritual Principle of the Atonement as a Satisfaction Made to God for the Sins of the World*. London: Kelly, 1898.

Seeberg, Reinhold. *Text-Book of the History of Doctrines*. Translated by Charles E. Hay. Reprint. Eugene, OR: Wipf & Stock, 1997.

Seet, C. "The Doctrine of Healing in the Atonement." *The Burning Bush* 2.2 (1996) 93–99.

Shapland, C. R. B. *The Letters of Saint Athanasius Concerning the Holy Spirit*. London: Epworth, 1951.

Shelton, R. Larry. *Cross and Covenant*. Milton Keynes, UK: Paternoster, 2006.

Siekawitch, Larry. "The Evolution of the Doctrine of the Atonement in the Medieval Church: Anselm, Abelard and Aquinas." *McMaster Journal of Theology and Ministry* 9 (2007–8) 3–30.

Smail, Thomas. "Can One Man Die for the People?" In *Atonement Today*, edited by John Goldingay, 73–92. London: SPCK, 1995.

———. "The Cross and the Spirit: Towards a Theology of Renewal." In *Charismatic Renewal: The Search for a Theology*, edited by Andrew Walker et al., 49–70. London: SPCK, 1995.

———. *The Forgotten Father*. London: Darton Longman & Todd, 1980.

———. *The Giving Gift: The Holy Spirit in Person*. London: Darton Longman & Todd, 1994.

———. *Once and for All: A Confession of the Cross*. London: Darton, Longman & Todd, 1998.

———. *Reflected Glory*. London: Hodder & Stoughton, 1975.

———. *Windows on the Cross*. London: Darton, Longman & Todd, 1995.

Smail, Thomas, Andrew Walker, and Nigel Wright. "'Revelation Knowledge' and Knowledge of Revelation: The Faith Movement and the Question of Heresy." In *Charismatic Renewal: The Search for a Theology*, edited by Thomas Smail, Andrew Walker, and Nigel Wright, 57–77. London: SPCK, 1995.

Smeaton, George. *The Apostles' Doctrine of the Atonement*. Edinburgh: Banner of Truth, 1991.

Smith, Christian et al. *Lost in Translation: The Dark Side of Emerging Adulthood*. Oxford: Oxford University Press, 2011.

Socinus, Faustus. *De Jesu Christo Servatore*. In *Bibliotheca Fratrum Polonorum* II. Edited by Andreas Wissowatius. Amsterdam: 1668.

———. *Paelectiones Theologicae*. In *Bibliotheca Fratrum Polonorum* I. Edited by Andreas Wissowatius. Amsterdam: 1668.

Solberg, Mary. *Compelling Knowledge: A Feminist Proposal for an Epistemology of the Cross*. Albany, NY: State University of New York Press, 1997.

Southern, Richard. *Saint Anselm: A Portrait in a Landscape*. Cambridge: Cambridge University Press, 1990.

Sowle Cahill, Lisa. "Quaesti Disputata: The Atonement Paradigm: Does It Still have Explanatory Value?" *Theological Studies* 68 (2007) 418–32.

Spencer, J. R. *Heresy Hunters: Character Assassination in the Church*. Lafayette, LA: Huntington House, 1993.

Spurgeon, C. H. *The Metropolitan Tabernacle*, Vol. 32. Edinburgh: Banner of Truth, 1991.

Stanton, Glenn, T. "Fact Checker: Are Millennials More Self-Sacrificing and Community-Minded Than Previous Generations?" *The Gospel Coalition*, February 8, 2013. Online http://thegospelcoalition.org/blogs/tgc/2013/02/08/factchecker-are-millennials-more-self-sacrificing-and-community-minded-than-previous-generations/.

Stapert, Calvin. "Christus Victor: Bach's St. John Passion." *Reformed Journal* 39 (1989) 17–23.

Steinbart, G. S. *System de reinen Philosophie oder Glücklichkeitslehre des Christenthums*. Zülichau: 1778.

Steinmetz, David. *Calvin in Context*. Oxford: Oxford University Press, 1995.

Stibbe, Mark. *O Brave New Church: Rescuing the Addictive Culture*. London: Darton, Longman & Todd, 1995.

———. "The Theology of Renewal and the Renewal of Theology." *Journal of Pentecostal Theology* 3 (1993) 71–90.

Stibbs, Alan. *His Blood Works: The Meaning of the Word "Blood" in Scripture*. Fearn, UK: Christian Focus, 2011.

———. *The Meaning of the Word 'Blood' in Scripture*. Cambridge: Tyndale, 1948.

Storkey, Elaine. "Atonement and Feminism." *Anvil* 11.3 (1994) 227–35.

Stott, John. *The Cross of Christ*. Leicester, UK: InterVarsity, 1986.

Strauss, William, and Neil Howe. *Generations: the History of America's Future, 1584–2069*. New York: Morrow/Quill, 1991.

Strehle, Stephen. "Universal Grace and Amyraldianism." *Westminster Theological Journal* 51 (1989) 345–57.

Strimple, Robert. "St. Anselm's *Cur Deus Homo* and John Calvin's Doctrine of the Atonement." In *Aosta, Bec and Canterbury*, edited by David Luscombe and Gillian Evans, 348–60. Sheffield, UK: Sheffield Academic, 1996.

Stump, Eleonore. "Atonement according to Aquinas." In *Oxford Readings in Philosophical Theology Vol. 1: Trinity, Incarnation and Atonement*, edited by Michael Rea, 267–93. Oxford: Oxford University Press, 2009.

———. "Atonement according to Aquinas." In *Philosophy and the Christian Faith*, edited by Thomas Morris, 61–91. Notre Dame, IN: Notre Dame University Press, 1988.

Synan, Vinson. "A Healer in the House? A Historical Perspective on Healing in the Pentecostal/Charismatic Tradition." *Asian Journal of Pentecostal Studies* 3.2 (2000) 189–201.

Taliaferro, Charles. "A Narnian Theory of the Atonement." *Scottish Journal of Theology* 41.1 (1988) 75–92.

Tabluteau, Emily. "Definitions of Feudal Military Obligations in Eleventh-Century Normandy." In *On the Laws and Customs of England: Essays in Honor of Samuel E. Thorne*, edited by M. S. Arnold, 18–59. Chapel Hill, NC: University of North Carolina Press, 1981.

Tamburello, Dennis. *Union with Christ: John Calvin and the Mysticism of St. Bernard*. Louisville: Westminster John Knox, 1994.

Taylor, R. O. P. "Was Abelard an Exemplarist?" *Theology* 31 (1935) 207–13.

Tee, A. B. "The Doctrine of Divine Healing." In *Pentecostal Doctrine*, edited by Percy Brewster, 197–209. No loc: P. S. Brewster, 1976.

TeSelle, Eugene. "The Cross as Ransom." *Journal of Early Christian Studies* 4.2 (1996) 147–70.

Thomas, G. Michael. *The Extent of the Atonement: A Dilemma for Reformed Theology from Calvin to the Consensus (1536–1675)*. Carlisle, UK: Paternoster, 1997.

Thomas, Owen. *The Atonement Controversy in Welsh Theological Literature and Debate, 1707–1841.* Edinburgh: Banner of Truth, 2002.

Thompson, M. *Epworth Commentaries: Isaiah 40–66.* Peterborough, UK: Epworth, 2001.

Tidball, Derek, David Hilborn, and Justin Thacker, eds. *The Atonement Debate.* Grand Rapids: Zondervan, 2008.

Tillich, Paul. *Systematic Theology,* Vol. II. London: Nisbet, 1957.

Tomlin, Graham. *Luther and His World.* Oxford: Lion, 2002.

———. *The Power of the Cross: Theology and the Death of Christ in Paul, Luther and Pascal.* Carlisle, UK: Paternoster, 1999.

———. "The Theology of the Cross: Subversive Theology for a Postmodern World?" *Themelios* 23.1 (1997) 59–73.

Torrance, James B. "The Contribution of McLeod Campbell to Scottish Theology." *Scottish Journal of Theology* 26.3 (1973) 295–311.

———. "The Incarnation and 'Limited Atonement.'" *Evangelical Quarterly* 55 (1983) 83–94.

Torrance, T. F. *Scottish Theology from John Knox to John McLeod Campbell.* Edinburgh: T. & T. Clark, 1996.

Tournier, Paul. *Guilt and Grace.* Crowborough, UK: Highland, 1986.

Trelstad, Marit, ed. *Cross Examinations: Readings on the Meaning of the Cross Today.* Minneapolis: Augsburg, 2006.

Trost, Lou Ann. "On Suffering, Violence, and Power." *Currents in Theology and Mission* 21 (1994) 35–40.

Trumbull, H. C. *The Blood Covenant: A Primitive Rite and Its Bearings on Scripture.* 2nd ed. Kirkwood, MO: Impact Christian, 1975.

Turner, H. E. W. *The Patristic Doctrine of Redemption: A Study of the Development of Doctrine during the First Five Centuries.* 1952. Reprint. Eugene, OR: Wipf & Stock, 2004.

Turretin, Francis. *Institutes of Elenctic Theology (1679–85).* Translated by Musgrave Giger. Edited by James T. George and James Dennison. Phillipsburg, NJ: P. & R., 1992–97.

Tuttle, George. *So Rich a Soil: John McLeod Campbell on Christian Atonement.* Edinburgh: Hansel, 1986.

Twenge, Jean, M. et al. "Generational Differences in Young Adults' Life Goals, Concern for Others and Civic Orientation, 1966–2009." *Journal of Personality and Social Psychology* 102.5 (2012) 1045–62.

Unger, Merrill. "Divine Healing." *Biblotheca Sacra* 128.511 (1971) 234–44.

Visser, Derk. "St. Anselm's *Cur Deus Homo* and the *Heidelberg Catechism* (1563)." *Anselm Studies* 2 (1998) 607–34.

Vlach, Michael. "Penal Substitution in Church History." *The Masters Seminary Journal* 20.2 (2009) 199–214.

Walker, Andrew G. "The Devil You Think You Know: Demonology and the Charismatic Movement." In *Charismatic Renewal: The Search for a Theology,* edited by Thomas Smail et al., 86–105. London: SPCK, 1995.

———. *Enemy Territory: The Christian Struggle for the World.* London: Hodder & Stoughton, 1987.

Wallace, A. J., and R. D. Rusk. *Moral Transformation: The Original Christian Paradigm of Salvation.* Auckland, New Zealand: Bridgehead, 2011.

Walters, G. M. "The Atonement in Medieval Theology." In *The Glory of the Atonement: Biblical, Historical & Practical Perspectives*, edited by Charles E. Hill and Frank A. James III, 239–62. Downers Grove, IL: InterVarsity, 2004.

Watson, Gordon. "A Study in St. Anselm's Soteriology and Karl Barth's Theological Method." *Scottish Journal of Theology* 42 (1989) 493–512.

Watson, Philip. *Let God Be God! An Interpretation of the Theology of Martin Luther*. Philadelphia: Muhlenberg, 1947.

Weaver, J. Denny. "Atonement and (Non)Violence." *Epworth Review* 36.1 (2009) 29–46.

———. "Atonement for the NonConstantinian Church." *Modern Theology* 6.4 (1990) 281–311.

———. "Christus Victor, Ecclesiology and Christology." *The Mennonite Quarterly Review* 68:3 (1994) 433–576.

———. *The Nonviolent Atonement*. Grand Rapids: Eerdmans, 2001.

———. "Some Theological Implications of Christus Victor." *The Mennonite Quarterly Review* 70 (1994) 483–99.

Webber, Robert. *Ancient-Future Faith: Rethinking Evangelicalism for a Postmodern World*. Grand Rapids: Baker, 1999.

Weingart, Richard. "The Atonement in the Writings of Peter Abailard." PhD diss., Yale University, 1965.

———. *The Logic of Divine Love: A Critical Analysis of the Soteriology of Peter Abelard*. Oxford: Clarendon, 1970.

Weisser, Michael. *Crime and Punishment in Early Modern Europe*. Hassocks, UK: Harvester, 1979.

Wells, Paul. "A Free Lunch at the End of the Universe? Sacrifice, Substitution and Penal Liability." *Themelios* 29.1 (2003) 38–51.

Westcott, B. F. *The Epistles of John: The Greek Text with Notes and Essays*. 2nd ed. London: John Murray, 1886.

Westerholm, Stephen. *Perspectives Old and New on Paul: The "Lutheran" Paul's Thought and His Critics*. Grand Rapids: Eerdmans, 2004.

Westermann, C. *Old Testament Library: Isaiah 40–66*. London: SCM, 1969.

Whale, J. S. *Victor and Victim*. Cambridge: Cambridge University Press, 1960.

Whidden, David. "The Alleged Feudalism of Anselm's *Cur Deus Homo* and the Benedictine Concepts of Obedience, Honor, and Order." *Nova et Vetera* 9.4 (2011) 1055–87.

Wicks, Jared. "Justification and Faith in Luther's Theology." *Theological Studies* 44 (1983) 3–29.

Wilkinson, J. "Physical Healing and the Atonement." *Evangelical Quarterly* 63.2 (1991) 149–67.

Williams, Garry. "Penal Substitution: A Response to Recent Criticisms." *Journal of the European Theological Society* 50.1 (2007) 71–86.

———. "Penal Substututionary Atonement in the Church Fathers." *Evangelical Quarterly* 83.3 (2011) 195–216.

Williams, George. *Anselm: Communion and Atonement*. Saint Louis, MO: Concordia, 1960.

Williams, S. N. "The Problem with Moltmann." *Evangelical Journal of Theology* 5.2 (1996) 158–59.

Wimber, John, and Kevin Springer. *Power Healing*. London: Hodder & Stoughton, 1986.

Wink, Walter. *Engaging the Powers*. Minneapolis, PA: Fortress, 1992.

————. "Facing the Myth of Redemptive Violence." *Ekklesia,* November 16, 2007. Online: http://www.ekklesia.co.uk/content/cpt/article_060823wink.shtml.

————. *Naming the Powers: The Language of Power in the New Testament.* Philadelphia: Fortress, 1984.

————. *Unmasking the Powers.* Philadelphia: Fortress, 1986.

Wolf, William. "Outline of Brunner's Theology." *Anglican Theological Review* 30.2 (1948) 129–35.

Wood, Maxwell. "Penal Substitution in the Construction of British Evangelical Identity: Controversies in the Doctrine of the Atonement in the Mid-2000s." PhD diss., University of Durham, 2011.

Wright, N. T. "Adam in Pauline Christology." *SBL Seminar Papers* (1983) 359–89.

————. *The Climax of the Covenant: Christ and the Law in Pauline Theology.* Edinburgh: T. & T. Clark, 1991.

————. "Jesus and the Identity of God." *Ex Auditu* 14 (1998) 42–56.

————. "Reasons for Jesus' Crucifixion." In *Stricken by God? Nonviolent Identification and the Victory of Christ,* edited by Brad Jersak and Michael Hardin, 78–149. Grand Rapids: Eerdmans, 2007.

Wright, Nigel. "The Charismatic Theology of Thomas Smail." *EPTA Bulletin* XVI (1996) 5–18.

————. *The Fair Face of Evil.* London: Marshall Pickering, 1989.

Yoder, John Howard. *The Politics of Jesus: Vicit Agnus Noster.* Grand Rapids: Eerdmans, 1972.

Yong, Amos, and Estrelda Y. Alexander, eds. *Afro-Pentecostalism: Black Pentecostal and Charismatic Christianity in History and Culture.* New York: New York University Press, 2011.

Yves Congar. *I Believe in the Holy Spirit,* Vol. II. London: Chapman, 1983.

Ziesler, John. *Pauline Christianity.* Oxford: Oxford University Press, 1990.

Zizioulas, John. *Being as Communion.* London: Darton, Longman & Todd, 1985.

Index

Abelard, Peter, xiii, 129–33, 149, 163
Addiction, 71
Anselm of Canterbury, xiii, 1, 7, 10–12, 43, 45–62, 64, 70, 73, 86, 88–90, 106, 107, 119–20, 125–26, 129–30, 132–34, 145, 149, 154, 163
Apostolic Fathers, 126–29
Aquinas, Thomas, xiii, 49, 71, 132
Athanasius, 32–33, 40, 45, 49, 51, 57, 59, 60–61, 88, 90–91
Augustine of Hippo, xiii, 5, 16, 52, 78, 141
Aulén, Gustav, 1, 8–13, 17, 19, 47, 144, 162–63

Barth, Karl, 29, 49, 111, 139–41, 143, 147
Baudrillard, Jean, 72–73
Boyd, Greg, 11, 13, 22, 25
Brunner, Emil, 105–7, 119, 163

Calvin, John, 8, 50, 63, 73–82, 118, 163
Calvinism, 74, 76–77, 79–83, 86, 88–89, 119, 133, 135
Campbell, John McLeod, 49, 88–92, 96–97, 105, 119–20, 145, 163
Chalcedon, 49, 52, 58, 60, 89, 96, 105, 119, 130
Christus Victor, 3–41, 45, 47, 68, 72, 79, 101, 123, 144, 153
Criminal Justice, 73–76, 83–84, 86, 145
Crucicentrism, 64–65, 76

Deification. See *Theosis*
Dodd, Charles Harold, 109–11
Dunn, James, D. G. 28, 33, 146

Emerging Church, 1, 11, 13, 21–23, 30

Enlightenment, the, 13, 83, 136, 149
Eucharist, 50, 64, 80, 128
Exemplarist view of the cross, 25, 84, 126, 130–32

Feminist theology, 1, 6, 11, 16–18, 20, 23, 116, 154
Feudalism, 50, 53–55, 60–61
Finnish School, 35–36
Forsyth, Peter Taylor, 88, 94–97, 104, 107–8, 119, 120, 163
Franks, Robert, S. 4, 5, 9, 27, 131, 134, 136–37

Generation Y. See Millennials.
Girard, Réné, xiii, 20, 48–49, 153–63
Gnosticism, 3–5, 7
Governmental Theory, 133–36
Gregory of Nazianzus, 31–32, 40, 163
Gregory of Nyssa, 4, 5, 7, 16
Grensted, Lawrence William, 4, 6, 9, 45, 53, 125, 134, 138
Grotius, Hugo, 133–36, 149, 163
Gunton, Colin, 10–12, 52, 56, 110, 160

Hagin, Kenneth. See Word of Faith.
Healing, Atonement and, 43, 48, 97–105
Heim, S. Mark, 49, 156–58, 161, 163
Hodge, Charles, 63, 85–87, 107, 134–36, 163
Holy Spirit. See Pneumatology.

Incarnation, 10, 12, 26–7, 32, 49, 50–51, 53, 55, 59, 65, 77, 80–81, 84, 89–90, 92, 96–97, 105–6, 141, 163, 166
Irenaeus, xiii, 4–6, 10, 14, 16, 18, 24–28, 31–32, 34, 40, 47, 51, 57, 60, 64, 72, 90, 119, 128

Jesus Died Spiritually (JDS), see Word of Faith

Limited Atonement, 79–82
Luther, Martin, 8–10, 35–36, 50, 63–77, 82–83, 85, 112, 118, 120, 140, 162–63

McKnight, Scot, 30–31, 36, 40
Millennials, 23, 36–40
Moberly, Robert, C. 87–88, 91, 138, 144–45, 147, 150, 161, 163
Möltmann, Jürgen, 121, 141–43, 147, 149, 150, 162–63
Moral Influence theory, 123–39, 144–45, 153, 161, 163
Morris, Leon, 109–11

Neo-Orthodox, 105, 138–43, 149–50
Nonviolent Atonement, 1, 11, 16, 18–21, 23–24, 57, 59, 153–61

Objective theories, 8, 43–121
Origen, 1, 4–6, 13, 16

Packer, James, I. 62, 100, 118, 133
Participation in Christ, 28, 78, 110, 130
Passion Mysticism, 64–66
Penal Substitution, 8, 11, 15, 29, 48, 56–57, 63–64, 70–71, 73–76, 83–87, 93, 101, 106–8, 112, 114–20, 126–27, 133, 136, 146, 154, 159, 161

Platonism, 158–60
Pneumatology, 32–33, 123, 138, 143–50
Postmodernity, 13, 38–39
Prince, Derek, 99, 103–5, 107, 120

Ransom to Satan, 3–25, 52, 57, 128
Rashdall, Hastings, 4, 9, 16, 131–32
Recapitulation theory, 1–2, 7, 25–32, 35–36, 41, 58–59, 77, 102, 120, 128
Reformation, 8, 51, 60–61, 63, 65, 68, 73–76, 80–82, 83, 119
Ritschl, Albrecht, 84, 94, 136–38, 163

Sanders, Ed Parish, 111–14
Satisfaction theory, 1, 8, 43–63, 71, 75, 77, 85–87, 118–20, 132–135, 137, 145, 147, 154
Socinus, Faustus, 133–34, 149, 163
Stott, John, 103, 106–8
Subjective theories, 8, 108, 115, 123–50

Theosis, 25–27, 31–41, 68, 120
Tillich, Paul, 10, 13

Vicarious Repentance. See Campbell, John McLeod.

Weaver, J. Denny, 10–11, 13, 18, 20–21, 48, 163
Wink, Walter, 14, 18–20, 24, 153
Word of Faith, 1, 13–16, 23–24, 34–35, 111
Wright, N. T., 28, 114, 163